More!
Wonderful
from
dog-friendly c
throughout Great Britain, with dog-friendly pubs nearby!

Walkers
Muddy Boots
& Dogs
Welcome!

Anna Chelmicka

Hubble & Hattie

The Hubble & Hattie imprint was launched in 2009 and is named in memory of two very special Westies owned by Veloce's proprietors. Since the first book, many more have been added to the list, all with the same underlying objective: to be of real benefit to the species they cover, at the same time promoting compassion, understanding and respect between all animals (including human ones!)

Hubble & Hattie is the home of a range of books that cover all-things animal, produced to the same high quality of content and presentation as our motoring books, and offering the same great value for money.

www.hubbleandhattie.com

First published in April 2022 by Veloce Publishing Limited, Veloce House, Parkway Farm Business Park, Middle Farm Way, Poundbury, Dorchester, Dorset, DT1 3AR, England. Tel 01305 260068/fax 01305 250479/e-mail info@hubbleandhattie.com/web www.hubbleandhattie.com. ISBN: 978-1-787117-21-1 UPC: 6-36847-01721-7. © Anna Chelmicka & Veloce Publishing Ltd 2022. All rights reserved. With the exception of quoting brief passages for the purpose of review, no part of this publication may be recorded, reproduced or transmitted by any means, including photocopying, without the written permission of Veloce Publishing Ltd. Throughout this book logos, model names and designations, etc, have been used for the purposes of identification, illustration and decoration. Such names are the property of the trademark holder as this is not an official publication. Readers with ideas for books about animals, or animal-related topics, are invited to write to the editorial director of Veloce Publishing at the above address. British Library Cataloguing in Publication Data - A catalogue record for this book is available from the British Library. Typesetting, design and page make-up all by Veloce Publishing Ltd on Apple Mac. Printed and bound by Parksons Graphics, India

Contents

Introduction

I travel about Great Britain and Europe in my motorhome finding walks and exploring the countryside. When I began doing this my dog, Ruby, accompanied me; later, her daughter, Amber, joined us. Nowadays I am accompanied by my Labrador, Pearl, another well-behaved dog (I believe going to training classes is imperative).

Pearl is a very special dog because she is the direct descendant of my wonderful dog Ruby who helped me recover from a life-changing illness, and adjust to the changed circumstances in which I found myself. As I slowly adapted to my new situation, Ruby was always there, supporting and encouraging me. She was such a special dog and had such a profound effect on my life: my first book, *My Friend Ruby*, is about her.

It was with Ruby I began my travels in my motorhome; very much a novice. We learnt together. Ruby was so good. I began some research about camping with dogs, taking photographs and recording my findings. I submitted articles to various magazines, some of which were published. Seeing my work in print still gives me an enormous thrill.

I did not anticipate owning two dogs at the same time, but I so enjoyed the whole experience of Ruby having a litter that I did it again. Therefore, when she had her second litter I kept the darkest bitch. She was a rich golden colour that it seemed appropriate to call her Amber. Ruby and Amber were very close, and, for several years, the three of us – Ruby, Amber and I – had a wonderful time travelling about all over Europe; Switzerland, Italy, Poland, Germany, as well as France and Luxembourg. We also travelled extensively throughout Great Britain, looking for places we could all enjoy.

When Ruby died it took many months for Amber to adjust and she was never quite the same dog. The time she and I spent without Ruby was very special. We went out and about in the motorhome, tramping all over the countryside discovering some amazing places.

Just 18 months after Ruby went, at a routine vaccination visit the vet diagnosed Amber

Ruby and Amber at Pisa in Italy.

as terminally ill. So very quickly she changed from a fit, active dog effortlessly leaping stiles to an old, slow, sorrowful animal. What was I going to do? It seemed as if in just a short time I would be without a dog. I could not imagine that.

Then I received a marvellous message from the owner of one of Amber's puppies who had had her mated. The mating had been successful, and Amber would shortly be a grandmother. So it was, not long after Amber's diagnosis, I collected the darkest bitch from the litter. She was much lighter in colour than either her great-grandmother, Ruby, or her grandmother, Amber, so in keeping with the precious stone theme it seemed appropriate to call her Pearl, though her coat has darkened considerably over the years to the extent that now her name is a misnomer.

Amber teaching Pearl campsite etiquette.

She and Amber got on well together. Pearl copied her grandmother and just loved curling up with her. They had six months together. I believe having her granddaughter around prolonged Amber's life as teaching the puppy gave her an added interest. We even, all three of us, managed to go out in the motorhome to a couple of campsites and find some different walks, with Amber instructing Pearl in campsite etiquette.

Pearl and I have carried on the tradition established first with Ruby then with Amber, of travelling about in my motorhome exploring Great Britain and Europe, finding walks and enjoying the countryside. Just like her ancestors, Pearl enjoys our jaunts. Whenever I am preparing for a trip, just as Ruby and Amber did, she slips quietly into the motorhome to be certain she comes along.

Pearl enjoying the great British countryside.

We have discovered some amazing places, especially whilst researching for my previous book, *Wonderful walks from dog-friendly campsites throughout Great Britain*. It made me realize just how special the British landscape is, and how fortunate we are to be able to access so much of it. In this book Pearl and I continue to explore the fantastic British countryside.

Walking and motorhoming
(or camping and caravanning)

The hurly burly of modern life – especially in this technological age – can be stressful, but time in the countryside surrounded by nature is a perfect solution, as has been demonstrated in many studies. As Grace Grant says in her poem *Why Walk?* –

... no traffic/just fresh air/with varying landscapes ...
(2016, https://www.knowledge.me.uk/poems/why_walk.html)

Chilling out beside the motorhome, drink in hand, and wandering country paths with a four-legged companion sounds sublime, but considerable preparation is necessary to achieve this: a campsite has to be found and the journey planned.

The quest to find suitable campsites began the moment I first acquired my motorhome. One of the reasons I decided to get a motorhome was so that I could take my wonderful dog, Ruby, with me when travelling about. Camping with a motorhome seemed the perfect solution as she could come, too. As a consequence, what facilities were provided for dogs was a significant factor in ascertaining a good campsite.

At the time, with so many campsite books available and the added perk of exciting new technology in the fast burgeoning internet, I thought this would be easy. Yes, there were many references to dogs, but only with regard to them being welcome. Occasionally in the small print, mention was made of a dog exercise area but no other information was offered, and it was only by careful study of the description of various campsites, and reading between the lines, that I was able to find relevant detail. Then off I would go with Ruby, not only to visit different parts of the country, but also to check out the campsites to be found there.

It was very hit and miss. Sometimes there was nothing specific for dogs; it was just that the campsite allowed dogs on site. On other occasions dog exercise areas were provided, but these were equally as unpredictable: I recall one that was the size of a postage stamp (or seemed to be), for example. After only a few minutes of wandering around it, Ruby looked quizzically at me as if to say, "Okay, where do we go now?" Some sites have small wooded areas or large grassy fields with plenty of space for dogs of all sizes to walk and chase balls, whilst others have nothing specifically designated for dogs, but are near fields or parks where they can be exercised.

There are even campsites that provide washing facilities for dogs, so they can be cleaned up before entering the living space, which is useful, especially if the ground is wet and muddy. If my dog is dirty, however, I put some water in a bucket, wash her with a sponge, then rub her down with a towel. Labradors are easy to clean as they are 'Teflon' dogs: their short coats mean that dirt and wet comes off easily.

Unfortunately, it wasn't until I had arrived and booked into a campsite that I knew whether or not Ruby was going to be as well catered for as I was, and it was as a direct result of travelling with her that I began to do some research into campsite facilities for dogs. I developed the habit of booking sites at the last minute and for very short periods because of not knowing what facilities might be available, and on some occasions I found it was practical to stay for only a day or two and then move on because of the lack of amenities for my dog.

Not long after I started my investigations a new camping and caravanning magazine, *Out and About*, was launched. Realizing there was little reliable information regarding facilities for dogs on campsites, I submitted articles based upon my findings, and was thrilled when several were published. Unfortunately, after a couple of years the magazine folded; nevertheless I continued my research.

Having a dog – especially one as active as a Labrador – necessitates lots of walking, and so it was that Ruby re-ignited my interest in country walking, and I even, for a time, subscribed to the magazine *Country Walking*. Besides related articles the magazine published instructions for lots of walks of varying lengths, which hugely appealed to me although, regrettably, I did not do many of them. Why not? Well, firstly, because most of the walks were in popular walking areas, and finding a place to park a fairly large motorhome is often problematic. Secondly, breaking camp and preparing the motorhome for a journey, then having to drive back afterwards and re-pitch, rather spoils the outing.

I continued going to campsites and receiving the *Country Walking* magazine, but it seemed 'never the twain shall meet.' The solution appeared to be to create my own walks using an Ordnance Survey Map. As it had been many years since I had last used my map-reading skills. I needed to update them, and began by practising reading maps and finding my way about in familiar places.

I prepared several walks close to home using OS Maps, and, whilst things did not always go according to plan, this was an important learning experience, and I soon gained enough confidence to try out my newly-acquired skills in new and unfamiliar places.

During my research for magazine articles I noticed that some campsites were very close to footpaths and bridleways, so quite long walks seemed possible. Unfortunately, yet again, there was little information and few instructions about any walks in the locality of the campsites, even though in the intervening years the internet had improved enormously and now provided a mountain of information. The problems I encountered trying to find really good sites for Ruby were replicated trying to find sites close to walking trails. Again, while walks were often mentioned, more detailed information was rarely forthcoming until registering at a campsite, by which time, of course, this information – though useful – was too late.

This time my newly-acquired map reading skills and the internet were extremely useful. Once I had found a campsite that suited Ruby I put the location into the OS Maps search box to bring up the appropriate map, from which I could see what footpaths, bridleways and trails were nearby. It was really useful in helping me make an informed decision, but was very time-consuming and convoluted. Even then, the choice sometimes proved unsuitable. Footpaths might be so overgrown that they were unusable, or had simply disappeared. At other times the trail was on a minor road that was very busy and made for unpleasant walking. Occasionally, there were no stiles or gates, and accessing the route required scrambling over walls and fences. Every now and then the campsite was further away from the footpaths than appeared on the map.

Even so, I did find some excellent sites and lovely walks of varying lengths, and discovered parts of the country that were totally new to me. In the process I learned a lot and my map-reading skills hugely improved, giving me the confidence to be even more adventurous.

As my experience of camping with a dog increased, so my requirements from a campsite changed. Now, I not only wanted a campsite that suited me and my dog, I also wanted one near footpaths so that I could go for long walks through the countryside accompanied by my four-legged companion.

By this time I had two dogs – Ruby and her daughter, Amber – and we travelled about in the motorhome having a wonderful time exploring Great Britain. However, it still took a considerable amount of time and organization to ensure that the campsites we stayed at fulfilled our requirements satisfactorily. Again, I kept notes and took photographs of my findings.

Even though Ruby was quite old and not in the best of health she still enjoyed going out in the motorhome with Amber and me. The walks, though shorter, took longer. Eventually, in the May I was forced to make the sad decision to have her put to sleep ... now it was just me and Amber. To help us adjust to the huge loss we both felt I took Amber in the motorhome to new and different places, and we walked and walked and walked. It was just what we both needed. Fortunately, the weather was kind and Amber was fit, leaping nimbly over stiles and enjoying the outings. We discovered some amazing places.

It was whilst stopping for lunch at the top of a hill next to a trig point (a fixed surveying station used in geodetic surveying and other surveying projects in its vicinity), admiring the view, with Amber leaning against me, completely ignoring my food (very unusual in a Labrador), that I had a flash of inspiration. I would note down the route of the walks I did from the campsites and compile a set of directions accompanied by photographs, then submit them to relevant magazines.

In 2016 I was delighted when *MMM (Motorhome Monthly Magazine)* agreed to publish a monthly series of my campsite walks. The editor had a clear plan for how the set of articles would appear in the magazine, and the specifications were very precise, so required a substantial amount of work, but I thoroughly enjoyed the whole experience.

Seeing my work in print was exhilarating and exciting; even more so when Hubble and Hattie published my first walking book that, as well as containing many of the campsites and walks in *MMM,* includes additional trails from other campsites.

Amber and me – just feet and paws – having lunch at a trig point.
This was a lightbulb moment for me.

The book you are reading now also details walks from dog-friendly campsites, many of which are in counties not included in the first book. There is an added ingredient, however, in that all of the campsites are near at least one pub offering good food and a warm welcome.

I hope you enjoy my book, find it useful, and have as much fun as I did with all of my dogs – Ruby, Amber and Pearl – trying out the wonderful walks contained in it.

Happy walking!

Respecting the countryside

In Great Britain we are very lucky to have access to so much of the countryside: a consequence of the 1949 National Parks and Access to the Countryside Act, which many, many people were involved in ensuring was ratified. Its objectives are to protect the countryside and to ensure that it is free for all to enjoy; achieved with the establishment of National Parks and other agencies such as nature reserves.

As times and circumstances have changed, so, over the years, the Act has been modified. Nevertheless, the basic principles have remained the same.

As stipulated by the UK Government's 'Countryside and Rights of Way (CROW) Act 2000,' walkers have the right to –

- Access specified areas of the countryside for walking
- Use public roads and pavements or public rights of way such as footpaths and bridleways
- Use the 'right to roam' on open access land such as mountains and moors, etc
- Access private land if the landowner gives permission
- Access private land if there is a local tradition or right of access

See https://www.gov.uk/right-of-way-open-access-land for more detail about the exact entitlements and restrictions for walkers, horseriders, and outdoor users (and also Appendix i).

In Scotland the Outdoor Access Code is slightly different. The 'Land Reform (Scotland) Act' came into force in 2003, and established a statutory right of responsible access over most areas of land and inland water. The main points of the 'Scottish Outdoor Access Code (SOAC)' are –

- Take responsibility for your own actions
- Respect the interests of other people
- Care for the environment

Essentially, there are very few restrictions as to where you can walk, ride a bicycle, swim, canoe, kayak or wild camp in Scotland's countryside. The Code leaves it for individuals to use the countryside as they wish whilst respecting their surroundings, the land, people, and, most importantly, to leave it in perfect condition for others to also use (see Appendix i for details).

These extensive and, to my mind, amazing and unique rights over our land carry with them huge responsibilities, which are set out in the Country Code.

Shortly after the 1949 act was passed it was decided that officially formulated guidance was needed for those accessing the land, even though common sense mostly sufficed. So, in 1950, a Country Code was devised, which has been updated over the years, with the most recent modification in 2012.

When walking, please do observe the Country Code, which states –

RESPECT OTHER PEOPLE
- Consider the local community and other people when enjoying the outdoors
- Leave gates and property as you find them, and always try to follow paths and trails

PROTECT THE NATURAL ENVIRONMENT
- Leave no trace of your visit and take home your litter
- Keep dogs under effective control

ENJOY THE OUTDOORS
- Plan ahead and be prepared
- Follow advice and local signs

See Appendix i for detailed and inclusive countryside codes.

Enjoy the right we have to explore our wonderful, diverse countryside and appreciate it, but remember your responsibilities and adhere to the Country Code.

We also have the responsibility to keep ourselves safe. Though we do not have wild animals such as wolves (yet) or bears in Great Britain, there are dangers. The weather can, in an instant, change a pleasant outing into an emergency, especially if walking in the hills and more remote parts of the country. And accidents can happen. It is advisable to follow the motto of the Scouts and Guides and 'be prepared.'

The walks in this book are not especially challenging so it is easy to be prepared and stay safe. My suggestions are not definitive or applicable to all situations, and they will certainly not prevent accidents, though will help in this regard, and allow you to enjoy the walks more, hopefully.

Maps

Although there are maps of each walk in the book these are for general guidance only, and it is absolutely essential that they are used in conjunction with the relevant Ordnance Survey Map.

In today's digital age there are many ways of accessing OS Maps. I still buy and use the paper version and, as I have been walking all over Great Britain, I have a shelf full of Explorer Maps, many of which have become quite tatty with use. However, I do not find it necessary to buy the weatherproof versions as I rarely walk in the rain.

Paper maps should be used for several reasons –
- The walk can be seen in the context of surrounding locality
- If the view is extensive it is possible to identify distant landmarks with a map of a larger area
- It is possible to turn a paper map in the direction of the walk. Digital devices usually

automatically revert to a north/south orientation when the device is turned
- With a paper version there are no worries about the battery getting low
- Having a signal is not a necessity. In more remote areas, the lack of a signal is a fairly regular occurrence
- They are vital in case of emergencies, even if digital maps are preferred

Nowadays, OS Maps supplies not only paper maps but also digital versions, and provides a range of products and services to suit various devices: this is THE place to go for mapping needs.

To access OS Landranger and Explorer Maps digitally an annual subscription is necessary, which also allows OS Maps to be downloaded onto other devices via the OS Map App. The Map App is free but some of the features – such as Explorer and Landranger Maps – have to be purchased. Also available to purchase are dedicated GPS units with Landranger or Explorer Maps of the whole of the UK, together with a variety of accessories. More information about Ordnance Survey Maps and the services it provides can be found on the website (https://www.ordnancesurvey.co.uk/).

Surprisingly, Ordnance Survey Maps has a long history as part of the Board of Ordnance from way back in the 1700s during the reign of George III, providing detailed maps to the military that would be useful in times of war. There was a very real threat of invasion by Napoleon in the late 1700s, and the defending forces needed very detailed information about the south coast area of England.

It was in 1801 that the first one-inch-to-the-mile map was produced – of the county of Kent – and thus began mapping of the country using the effective Principle of Triangulation, which has resulted in trig points on the top of so many hills. It took many,

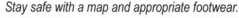

Stay safe with a map and appropriate footwear.

many years and a veritable army of people to produce the maps. Over time, other people and organizations discovered just how useful the maps were and, eventually, in the 1900s, maps were produced for the leisure market and general public. They became extremely popular, especially with walkers, and Ordnance Survey began producing leisure metric maps as early as the 1970s.

Today, Ordnance Survey Maps, or OS Maps, as the organisation has been re-branded, produces two kinds of detailed map for outdoor enthusiasts. The one with the purple cover is the Landranger Series with a scale of 1:50 000, which means that every 1cm on the map represents 500m on the ground. The series with the orange cover is the Explorer Map with a scale of 1: 25 000: every 1cm on the map is 250m on the ground, which is the same as 4cm on the map to 1km on the ground. The imperial equivalent is 2½in on the map to one mile on the ground. These Explorer Maps are by far the best for walking as they show more detail, including field boundaries.

The service that Ordnance Survey Maps provides is unique, and it continues to embrace new technology to improve the products it is able to offer the general public. It is important that we support OS Maps so that it can continue with this work.

Mobile phone

Nowadays, mobile phones greatly reduce risk if used properly, especially for walkers. As a lone walker it is a vital piece of equipment. When setting out, make sure your phone is fully charged, and be aware that some places have only a weak signal or even none at all. If you use apps on the phone, such as mapping or fitness monitoring, be especially mindful of battery usage. Various options exist to ensure battery life. For example, you can carry a power bank (a portable charger designed to recharge your electronic gadgets when on the move), some of which will allow you to recharge your phone two or even more times before they themselves need to be recharged. If excursions are inclined to be long, the weight and physical size of the power bank is a factor. Alternatively, you could take along a dedicated phone with a pay-as-you-go sim card just for calls and texts.

So, keep safe. Take a mobile phone with you with sufficient battery charge to last for your excursion, irrespective of the length of the outing and size of the group.

Clothing

Although expensive specialist attire is not necessary for general walking, it is essential to wear sensible clothing. Trousers are a better option than shorts, even if it is hot, for protection against prickly plants and stinging nettles. These should be comfortable and, if possible, of a light material so that, should they get wet, they will not become too heavy and will dry quickly (unlike most denim). It is best to wear several layers of thinner garments as this is easier to adjust for a sudden spell of warm weather. I find it useful to take a wool hat, scarf and gloves in case the temperature suddenly drops; it's surprising how much these help. Of course, rain gear is nearly always a requirement as there are often rain clouds just over the horizon.

The one thing that is vital is appropriate footwear. Bespoke walking boots or shoes are essential, as these support the foot and have a good grip: crucial for muddy and uneven surfaces. Most outdoor shops sell a range of specialized walking footwear, ranging from the incredibly expensive to the reasonably priced.

Check the weather forecast

Some people are of the opinion that Great Britain doesn't have climate, only weather, because conditions change so much; not just day-to-day but hour-to-hour. Even though walking in this country is generally a safe, everyday pastime, it can, on occasion, turn into an extremely unpleasant and even dangerous activity if the weather should become inclement. I do not like walking in the rain and mist, and do too much of this type of walking on a regular basis with my dog. I much prefer it to be clear and, if possible, sunny, when I can see more and really appreciate the variety and beauty of the countryside.

Nowadays, with access to a range of weather forecast apps and programmes for various devices, it is much easier to ascertain the weather hour-by-hour as opposed to daily forecasts. Also, as technology has enabled the gathering of more data and made tracking of weather patterns easier, so the forecasts have become more accurate.

Before setting out, check the weather. Too often people venture out unprepared, and mountain rescue teams or the coastguard have to be called out as a result. On two occasions when I have stayed at Glen Nevis Campsite at the foot of Ben Nevis I have witnessed possible emergency incidents, one of which even involved a helicopter hovering dangerously close to the mountainside. I have to confess to it being thrilling to watch, like a film.

If staying at Glen Nevis Campsite, do go down the road to the Ben Nevis visitor centre, which is unlike any other. Extremely interesting and informative, with the emphasis on being safe outdoors, it has a section on maps and navigating, the weather, and also appropriate clothing. There is also a large section about the mountain rescue teams, which are made up of volunteers who go out in all conditions to find walkers who get into difficulties. I was astounded to discover how many times they are called out; not only to Ben Nevis but also generally. To avoid being a mountain rescue statistic, assess conditions before setting out. Should you need assistance it is extremely helpful to all concerned if your precise location is known: easily ascertained with the OS Map and what3words apps, which give an accurate grid reference for the emergency services to use.

Control of dogs

Great Britain has another exceptional tradition, which is to allow dogs access to so many places with so few restrictions: it is not like this in many other countries. It is therefore the responsibility of all dog owners to ensure they have control over their animals, do not annoy or upset others, endanger livestock, or in any way jeopardize this freedom.

Owners need to help their dog be confident and relaxed with other dogs not known to them: at the very least they should be able to tolerate passing dogs. This is essential at campsites and on narrow footpaths. Sometimes, space is less than ideal, and dogs have to pass quite close to each other. I find it distressing when dogs react aggressively, barking ferociously and snarling as Pearl and I pass by along the route. On the other hand it is wonderful when Pearl finds a new companion to play with.

It is generally recognized as a necessity to have a dog on a lead at certain times – for example, near livestock; especially sheep. When it comes to larger animals, how a dog is managed depends on the circumstances. My present dog, Pearl, thinks horses are large dogs and wants to play with them, so she becomes rather skittish, which is not ideal behaviour. Ruby, however, was frightened of them as her first close encounter with a horse was beside an electric fence that she accidentally touched. As a consequence she was wary of all horses and stayed well clear.

Again, the situation with regard to cattle depends upon circumstances. I have been reassured many times that cattle are harmless except when cows have calves, and one accidentally gets between mother and offspring. Generally, the presence of a dog merely arouses their curiosity. Unfortunately, I have had some frightening experiences: having ten or more cows crowding round is rather alarming, and it is not unknown for walkers to be trampled to death by a herd of cows.

Advice is conflicting. On the occasions I have found myself in a field of high-spirited horses or cows I have quickly moved towards the edge of the field by a fence or hedge, because the self-preservation instincts of animals causes most cows and horses to slow down so as not to injure themselves by charging into the hedge or fence. This usually gives some space and time to move rapidly to the exit. I have scrambled over many a gate and stile, shoving my dog ahead of me, and I am extremely cautious when I encounter livestock. It is obviously important that you know your dog very well when out and about. It is also extremely important to be able to control him, both on- and off-lead. In my opinion the best way to really understand and know your dog, as well as to learn how best to control him, is with training.

Training should be a continual, ongoing process, and not just reserved for when he is a puppy. I took Ruby to classes every week for most of her life, and she loved them. She really enjoyed doing all the exercises and learning new tricks, even when she was quite old. Pearl is very young, and she, too, likes attending her classes. Like Ruby she is clever but a very different dog. She loves agility; especially running through the tunnels. Because my dogs are so good and well-behaved I feel confident about taking them with me in the motorhome and exploring the countryside. I have travelled extensively throughout Great Britain, and even been to several countries in mainland Europe.

Having a well-trained dog who reliably responds to cues makes outings more pleasurable for both of you.

Another responsibility of dog owners which I am happy to say is usually adhered to, is removal and correct disposal in an appropriate waste bin of dog poo. Unfortunately, recently, it has become commonplace for bags of dog faeces to be either tossed into the hedge, hung on the branch of a tree, or left on the side of tracks and footpaths. A disgusting and most objectionable habit. Firstly, it is an environmental act of vandalism: not only does it spoil the countryside but it takes many years for the bag and its contents to decay, even if the bag is biodegradable. Secondly, it is extremely selfish and inconsiderate. There is no provision for these bags to be collected and properly disposed of, and quite rightly there are few volunteers for such an unpleasant task.

So as not to walk several miles carrying a bag of dog poo, which no one likes to do, the 'stick and flick' method is recommended as an option. The idea is to find a stick and flick the poo out of the way into a verge or hedgerow. This is the method now recommended by the National Trust to visitors on some places it manages. This is not an ideal remedy but is far better than bags of poo decorating the trees and hedges, and littering the countryside.

With so many people taking their dogs with them when walking, a 'Dog Walking Code of Conduct' is becoming customary. The Kennel Club has always offered such advice (see Appendix i), and nowadays other organizations are reminding dog owners of their responsibilities. The most succinct and inclusive code I have come across is that advocated by the Pembrokeshire Coast National Park in the events magazine *Coast to Coast* –

LOOK AFTER YOUR DOG

- Keep your dog close and in sight: on the lead if necessary, and always if he won't recall on cue
- Ensure your dog wears a collar, identification disc, and is microchipped
- Don't allow your dog near cliff edges, rough seas or strong tidal currents
- Think of the weather – on warm/sunny days cars and beaches can be too hot for dogs

LOOK AFTER OUR COAST AND COUNTRYSIDE

- Always pick up your dog's poo: this is a legal requirement on beaches and places where people walk and play
- Take home your bagged dog waste or put it in a litter bin
- Ensure your dog is on a lead near livestock, and doesn't approach or chase birds or other wildlife
- When cattle are present keep your dog on a lead and away from the cows
- Follow signs and abide by bylaws such as dog restrictions on beaches
- Keep your dog on the path when walking in the countryside

BE CONSIDERATE OF OTHERS

- Show respect for other people and their dogs
- Keep your dog away from horseriders, cyclists and picnics
- Don't allow your dog to bark excessively

Remember that not everyone likes dogs, especially small children. For me, having an obedient four-legged companion adds an extra dimension to my walking. It is really enjoyable discovering the many wonderful places in this country. Having been given so many rights in regard to exploring the countryside, we must all make sure we accept and fulfil our responsibilities.

Campsites

Just as each person is unique and yet still part of the human race, so campsites come in all shapes and sizes, are distinctively different, and yet have a commonality. At one end of the spectrum are those sites that are just a flat field with maybe a tap, whilst at the other extreme are the all-singing, all-dancing sites providing a whole range of amenities, sometimes even including fitness centre and spa facilities, which are more like holiday parks. However, most campsites fall somewhere between these extremes.

Two main organizations cater specifically for anyone who likes camping: the Camping and Caravanning Club and the Caravan and Motorhome Club. Over the years, these clubs have grown from very small beginnings to the large organizations they are today, offering their members a whole range of services. Both clubs own and run a considerable number of campsites located throughout the country, which have a specific, easily recognised modus operandi. This has resulted in well-designed sites with premium facilities for showering, washing dishes, and doing the laundry, etc, in a neatly-kept and attractive setting. The wardens are always helpful and efficient. These campsites are usually the yardstick by which all others are judged, and even though they rarely have additional facilities such as bars, cafés or swimming pools, they generally represent excellent value for money.

As campsite requirements are particular to each individual, so reviews are not always helpful, whereas facts are, and I have endeavoured to provide factual information about each campsite. Because I have a dog, the suitability of a site for her is of paramount importance. Also, as we both like walking (especially my dog), it is also vital that there are footpaths close by to allow us to explore the countryside. These concerns occasionally supersede my own requirements.

What I look for in a campsite, in order of importance –
- Dogs are welcome
- A flattish site for the motorhome. I generally prefer this to be grass, though this can become so soft in wet weather the motorhome becomes bogged down and stuck: not a pleasant experience
- Footpaths handy to explore the countryside
- Electric hook-up so I have the luxury of using my electrical appliances, especially the heater in the winter and, of course, to charge my various devices. As technology develops so there is more and more demand for electricity. A solution for those who like 'wild camping' is a solar panel. I prefer the ease of an existing electric supply

- Toilet block so I don't have to empty my cassette so often
- Showers that are more spacious than mine in the van
- Wifi or mobile signal so the next stage of the trip can be planned

Then there are those amenities on-site or nearby that increase the comfort quotient –
- A dog exercise area large enough to allow a stretch first thing in the morning and last thing at night, or to chase a ball or frisbee
- A shop where provisions can be replenished
- A pub (an essential requirement for this book)
- A café to indulge in delicious cakes
- A TV connection (on occasion an enjoyable distraction)

Finally, there are those places, usually called 'Holiday Parks,' which provide a variety of entertainment facilities, such as –
- Swimming pool
- Children's play area
- Fitness centre
- Spa facilities
- Horseriding
- Crazy golf
- Evening entertainment such as bingo or live shows
- Animal petting centre

The range of amenities and facilities found on campsites is vast, thus making each place quite distinctive. One of the pleasures of travelling about is seeing how the campsite description corresponds to reality, and discovering the special characteristics of each site.

This book is slightly different from the first volume, *Wonderful walks from dog-friendly campsites throughout Great Britain*, inasmuch as the campsites are close to some kind of pub/restaurant. These vary as enormously as do the campsites: some are part of big commercial sites, whilst others just happen to be located next to or near a campsite. A few are a short walk away; sometimes across the fields, along a quiet road, or via a pavement.

Most of the campsites alongside pubs are classified as CL (Certificated Location) sites, which are affiliated to and endorsed by the Caravan and Motorhome Club, or CS (Certificated Site) linked to the Camping and Caravanning Club. To use these sites you have to be a member of the relevant club as these are small, private, five-unit sites run by members for members. They are often located in secluded places where access is via narrow country roads, making access difficult if not impossible for larger units. For this reason, some campsites limit the size of motorhomes and caravans that they will accept; so check this when booking, However, many of these types of site are more favourable for walking.

Some of them are very basic, whilst others have all the bells and whistles. The sites selected have my basic requirements as outlined above – dog-friendly, flat, electric, etc – though usually wifi is only available in the pub. Being able to nip 'next door' for a drink and

Campsites come in all shapes and sizes.

meal with your four-legged companion makes these sites especially attractive, particularly after a day's walking.

Fees for campsites are just as variable as the campsites themselves. Many places have different rates for different times of the year – high, medium and low season – with even a special high rate for bank holidays. Some have a concessionary 'mid-week' or OAP rate, and then there are those few sites that charge a straightforward flat rate.

How the fees are constructed also varies. Some, such as the two big clubs, charge separately for each facility – pitch, adult, electric, etc – which is best for sole travellers like me. Other places charge as a package: pitch + 2 adults. Sometimes the package includes other amenities such as electric hook-up and TV. Of course, campsite fees change year-to-year, particularly if they have upgraded their amenities. This is all very confusing. The only way to be certain of the charges is to check at the time of booking.

Then there is, for me, the issue of charges for dogs. Many campsites – including all of the 300+ sites that are run by the two main clubs – do not charge. I cannot understand why fees are as high as £3.00 per dog per night in some instances. Then there is the restriction on number of dogs campsites will accept, which also varies considerably. Some will allow a maximum of two dogs per unit whilst others have no restrictions at all. Again, check when booking.

I have noticed a recent trend for what is usually referred to as 'super' or 'service' pitches, which is generally a hardstanding with all services supplied to it. So, on the area's perimeter will be a water tap, electric hook-up, TV connection, wifi signal and waste drain.

Obviously, there is an extra charge for such pitches. As with campsites that provide swimming pools or bars, etc, these additional provisions are an enjoyable luxury, but not all of which I require.

I am happy with well-managed and maintained resources such as those provided by the 'club' campsites. Not all of the campsites I visited were of this standard, but they did all have electric hook-up, toilets and showers, whilst a

The additional ingredient of a nearby pub.

few had additional facilities such as a shop, etc. Similarly, the facilities for dogs varied, and Pearl has appraised these in her section, Pearls of wisdom.

With all the hustle and bustle of modern life it is a pleasure to experience a simpler, slower pace for a time, and be able to watch the flowers grow, hear the birds sing, and gaze at the sunsets as they splash the sky with colour ...

Finding the walks

The campsites are located throughout the country. Great Britain is divided into seven regions –

- Wales
Ceredigion, Denbighshire, Montgomeryshire

- North East
Durham, Lincolnshire, Norfolk, West Yorkshire

- North West
Cheshire, Cumbria, Lancashire

- Central
Leicestershire, Warwickshire, Worcestershire

- South East
Kent, East Sussex, Suffolk

- South West
Devon, Dorset, Gloucestershire, Hampshire

- Scotland
Aberdeenshire, Argyll and Bute, Dumfries and Galloway

The three campsites from each region are selected from different counties. I have included a couple of extra campsites because they are particularly special.

The book comprises 23 campsites with detailed instructions for 46 walks. Each of the chapters is a region of Great Britain, and the walks are in alphabetical order of the county in which the campsites are located.

First, there is a brief summary of the unique characteristics of the county, followed by a description of the campsite and the pub. Then there is the most important section: Pearls of wisdom, detailing what my dog thinks of the campsite, walks and pub.

Following this are directions for the walks. First, the short walk of between 4-6 miles (6-10km), which is divided into four sections, then come the directions for the longer walk of 8-11 miles (13-18km), which is divided into 8 sections.

The final section is a brief account of the activities and attractions in the immediate vicinity, within an approximate 10ml (16km) radius of the campsite. It may be possible to walk to some of these, although there is not always a convenient walking route.

The campsites and walks have been purposely selected to illustrate the huge variety and diversity to be found in Great Britain, and include campsites with basic facilities as well as some with a range of amenities. Similarly, the walks traverse a range of landscapes.

All of the walks in this book are possible with dogs, and if they are well-behaved the jaunts are easier and more enjoyable. Dogs need to be agile to manage the stiles, fences and walls, and there is the very occasional 'sheep-proof' stile which may require a helping haul and shove for them to get over if they are too big to lift.

These walks are not particularly challenging as most of the routes are along tracks and across fields. However, a reasonable degree of fitness is necessary, as is a moderate level of stamina, as there are stiles and gates to climb over and some quite steep hills. Consequently, these walks are not suitable for pushchairs and wheelchairs. As for children, parents need to decide which walks are appropriate for their child.

This book can be used on various trips –

- A weekend break to just one campsite, and doing the walks from that campsite

- Longer trips of about a week, exploring a region and visiting all three campsites and doing the six walks

- An extended expedition, visiting several regions and either doing all of the walks in each, or selecting just one campsite from which to walk and so experience a more in-depth taste of that region

However you use the book, please keep in mind that it contains only a selection of walks available from campsites.

Appendix i states in full the various Countryside Codes.

Appendix ii contains essential information for all of the campsites, such as contact details, directions, etc, and charges are correct at the time of publication.

Walks in Wales
(Ceredigion, Denbighshire, Montgomeryshire)

Ceredigion – real Wales
OS MAP EXPLORER 213 ABERYSTWYTH & CWM RHEIDOL

During the latter part of the 20th century the boundaries and names of many British counties were revised; Ceredigion was one of these. Initially, it was known as the county of Cardiganshire, but then was incorporated into the new county of Dyfed. Later, it was reinstated but with a name change to Ceredigion.

Ceredigion is a rural county but with a long coastline round Cardigan Bay of more than 50 miles (80km). With cliffs, coves, beaches and rock pools there is plenty to explore, and many of the coastal towns and villages have small coastal harbours once used for

The 'Green Desert,' with the Cambrian Mountains in the distance.

fishing or shipbuilding. Most of Wales' boats were built in Cardiganshire. Nowadays, the harbours are used to launch wildlife boat trips, spotting, among other things, the dolphins who frequent the area. The stunning coastal scenery is accessible via the Ceredigion coastal path that runs from Cardigan to Machynlleth. The southern part of the coastal path includes places frequented by the Welsh poet Dylan Thomas, and was the inspiration for his play *Under Milk Wood*.

Most of Ceredigion's settlements are located around Cardigan Bay, because the Cumbrian Mountains that run north to south down the middle of Wales overflow into the eastern edge of the county. This part of central Wales is known as the 'Green Desert of Wales' because it is so remote and inaccessible, with few roads and a small population. The amazing scenery makes for perfect for hiking, wild-camping and stargazing, and somewhere to experience peace and quiet.

Squeezed between the sea and the mountains, the county is rather isolated, and regarded as somewhat of a backwater. As a result, many significant historical happenings have had minimal impact – the Industrial Revolution, for example – but this proved useful during World War II when various important and sensitive enterprises were relocated to Ceredigion, as it was considered one of the safest places in Great Britain. The Queen's Hotel in Aberystwyth (now Swyddfa Sir) was the RAF Headquarters, and items from various national collections were stored in the National Library of Wales in Aberystwyth.

It is here, in this secluded county, that many of the traditions and customs of Wales survive, and with many of its residents being Welsh speakers, Ceredigion is regarded as the centre of Welsh culture, with Aberystwyth the capital.

Agriculture has been and still is important in Ceredigion, with dairy farming and some fishing along the coast, and sheep farming and some forestry inland. Of course, Aberystwyth University hugely enhances the region: tourism is vital to the economy of the area but there is fierce competition from the northern bulge of the Cambrian Mountains – Snowdonia and the southern spur of the Brecon Beacons – both of which are synonymous with Wales. The area has much to offer in this respect: walking, cycling, horseriding, sailing, and sea-fishing. I found the walking fabulous as it was so quiet and peaceful ... except for the noisy sheep!

Ceredigion may be somewhat overshadowed by surrounding counties, but is, nevertheless, a hidden gem.

CAMPSITE – WOODLANDS CARAVAN PARK

The hillside location of this campsite has been cleverly terraced so that each level is a separate self-contained section. On the lower terraces are the static caravans; then the administration block with a shop and café. The middle terrace is the entrance to the 400-acre sheep farm – so the baaing of sheep is particularly evident on occasion, especially at feeding time – and the top section is reserved for tourers. There are hardstanding pitches for bigger units, and also a large grassed area where smaller units and tents can choose to set up. This, together with picnic tables scattered about, creates a friendly, informal atmosphere.

The facilities block was completed in 2014 and looks really modern, though was

The Woodlands Campsite tucked into the hillside next to the sheep farm.

closed during my visit due to Covid regulations. There are walks of different lengths directly from the campsite, mostly over the adjacent farm. Though this is a large campsite, it is spacious and efficiently run.

Pub – Hafod Hotel

To comply with Covid regulations the hotel had set up an imaginative outside seating area in the lay-by on the opposite side of the road, where drinks and food were served.

Other refreshment facilities

Woodlands Tea Room

Normally available is breakfast, lunch and tea but, during my visit, a limited takeaway menu was the only option. The attached gift shop was also closed.

Two Hoots Tea Room

This is located in the station. Again, menu options were limited.

Pearls of Wisdom 🐎

Wow! Oodles of space; looks terrific. I hope we can start exploring soon. But wait ... what's that I hear? Sounds like .... baaing. Sheep ... is that sheep? I do hope not, they are such funny creatures: sometimes they dash away; other times they shadow me in a big group, stamping their feet irritably. Whenever we walk in a field that has sheep in it I am on a lead – not my preference, of course, but essential. Yes, there were a lot of sheep, but as there are so many paths to walk we found quite a few sheep-free ones, luckily!

Short walk – Panoramic stroll

Distance: 6mi (9.6km)

More wonderful walks from dog-friendly campsites

The Hafod Hotel opposite the lay-by.

Duration: 2.5hr (Easy)
Terrain: Footpaths, tracks, fields, gates, roads (mostly quiet), stiles, some gentle climbs

Section 1: 1.5mi (2.4km)
- Exit campsite via reception out to A4120
- Turn left along road over bridge, round right-hand bend past hotel to railway station
- Turn left along tarmac drive just before Chocolate Cabin shop
- Follow drive, taking right fork and passing houses on right
- Take right fork again, over stile in fence on right into field
- Turn left, keeping close to fence on left, then bear right, skirting copse on left to way-marker

Panoramic stroll route

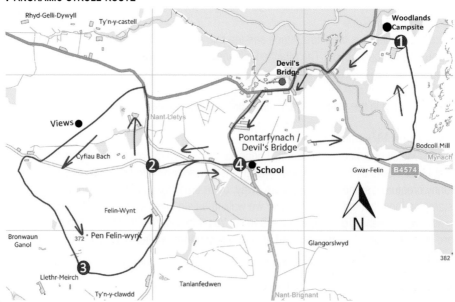

- Take right fork to way-marker by tree
- Turn left up steep slope onto wide, grassy track
- Turn right and follow track around edge of field, and through gate out to minor road by school on left
- Turn right to junction with B4343
- Turn left along minor road signposted 'Trisant'
- Follow road, taking left fork, turning right at bridle path, signposted, at next junction

Section 2: 1.5mi (2.4km)
- Continue along downhill track to road
- Straight on along road to A4120
- Continue straight ahead along main road, turning left in 50yd (45m) through gate onto track
- Follow stony track to corner, keeping close to fence on left
- Bear right uphill through gate in fence
- Keep bearing right, climbing uphill
- Bear left along wide footpath to way-marker
- Follow path along top of hill, keeping close to fence on right (views), through gate, over stile, through side garden of house on right to stony track
- Straight ahead along track to minor road by white house
- Turn right along road, then left through gate onto stony track
- Follow stony track round right-hand bend, keeping close to fence on left, passing mobile mast on right: through gate; downhill through second gate

Section 3: 1.5mi (2.4km)
- Turn right along track going around hill on left
- Bear right off track at white house on left, up slope through gate at top
- Follow path downhill through three gates onto road
- Turn left along road, turning right through gate between trees, signposted
- Bear left downhill, round to left through gate, over track through gate opposite into field
- Bear right across field, then through gate into next field
- Cross field to right corner, through kissing gate out to road
- Turn right along road, follow round left-hand bend to school

Section 4: 1.5mi (2.4km)
- Take path to left of school through gate
- Follow path round edge of field with school on right, keeping close to fence on right; through gate onto stony track
- Take right fork past buildings on left
- Continue along track through three gates
- Turn left at fence corner, down slope and over stile onto driveway
- Turn right through gate to road
- Continue up road past pink house on right
- Turn left at wide track going downhill

- Take left fork in 50yd (46m) onto narrow grass track, signposted
- Follow path downhill through woods and over footbridge
- Continue along path, way-marker, now going steeply uphill and over stile into field
- Straight ahead, still climbing to wide, stony track, over stile on right onto another stony track
- Follow track round left-hand bend through gate
- Turn right through another gate into campsite

LONG WALK – MOUNTAIN TASTER
Distance: 7mi (11.2km)
Duration: 3.5hr (Challenging in places)
Terrain: Long, steady climbs up and down, short steep climbs both ways, tracks, steps, kissing gates, gates, stiles (mostly sheep-proof), footpaths (some narrow and uneven). Not the usual long walk because it's more demanding

Pearl waiting to cross the bridge in the wood.

Section 1: 1mi (1.6km)
- Exit campsite via track in right corner of touring field, passing red telephone box on left; through gate
- Cross field, through gate opposite, down slope across stream, over stile opposite into woods
- Turn right along footpath, keeping corner then down to track
- Turn left along track, then sharp left again at fence corner
- Continue up slope to gate in fence on left
- Bear right up field to way-marker by tree
- Turn right to follow path uphill (steep) to wooden post (rotten) on skyline
- Continue along narrow footpath, taking left fork heading towards another wooden way-marker on skyline
- Straight ahead along narrow footpath to hill edge (amazing views!)

Section 2: 0.75mi (1.2km)
- Bear left along narrow path going downhill to way-marker by junction
- Turn left along path round hill on left, then over stile into wood
- Continue straight ahead along path over stile
- Turn right down to stony track

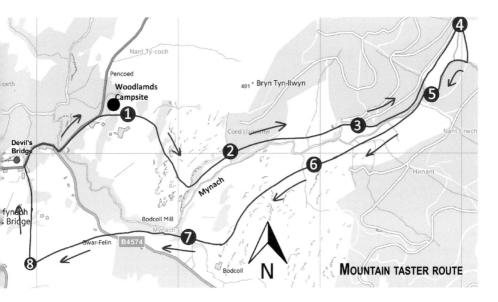

Mountain Taster Route

- Turn left along track
- Turn right before gate across track, through small gate of house on right into the garden
- Follow path around house through gate ahead and past building to track between stone walls
- Turn left over stile in fence on left
- Follow path up steep climb (short) round to right and left over stile onto wide, stony track

Section 3: 1.25mi (2km)
- Continue along track through woods

Section 4: 0.5mi (0.8km)
- Turn right off track over stile in fence and onto footpath
- Follow path down steps to left and right over footbridge
- Continue along path ahead, going slightly uphill towards trees and over footbridge

Section 5: 1mi (1.6km)
- Turn right through gate onto path
- Follow path, keeping close to river on right, through a second and then third gate, then gates four and five in quick succession out onto hillside

Section 6: 1mi (1.6km)
- Straight ahead across hillside away from river and through gate
- Follow path, keeping close to fence on right as it winds up and down the hill, then through another gate onto a stony track

The valley of upper Afon Rheidol.

- Continue along track, this time passing a gate on right but through second gate on right into field
- Straight ahead, keeping close to fence on right to river in right corner, then through gate over footbridge

Section 7: 0.75mi (1.2km)
- Follow footpath diversion to right onto wide track; through gate out to road
- Turn right along road through second gate on left just past pink house
- In 25yd (22.8m) turn left up slope and over stile into field, signposted
- Continue up slope; sharp right at fence corner onto wide, stony track
- Follow track through three gates

Section 8: 0.75mi (1.2km)
- Turn right into field just past copse, descending slope to way-marker
- Turn right to follow path towards fence, skirting copse on right
- Turn left to continue along path beside fence and over stile in fence on right onto stony track
- Turn left along track, passing houses, to A4120 (refreshments available at various outlets along main road)
- Turn right along road, passing through village to campsite entrance

IN THE VICINITY
BIRDWATCHING
In this part of Wales raptor birds are commonplace. These are birds, such as kites and buzzards, who hunt live prey for food, and, of course, the red kites feeding displays at the Forest Visitor Centre (see opposite) guarantees a sighting.

CYCLING
There are many cycle trails in the area as the roads are quiet. Several start at the Forest Visitor Centre.

Devil's Bridge Falls

This bridge is important because it is one of the few places where the Afon Rheidol can be crossed, and is so unusual and spectacular that it has long been a popular tourist attraction: a small settlement has grown up around it.

The bridge – which spans the spectacular waterfall where the River Mynach plunges 300 feet (90 metres) to the River Rheidol below – is very unusual because it is, in fact, three bridges, one on top of the other. Apparently, it was not considered necessary to demolish the previous two, even though they were considered unsafe. The top bridge is the most recent, built of iron in 1909; the stone one beneath it was built in 1753, and the bottom one was built in 1075 – by the devil, according to legend. He must have been very busy as there are over 20 such bridges attributed to him throughout Europe! Maybe this explains how he came to be outsmarted by an old woman ...?

Visitors have been coming to see the falls for centuries; some of them, such as William Wordsworth, well-known figures. Nowadays, the bridges and falls can be viewed from the nature trails that criss-cross the gorge, but be aware that the walks are challenging, with hundreds of steps. Dogs can accompany their owners but do need to be obedient – and fit.

Bwlch Nant yr Arian Forest Visitor Centre

Also close to the campsite and Llywernog mine is this visitor centre, owned and managed by the Forestry Commission and part of the National Forest for Wales. Though it is renowned for the regular feeding of red kites, it is also the focus of a range of activities including walking, cycling of all kinds, horseriding, and so much more.

Rheidol Reservoir, Staatkraft Visitor Centre

Also situated in the Rheidol Valley, just over 5 miles (8km) from the campsite, is Rheidol Reservoir and power station; owned and operated by the hydro-power company Statkraft. Renewable energy has been provided by this complex since 1962, using the geography of the surrounding mountains and rain. The interaction between the environment and energy needs are intricate and incredible. Entrance to the visitor centre and tours is

One flight of the many steps in the Devil's Bridge gorge.

free, although guided tours have to be pre-arranged. Unfortunately, dogs are not allowed.

THE MAGIC OF LIFE BUTTERFLY HOUSE
This is situated just 5 miles (8km) along the Rheidol Valley, close to a railway station. Here, you can walk among hundreds of butterflies in the tropical displays, or be inspired by the butterfly-friendly plants in the wildlife garden. Dogs are welcome.

VALE OF RHEIDOL RAILWAY
Take a trip to Aberystwyth on the Vale off Rheidol railway, which terminates at Devil's Bridge. This is a unique way to see the spectacular Rheidol Valley, especially since the recent major maintenance work.

The line was built in 1902 to transport goods from the lead mines and forestry businesses in the Rheidol Valley. It was an amazing feat of engineering in its day as the route drops around 700ft (213m), twisting and turning, to Aberystwyth. The train continued to run even when the mines closed due to its popularity with people wishing to visit Devil's Bridge. In 1989 it was sold, and is now a heritage charity.

The journey to Devil's Bridge is 12 miles (19.3km) long, and takes about an hour. Tickets can be obtained online or from the booking office at either Devil's Bridge or Aberystwyth. As in days past, there are different classes of carriage. The charge for dogs is £3.00 for the day in third class only. Bicycles can also be taken on the train if space is reserved in advance.

SILVER MOUNTAIN EXPERIENCE
In 1742, during the reign of George III, silver was discovered at Llywernog, just 4.5 miles (7.2km) away from the campsite on the A44. The original mine was a simple affair that gradually grew, burrowing ever-deeper into the mountain. Its heyday was the early 1800s but, by 1910, it had become unprofitable and was abandoned, becoming derelict. In 1973 it was reborn as a mining museum, and has been carefully restored: now offering a fascinating insight into the lives of early miners. Dogs are not allowed underground on the mine tours, although well-behaved, social dogs are welcome above ground.

CAMBRIAN SAFARIS
These excursions provide the opportunity to explore the 'Green Desert' of central Wales in Land Rovers that provide access to the remote parts of the area. A range of guided tours are on offer, from two hours to the whole day.

YSBYTY CYNFYN CHURCH
This small, unusual church is only a mile north of the campsite, tucked away next to an old mine. Its history is somewhat hazy as records are relatively recent, and it is assumed to be older because of the standing stones that surround it, and are built into the walls: it was even once occupied by the Knights Hospitaller (the Order of Knights of the Hospital of Saint John of Jerusalem). Nowadays, it is on the Heritage Trail of Ceredigion's Peaceful Places.

ABERYSTWYTH

This seaside university town is situated at Cardigan Bay, and is easy to get to from Devil's Bridge via the Vale of Rheindol Railway. Aberystwyth is a lively place with plenty to see and do, such as the Camera Obscura, Arts Centre, and National Library of Wales. For the more active there is the Cliff Railway, a hill fort at Pen Dinas where there is a monument to the Duke of Wellington, and, of course, Aberystwyth Castle.

Denbighshire – offbeat North Wales
OS MAP EXPLORER 264 VALE OF CLWYD/DYFFRYN CLWYN

For such a compact county its range of scenery and landscape is surprising, and the most significant features are the rivers that flow through the area. The largest is the River Clwyd and its many tributaries, which flows south to north through the centre of the county, collecting other, smaller rivers on the way and eventually flowing into the Irish Sea at Rhyl, where there is a large, sandy beach that stretches for almost 2 miles (3.2km).

The River Clwyd has carved out a wide, fertile valley – the Vale of Clwyd. Mostly rural, the typical patchwork of fields separated by hedgerows underlines the importance of agriculture in the area. Slicing across the south of the county is the River Dee on its way to Chester in England.

Bordering the Vale of Clwyd to the west are the uplands of Mynydd Hiraethog, or Denbigh Moors as they are more commonly known. Located here are two reservoirs, a forest where red squirrels are to be seen, Gwylfa Hiraethog – the ruins of an historic hunting lodge – and the highest pub in Wales, The Sportsman's Arms.

East of the Vale of Clwyd, rising steeply from the valley is the Clwydian Range of hills, stretching from the coastal town of Prestatyn in the north to the River Dee in the south. With amazing views, imposing hill forts, and a carpet of purple heather, the hills are exceptional; so much so that the region, together with the Upper Dee Valley in the south of the county, has been designated an Area of Outstanding Natural Beauty (AONB). Contrary to expectation, this happened only recently: the Clwydian Range in the summer of 1985, which then grew to include the Upper Dee Valley in 2011.

Denbighshire occupies a small area of northeast Wales, and stretches down the valley from the popular seaside towns of Rhyl and Prestatyn, hemmed in between the hills and uplands to the River Dee. The most densely populated area is along the coast, with smaller, rural settlements dotted about inland.

One such place is Dyserth, lying on the lower slopes of Moel Hiraddug in the shadow of the Clwydian Range. Although Dyserth has actually stayed in the same location for centuries, it has, since 1974, 'wandered' around North Wales as a result of various Parliamentary Acts. Originally in Flintshire, it initially moved to Clwyd, then in 1996 to Denbighshire, its current locality.

Like many of the towns and villages in the county, Dyserth has a long and interesting history, and is mentioned in the Domesday Book, as is a nearby mill, so obviously the village had been a thriving community at one point. Dyserth Castle was constructed by Henry III from 1241, and sits on a promontory high above the village. It was attacked and destroyed by Llywelyn ap Gruffydd (Llywelyn the Last) in 1263, leaving it in ruins, and all that now remains is a green mound as the ruins were quarried away during WWI.

Dyserth has been the centre of many commercial enterprises over the years, but mining and quarrying had the greatest impact on the village for the longest period of time, with evidence of mining from as early as 1303. The mines finally closed in 1884, but it wasn't until the 1980s that the lime-works

Agriculture is very important to the area.

and quarrying ceased. Milling was also important, with as many as seven mills sited along the River Ffyddion: most of these were for flour but some were for cloth making as there was a significant woollen trade. Some time during the 18th century these closed, too. Many of the buildings remain, although some have been re-purposed.

With the advent of railways a branch line to the village was opened in 1869 for transporting goods from the mines and quarries. Then, in 1905, services were extended to include passengers. Closure of various industries and competition from roads meant rail services were gradually reduced until, finally, the line was closed in 1973. This, too, has been re-purposed as a footpath and bridleway.

Denbighshire in northeast Wales delivers an amazing number of experiences for such a compact and easily accessible area. Stunning countryside, bustling market towns, two of Britain's best-known seaside resorts, and many centuries of rich heritage combine to make Denbighshire a destination with a difference.

CAMPSITE – FUNDRAISING (PET RESCUE) CAMPSITE

A campsite that all animal/dog-lovers should visit to support the amazing work that Marg, the owner, does in the community. Marg takes in and looks after unwanted animals – mostly dogs – and looks for long-term foster homes for them so that if there are any issues with a placement the animals come back to her. The dogs she currently has are a sorry lot, but the man who helps her look after them is wonderful.

Marg also runs a pet food bank and vet consultations. When school holidays end she expects the usual influx of dogs. To fund this work she runs a boarding kennel as well as the campsite: she's a very busy lady but considerate of others, especially dogs.

The campsite is a large, fairly level field with all the usual facilities. Yes, these are basic – showers and toilets are housed in portacabins – but they are serviceable. Along the side that has electric hook-up are glamping pods adjacent to their ubiquitous hot tubs; bell tents and pitches for tourers, plus a catering van. Due to Covid restrictions this wasn't open when I visited so I have no information about it. A unique campsite and owner.

The Fundraising (Pet Rescue campsite) is run by an amazing woman.

Pub – The New Inn

From the campsite, just ten minutes' walk across the road through the new housing estate and past the playing field, is The New Inn, an imposing, red-and-white building on the corner opposite the church.

Because it has a large, outdoor area the pub was able to open. The food was standard 'pub-grub' (which suits me) but locally sourced, so delicious.

Pearls of wisdom

True, there was no specific area for me to play, but I was allowed to chase my Frisbee nearby if there was room. My owner also found me an adjacent field to explore and play in, but I had to jump the stile; there wasn't a gap big enough for me to squeeze through. Occasionally we met other dogs there, but they seemed sad and subdued so I left them alone. There was quite a pleasant daily walk along a field and exciting wooded lane, but also along a busy road. Fortunately, it had a grass verge so was worth checking out.

The other walks were fabulous: a swim in the sea, wind ruffling my coat on hilltops. Unfortunately, there were some cows and rather a lot of roads. Whilst there I often heard dogs barking and whining, but I couldn't see them. It was such a sad sound: not at all threatening but it made me a little uneasy.

Short Walk – Waterfalls and trig point

Distance: 4.5mi (7.2km)
Duration: 2hr (Moderate)
Terrain: Roads with pavements, footpaths, tracks, steps (lots), cyclepath, green, open spaces, kissing gates, stiles (two sheep-proof), some long, steep climbs up and down

Section 1: 1.25mi (2km)
- Exit campsite via entrance
- Bear right to turn into car park

The New Inn with its lovely outdoor space.

- Straight ahead over stile into field
- Follow path along edge of field with stream on left, through gate in corner onto footpath
- Turn left over footbridge
- Follow path through gate to A547
- Turn left along road (there is a pavement)
- Turn right through second gate into field, signposted
- Turn left, then sharp right through small gap in hedge into another field
- Follow the footpath along the edge of field, keeping close to hedge on right
- At hedge corner bear right across field to row of trees
- Continue along edge of field, keeping close to trees on right, then over stile into next field
- Bear slightly right across field, over stile opposite, between houses into lane on to minor road
- Turn right along road round bend to steps at next bend
- Take steps down to Waterfall Road
- Turn left along road (narrow, no pavement) to Waterfall shop and café (stop here and take time to give your dog a special ice cream and look at the waterfall: it's impressive)

The waterfall in the centre of Dyserth. The railings at the bottom of the photo give an indication of its size.

WATERFALLS & TRIG POINT

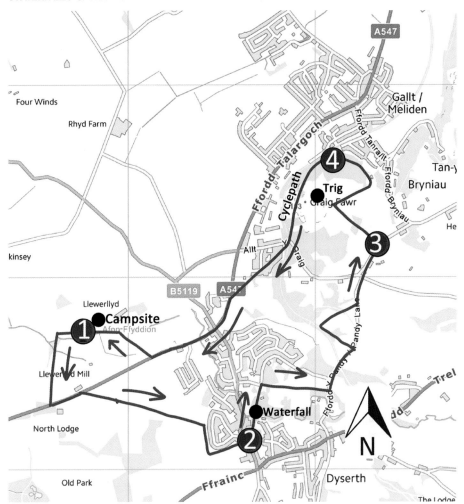

Section 2: 1.25mi (2km)

- Turn left up the road, passing café and shop on right
- Turn sharp left onto stony driveway, signposted
- Follow track, passing big, square house on right; up steps between wooden fence
- Continue up long, steep flight, taking left fork at top to tarmac path, then up more steps to minor road passing several houses
- Turn left, keeping close to house on left, down more steps with metal handrail and cross large, broken stone footbridge over stream
- Continue straight past footbridge on left and through kissing gate
- In 25yd (23m) turn right up steep path and out onto wide, open green
- Straight ahead across green, through gate in hedge opposite and out to road junction

- Take second exit on left along minor road beside dog poo bin
- Take right fork along road
- Turn right down slope, then right again onto cyclepath
- Turn right off cyclepath by bridge (by another dog poo bin); down slope to footpath
- Turn left and follow path up hill
- Turn right at junction, over stile onto track
- Follow track going up, over another stile and out to road
- Turn left along road to junction
- Take second exit to car park, signposted
- Cross car park and through kissing gate to open green

Section 3: 0.75mi (1.2km)

- Turn right to follow wide, grassy path to trigpoint (it's an easier climb to the very top on the opposite side: spectacular views of coast and mountains)
- Just before trigpoint turn right along wide, grassy path
- Follow well-defined track going down (this becomes a narrow earth footpath between gorse bushes) and descend flight of steps by wooden fence
- Turn left at bottom onto path
- Follow path through wood to Y Shed on cyclepath
  (The café in Y Shed is a good place to stop for refreshments, including more doggie icecream)

Section 4: 1.25mi (2km)

- Exit Y Shed onto cyclepath
- Turn right, passing Y Shed on right
- Continue along cyclepath to 'Village of Meliden' signpost
- Turn right through kissing gate, then immediate left onto path
- Follow path parallel to cyclepath
- Take left fork at junction, keeping close to tall, metal fence on right
- Continue along path across road, through kissing gate and over stile (broken) with fence still on right
- Turn right off track down wooden steps towards buildings
- Follow path, bearing left then right round fence onto wide, open green
- Take path on right, keeping close to buildings on right
- Continue along path, heading to road sign above hedge
- Bear left, keeping close to hedge on right
- Turn right through kissing gate onto A547
- Turn left along pavement to cross both junctions at traffic lights
- Continue along A547; through kissing gate after sewage works into field
- Bear left across field and over stile (sheep-proof) in opposite corner to campsite entrance

LONG WALK – TO THE BEACH
Distance: 10mi (16km)
Duration: 5hr (Easy)
Terrain: Roads, footpaths, tracks, lanes, cyclepath, fields, woods, beaches, gates, kissing gates, stiles (some sheep-proof); some short, steep climbs

Section 1: 1mi (1.6km)

- Exit campsite via entrance
- Bear right into car park
- Straight ahead over stile (sheep-proof) into field
- Follow path along edge of field with stream on left, then through gate in corner onto footpath
- Turn right along track between fields and around left-hand bend
- Turn right at junction (beside collapsed stile), signposted
- Continue along path to tarmac lane
- Turn right along lane to road junction

Section 2: 1.25mi (2km)

- Turn left along Dyserth Road (take care as busy with several bends)
- In a quarter-mile (0.4km), immediately after a sharp bend turn right through gate onto grassy track
- Follow track round left-hand bend and through gate onto tarmac drive
- Continue along drive, passing house on left, round right-hand bend passing animal sanctuary and

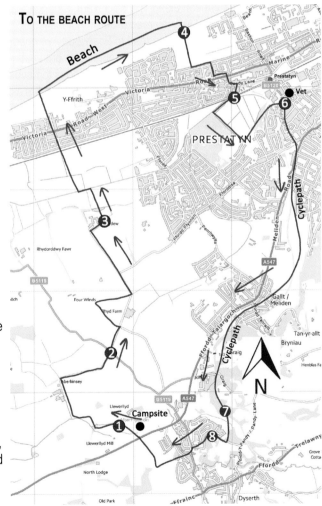

TO THE BEACH ROUTE

caravan park on left, and through gates to junction
- Turn left along another driveway to Pydew Farm
- Follow driveway past farmhouse to bend, signposted
  (The actual footpath goes left through a gate to turn right along edge of field; over a stile, turn right again and through gate onto footpath. I did not take this route because of cows by the first gate. The farmer allowed me to go right then left through his farmyard to join footpath at gate on left. Be considerate. Ask him first and check for farm dogs: we did not meet them)
- Follow stony track through gate into field

Section 3: 1.75mi (2.8km)
- Turn left, keeping to edge of field, then right at corner and through gate over rail track (take care); then through another gate, past houses and out to road
- Continue straight ahead along The Boulevard, around the grass square, across Christina Ave and out to main road (A548), Victoria Road
- Via traffic lights on right, cross road to Eastwood Ave opposite
- Continue along Eastwood Ave and through gate onto path, then through dunes to beach (there is plenty of opportunity here for dogs to have a swim in the sea)
- Turn right along beach (there are several different paths along the shoreline)

Section 4: 1.25mi (2km)
- Exit beach area on right, via concrete path beside red lifebuoy just before car park
- Continue along path and through holiday park, following yellow footprints as indicated
- Go straight on at bend onto narrow lane and through tall gates to road
- Turn left along road, passing two-tone houses on right
- Turn right past houses to A548, with Co-Op on right
- Turn left, cross main road at lights, and turn left along road
- Turn right after Fish Bar, continue along road around left-hand bend

The beaches are amazing,- with lots of opportunity for Pearl to swim.

Section 5: 0.75mi (1.2km)
- Turn sharp right along path beside stream, and through gates over rail track
- Follow path with stream on right
- Turn left along footpath, taking left fork passing playing fields on right
- Turn left along path to town centre, signposted, passing school on right
- Continue straight ahead along concrete path, taking right fork through gate onto road, Banastre Avenue
- Continue straight ahead, crossing Conwy Grove towards veterinary practice

Section 6: 2.25mi (3.6km)
- Turn right at veterinary car park to entrance of Prestatyn-Dyserth Walkway (cyclepath)
- Follow cyclepath, passing several footpaths leading off to left and right, and also passing Offa's Paddock café at the golf club (potential refreshment stop), and the Y Shed café (another potential refreshment stop)

Section 7: 0.75mi (1.2km)
- Turn left off cyclepath at bridge with dog bin, onto narrow footpath going downhill
- Turn right at junction and under arch
- Turn right along footpath, bearing left and descending
- Turn left at bottom onto narrow path
- Continue straight ahead through kissing gate opposite, and between houses into lane
- Follow lane to road
- Cross road and turn left, then right at junction, and left up steps between houses
- Follow lane to road

Section 8: 1mi (1.6km)
- Turn right (look out for delightful garden across road); follow road to main road
- Cross road; turn left and then right with pub on left and stream on right
- Straight ahead beside stream
- Bear left across small green through gap between wooden fence and brick wall
- Continue up slope to pavement
- Turn right along road onto footpath beside playing field
- Follow path past play area and new houses on left to driveway
- Turn right to A547
- Cross road; turn left along road
- Turn right through kissing gate beside sewage works into field
- Bear left across field and over stile (sheep-proof) in opposite corner to campsite entrance

IN THE VICINITY

LLEWERLLYD FARM

Today, this is no longer a farm but an animal rescue centre, with the on-site campsite funding the work there; an unusual setup, to be sure.

More wonderful walks from **dog-friendly campsites**

CYCLING
Denbighshire is ideal for all kinds of cycling as it is part of North Wales Cycling Centre of Excellence. Besides the cyclepath along the disused railway there are many bridleways in the Clwydian Range, plus special venues in the county for BMX and mountain biking. Details can be found online.

FRANKIE'S FARM SHOP
Situated right on Dyserth High Street, this family-run farm shop-cum-café's menu includes sumptuous English breakfasts and classic Afternoon Teas, and is open seven days a week from 9am until 4pm.

WATERFALL
Dyserth's must-see attraction is the incredible waterfall right in the centre of the village near the church, which has had huge impact. As the River Ffyddion flows westward, it cascades some 70ft (21.3m) over the waterfall to join the River Clwyd.

A significant feature in the success of mining and milling in the area, over the years people have flocked to see it – and are still doing so. All kinds of legends surround the waterfall and the two huge walls nearby, which some think might be the remains of a water wheel. The path between the walls is steep with lots of steps, but eventually it scales the hill to join other footpaths.

BODRHYDDAN HALL
This magnificent stately house, just 1.5 miles (2.4km) from the campsite, is the home of the Lords Longford, and has been for the past 500 years. The current building, which is Grade I listed, is a modified version of an already old building from the 1690s, and the Victorian era witnessed further changes. The house contains an extensive collection that includes portraits, armour, and an Egyptian mummy, and is surrounded by woodland and amazing gardens. It is open to the public for just two days a week as it is still a family home.

ST BRIDGET PARISH CHURCH
There has been a church of some kind on this site for around 1500 years. The first building was probably constructed of wood, since when the church has been modified and renovated many times, with major changes instigated by George Gilbert Scott in the 1870s. Parts of the current church date from the 13th century, whilst the famous 'Jesse' window is 16th century, and claimed to be 'the finest example of a medieval Jesse window in North Wales.'

RHYL AND PRESTATYN
The beaches of these seaside towns are long and sandy; wonderful for dogs, although they are allowed in certain areas only from May to September as restrictions are in place at other times. Signs and maps on the beach indicate where dogs are allowed during the summer months.

FRITH BEACH

Just one of the lovely sandy beaches along the North Wales coast, situated between Prestatyn and Rhyl. Access to the beach is easy because there is a gentle slope from the promenade, but access to the water can take a while at low tide as the sea goes out a long way. Dogs are free to use the main beach anytime, but there are restrictions at each end from May to September.

Montgomeryshire – extraordinary border

OS MAPS EXPLORER 216 WELSHPOOL & MONTGOMERY – Y TRALLWNG A TREFALDWYN

Montgomeryshire is one of the old counties of Wales that was incorporated into the larger county of Powys in the 1970s. Like much of Wales, mountains and hills are a significant feature here: the Cambrian Mountains rise upward in the west of the county, with rivers slashing through them, especially the infamous River Severn.

Much of the land is only suitable for sheep, and during the 15th century Montgomeryshire was renowned for its production of wool flannel. There was also some lead mining. Nowadays, tourism is its main industry, although hill farming is still important. The county is sparsely populated, and several towns and villages are squashed into the hillside, sometimes overseen by castle ruins. Eastward, the landscape becomes less severe as it crosses Offa's Dyke into England.

Roughly following the Welsh/English border, Offa's Dyke stretches over 150 miles (241km) across the countryside from coast to coast, from Sedbury in the south to Prestatyn in the north, so slicing through the eastern section of Montgomeryshire. As its name suggests, the dyke was built by Offa, king from 757 to 796 AD of a huge chunk of central England known as Mercia. In order to protect his kingdom from marauding Welsh tribes, Offa built a dyke along his western border. It was an imposing earthwork embankment, and stood 12ft (3.6m) high and 60ft (18m) wide. The earth excavated from the Welsh side was piled onto the English side, so creating a flattened ridge (the 'Dyke'), with a large ditch on the Welsh side. When hills were encountered during construction, the dyke was built to the west of them; as a consequence, the view of Wales from the dyke was clear and unimpeded along its entire length.

The striking structure suggests that Offa was an affluent and powerful king, able to commission the necessary manpower and resources to construct and complete the dyke. Though there appears not to have been a specific defence force, the dyke was nevertheless an effective deterrent, demonstrating the supremacy of Mercia and signalling its importance as a major power. Besides keeping the Welsh at bay, it was probably also useful as a means for checking local movement, and raising taxes from cross border trade and exchange.

Many decades of research and study have revealed much information about this impressive structure. Modern technology and ongoing archaeological work on the dyke indicate it may have been more complex than is evident now, and recent findings have resulted in a re-evaluation of facts and theories about it: its precise purpose and function are still hotly debated. Offa's Dyke exudes an air of mystery – and even magic – and, as a result, is safeguarded; classified as a scheduled monument.

Throughout the intervening centuries the dyke has been an important, immutable structure marking the boundary between England and Wales, although not so nowadays. Only in a few places does the dyke mark the actual border, though it does run within a few miles of it.

Thanks to this Anglo-Saxon king who authorized the building of the dyke, now, in the 21st century, we have access to another long-distant walking trail that stretches north/south from coast to coast: the appropriately named 'Offa's Dyke Path' that opened in 1971. Some sections of the 177-mile (285km) route run along the top of the dyke, whilst others are close by. In places, there is little evidence of the dyke. The trail passes through some spectacular countryside as it crosses eight counties and three AONB (Areas of Outstanding Natural Beauty), and offers the opportunity to experience a changing landscape and the chance of seeing a variety of wildlife. What a marvellous inheritance the ancient kings left us!

CAMPSITE – MELLINGTON HALL HOLIDAY HOME PARK

The long, narrow drive with clearly signposted passing places suggests a well organized, stylish establishment, which is affirmed as the imposing building slowly comes into view. The 'Hall' in the name is entirely apt.

Directions for registration lead to the right of the Hall through an impressive arch and round to the back, where, located in a small room at the end of the drive, is reception. Here, too, at the rear, the Hall exudes an air of magnificence, with a large grass terrace overlooking the grounds.

The field for tourers is located past the 95 statics, over a stream and into a meadow:

Offa's Dyke is a popular long-distance walking trail.

The campsite is in a meadow over a stream.

The Hall, where there is a bar, restaurant and other places to relax.

a small, intimate area with space for just 30 units. The views are glorious. All of the pitches have hardstanding, electricity and water. The modern amenities block is some distance from the site, via a footbridge across the stream.

Situated in 270 acres, the estate is substantial, and besides the lovely landscaped grounds with ponds and streams there is also extensive woodland with signposted walks snaking through it (necessary, as it is very easy to get lost). Slicing through the woodland is Offa's Dyke Path, as well as a section of the dyke itself. There are ample places to relax with your dog and enjoy the peace, tranquillity and amazing views of the countryside.

Bar and restaurant in the Hall

The Hall, astride a slight rise, benignly oversees the campsite and accompanying land. Because the main building is an hotel, it also houses a bar, which, though small, is both comprehensive and intimate, and a restaurant that serves a varied range of meals. As befits a grand mansion, the rooms, too, are impressive. Astute arrangement of furniture, both inside and outside on the grass terrace, has created inviting cosy spaces in which to relax, eat and drink, read, and enjoy the ambience. All guests of the two-legged and four-legged variety are welcome to use the many spacious and sumptuous communal areas, although the restaurant is reserved for two-legged guests.

PEARLS OF WISDOM 🐾

I found this campsite baffling. The walks in the woods were brilliant: so much to discover, and so many intriguing smells. I couldn't wait to get to them, but it seemed to take a long time along tarmac. Mind you, there was no road to negotiate, no traffic to worry about, and no sheep or cows!

Once we had arrived I was impatient to find out which way we were going. The woods appeared to go on and on. I was very disappointed I could not swim in any of the lakes and ponds, though I could go into the big building, where I was made a fuss of and got lots of treats.

Setting out on our walks was such fun, although occasionally there were cows. Whenever we meet cows they always want to check me out: I find this a bit frightening as they are so big!

SHORT WALK – ROUND AND ABOUT
Distance: 4mi (6.4km)
Duration: 2.5hr (Moderate)
Terrain: Footpaths, tracks, fields, roads, lanes, gates, stiles, some steady climbs

Section 1: 1mi (1.6km)
- From toilet block take path straight ahead with hotel on right
- Continue on past Hall, following path round right-hand bend
- Turn left immediately after large shed and follow track into woods, passing recycling area on left and garages on right
- Continue straight ahead along wide, muddy track, up steps onto embankment (Offa's Dyke), and round to the left
- Continue along top of dyke, going up and down and passing campsite on left; through a gate and up slope opposite
- Follow path down and through second gate
- Straight ahead across field, through gate opposite, cross track, through fourth gate and up bank onto clearly-marked footpath between trees
- Continue along path and through fifth gate out to road
- Turn right, climbing steadily along minor road
- Turn right just past buildings on right, through gate into field, signposted (pic overleaf)

Section 2: 1mi (1.6km)
- Bear left across top of field and through gate into next field
- Straight ahead towards large tree and telegraph pole
- Continue across top of field to gap in hedge by wood
- Bear right, going downhill through gate onto wide, stony track

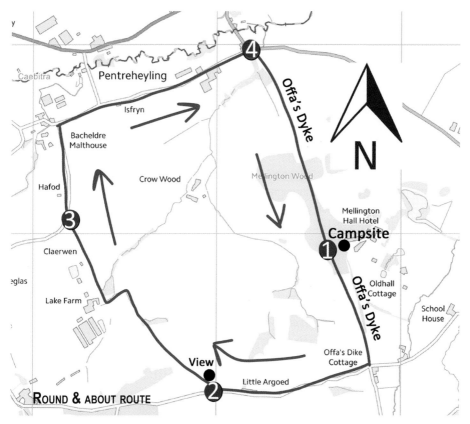

ROUND & ABOUT ROUTE

Turn off the road and into a field.

- Follow track towards farm, going first round to right then round to left and through farmyard
- Continue along farm driveway to road

Section 3: 1mi (1.6km)
- Turn right and follow road to junction and round right-hand bend
- Take right fork at next junction
- Continue along road, ignoring all tracks and path, to junction with B4385

Section 4: 1mi (1.6km)
- Turn right through large black gates onto wide path
- Follow path, passing house on left, and onto track between magnificent large fir trees and round large stone out to driveway
- Turn right in 20 paces and go through small gate into wood

- Continue along path through wood, up along dyke and through gate into field
- Follow path along edge of field with hedging on right; through gate on right back into wood
- Continue along path through wood, turning right off dyke across stone slabs by large tree stump, and post with a small blue-and-orange disc
- Turn left towards post with orange disc, passing bench on right
- Continue along path parallel to dyke on left
- Follow path past post with orange disc round to right and up onto path(this is narrow but space between trees is wide)
- Turn left along path, passing tables and chairs on right
- Continue along wide track through woods to large junction
- Turn left along wide track, passing between steps, up to dyke and recycling area on right, with garages on left, to path at side of Hall
- Turn right for path to touring section

LONG WALK – IN OFFA'S FOOTSTEPS
Distance: 9.5mi (14.4km)
Duration: 4.5hr (longer with castle visit) (Moderate)
Terrain: Wide and narrow woodland tracks, footpaths; gates and kissing gates, stiles some sheep proofed, fields, quiet roads, steady climbs and short, steep climb to castle

Section 1: 1.25mi (2km)
- From toilet block take path straight ahead with hotel on right
- Continue on past Hall, following path around right-hand bend
- Turn left immediately after large shed and follow track into woods, passing recycling area on left and garages on right
- Continue straight ahead along wide, muddy track and up steps onto embankment (Offa's Dyke); then round to right
- Follow path through wood and gate out into field
- Bearing slightly right, continue ahead, keeping close to hedge on left, and go through gate back into wood
- Continue along woodland path and through gate onto driveway
- Turn left onto path between trees, and through large, impressive black gates onto road
- Continue straight ahead along road, over humpback bridge to Blue Bell Hotel and A489
- Cross main road onto grass verge, turn left, then immediate right along road signposted Montgomery B4385
- Turn right in 50yd (46m), signposted, and through gate onto tarmac driveway

Section 2: 1mi (1.6km)
- Turn left in 50yd (46m) and go through gate into field
- Continue along edge of threefields – through gates where necessary – keeping close to fence/hedge on right

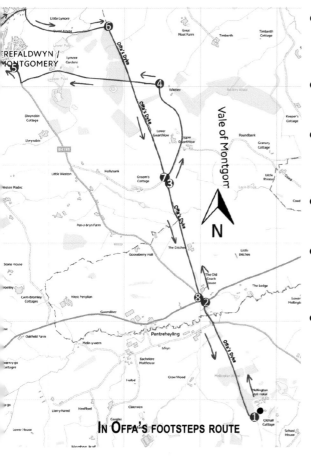

IN OFFA'S FOOTSTEPS ROUTE

- Continue ahead, bearing slightly right through hedge and over two stiles, (sheep-proof) into farmyard
- Straight across farmyard and through wooden gate to right of trees
- Continue ahead over stile into field, keeping close to hedge on right and ignoring stile in hedge
- Keeping to edge of field, go up embankment and through kissing gate
- Keeping to edge of field over stile, cross footbridge and go through another kissing gate into field
- Straight ahead, keeping close to hedge on right along edge of field, following path round to right and over stile onto minor road

Section 3: 1mi (1.6km)
- Turn right along road; at junction cross stile in hedge ahead into field
- Straight ahead over stile opposite
- Continue straight across field towards trees, and take left fork at edge of field, keeping close to copse on right
- Follow path at corner round to left along second side of field
- Turn right in 30yd (27m) and cross stile into field
- Straight ahead along edge of field through gate in corner
- Continue along edge of this field, hedge on right, to cross stile onto tarmac driveway

Section 4: 1.5mi (2.4km)
- Turn left along driveway, crossing two cattle grids (first has no gate), to junction of Offa's Dyke and over a third cattle grid into Lymore Park
- Continue along tarmac driveway over fourth cattle grid, with cricket pitch on right, and round right-hand bend

- Turn left just past farm; go through gate onto stony track, signposted
- Follow track, keeping close to hedge on right, and through gate
- Continue along track close to hedge, towards gate leading to busy road
- Turn right just before large, metal gate, through kissing-gate and over wooden footbridge on right
- Follow stony footpath out to small car park and recycling area
- Cross road towards play area
- Turn left, keeping play area on right, and follow pavement to B4385
- Turn right along B3458 into centre of Montgomery
(An interesting market town built into the hillside, so with some very steep streets. Refreshments are available from the local pubs. There's also an amazing castle ruin that is well worth visiting for the spectacular views. The return route via Offa's Dyke begins from the castle ruins.)

Section 5: 1.25mi (2km)
- Take path on left, with castle ruin behind, going down a steep, gravelly footpath
- Take left fork down to Market Square, turning right into Arthur Street
- Continue along Arthur Street, taking right fork to crossroads
- Bearing slightly left, cross to road opposite (B3486)
- Follow B3486 past fire station on right to another crossroads road to cattle grid
- urn left along driveway before cattle grid
- Turn right through gate in 50yd (46m), just before house
- Straight on, keeping close to hedge on right, and through gate into field
- Continue along edge of field and through gate opposite into another field
- Straight on along edge of this field and through gate opposite into garden
- Turn immediately right and through gate into field
- Turn left and follow path around garden with fence on left, towards trees and cross stile
- Continue along path around copse and cross wooden bridge, then stile, and follow path out into field
- Straight ahead along edge of field with hedge on right to corner, and cross stile onto Offa's Dyke

Section 6: 1.25mi (2km)
- Follow path with wood on right and cross stile into field
- Straight ahead and cross stile opposite
- Continue along edge of field close to wood on right to road
- Cross road; through gate opposite
- Turn left and follow track along edge of field with hedge now on left, and cross stile into second field
- Continue along path, hedge still on left, and cross stile into third field
- Follow path along edge of field, still beside hedge, to driveway
- Cross driveway through gate and along path into field
- Continue on path along edge of next two fields and over stiles out to road

Section 7: 1mi (1.6km)

- Cross road, over stile, and follow path round to left into field
- Continue straight ahead to corner and through gate over footbridge; then cross stile into another field through gate into another field
- Along edge of field and over stile into farmyard
- Bearing slightly left, cross farmyard and into field through wooden gate to left of trees
- Continue along edge of three fields, keeping close to hedge on left, going though gates were necessary to farm driveway

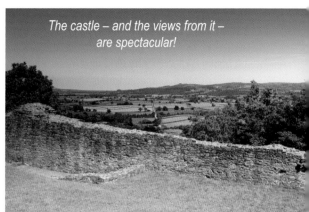

The castle – and the views from it – are spectacular!

Section 8: 1.25mi (2km)

- Turn right along driveway and out to B4385
- Turn left along road to junction
- Go straight across A489, along road and over humpback bridge
- Continue along B4385, going straight ahead at bend through large, black gates onto wide path
- Follow path, passing house on left, onto track between magnificent large fir trees and round large stone out to driveway
- Turn right in 20 paces through small gate into wood
- Continue along path through wood, up along dyke and through gate into field
- Follow path along edge of field with hedging on right; through gate on right into wood
- Continue along path through wood, turning right off dyke and across stone slabs by large tree stump, and post with small blue and small orange discs
- Turn left towards post with orange disc, passing bench on right
- Continue along path parallel to dyke on left
- Follow path past post with orange disc, round to right up onto path (this is narrow but wide space between trees)
- Turn left along path, passing tables and chairs on right
- Continue along wide track, through woods to large junction
- Turn left along wide track, passing between steps up to dyke and recycling area on right with garages on left, to path at side of Hall
- Turn right to path to touring section

In the vicinity

Mellington Hall

This establishment has been owned and run by the same family for several generations. Interestingly, though the main building is very stately, it was, in fact, only built in 1873 by

Philip Wright, whose family made its fortune from coal and steel. Unfortunately, Philip was a spendthrift, and was forced to sell the house and estate in 1901. Purchased by Sidney Heap and his American wife, Frances, the pair modernized and sumptuously decorated the house. When Sidney died nine years after his wife in 1957, it was sold again, and John Evans bought it, primarily for his wife, who had worked for Sidney Heap at the hall. The building was dilapidated and demolition was recommended. The caravan park was set up to fund the restoration and help with the upkeep.

The estate is now run by John Evans' grandson, Alistair Evans, and his wife, Claire. There is still a caravan park in the grounds but the 'Hall' is now an hotel.

BIRDWATCHING

Though there are no hides on the estate, there are several seats dotted about – in the woodlands, beside the lakes, and throughout the grounds – which are ideal for spotting the huge variety of birds who visit, so remember the binoculars!

CYCLING

With bikes, including E-bikes, available for hire from the Hall, it's possible to explore further afield along the quiet lanes, and even to tackle nearby hills. Suggested cycle rides based on the nearby town of Montgomery are available on the internet.

FISHING

The lakes on the estate are suitable for coarse fishing: details and advice are available from the Hall.

MONTGOMERY

This charming county town is wedged against the hillside beneath the castle ruins. Because it is located in the Welsh Marches (the lands along the English and Welsh border), it has a long and momentous history.

It acquired its name in the 11th century when William the Conqueror gave his supporter Roger de Montgomery a swathe of the Welsh Marches. He then built a castle nearby as protection.

However, it was Henry III who, in 1223, built a magnificent stone structure on a craggy outcrop to safeguard an important ford across the River Severn, and the town grew up on the slopes below this imposing structure. By 1227, there existed a thriving medieval town, which was granted a Royal Charter to erect protective structures and hold fairs and markets, and every Thursday, still, a market is held in the Town Hall.

Over the centuries the layout of the streets has changed very little, but the Georgian buildings reflect the town's prosperity during the 18th and 19th centuries. In 1974, the status of the town was downgraded with the assimilation of Montgomeryshire into the county of Powys.

Even so, the town is a lively place, delightful to explore, albeit this is somewhat time-consuming to do due to its steep streets.

Montgomery Castle

The stone castle built by Henry III survived several attacks by the Welsh. The 1267 Treaty of Montgomery downplayed the strategic importance of the castle, and it fell into some disrepair as a result. It nevertheless succeeded in repelling Owen Glyendower's (Owain Glyndŵr) assault in 1402, however, and was refurbished by Roger Mortimer, the Earl of March, several times. It was eventually destroyed in 1644 after being captured by the Parliamentarians during the English Civil War. Even so, the ruins are truly monumental and the views are stunning, making it well worth climbing up to visit. There is no charge and dogs are free to roam.

St Nicholas Church

Built in 1266, the same time as the stone castle, the church, too, is an impressive building, and, surprisingly, has many interesting historical features from both Norman and Tudor times. The large, rectangular churchyard contains notable monuments and graves, including some Commonwealth graves. Unfortunately, when I visited, although the building was still magnificent, the churchyard was very overgrown and unkempt. Dogs are allowed in the churchyard.

The Robber's Grave

According to legend, in 1821 upon his execution for robbery, John Davies cursed those he thought responsible for accusing him of robbery, and prophesied that, for a hundred years, grass would not grow on his grave. Though grass is now growing around the simple cross that marks The Robber's Grave in St Nicholas churchyard, this appears to be a recent phenomenon, and there are those who attest that the place is haunted, presumably by Davies' restless sprit ...

Old Bell Museum

The building on Arthur Street was once a 16th century inn, but is now a museum run by volunteers, that houses many exhibits and artefacts about the local area over the last one thousand years. It's an ideal place to visit to learn more about the town and castle.

Cloverlands Model Car Museum

Opened in 2015 at the Montgomery Institute on Arthur Street, many of the exhibits in this musuem were collected, commissioned or built over 60 years by a Miss Rogers. With an extensive display of over 5000 model cars, this is perfect for the motoring enthusiast.

The Cottage – The Monty's Brewery Visitor Centre

The centre provides an opportunity to stop off for nibbles and a beer; learn about this local brewery; sample its beers; ask questions, and even, if you wish, place an order!

Bishop Castle

Situated 7 miles (11.2km) south east of the campsite is this delightful market town with its network of narrow, quirky streets and some impressive historical buildings and museums.

Several shops, cafés and pubs are dotted about, and the many outdoor music events in the evening create a quite lively and energetic atmosphere. Several long-distance trails lead to the town, but large sections of them are along single track roads; not the best for walking with your dog.

THE HOUSE ON CRUTCHES MUSEUM
Housed in a stunning, typical black-and-white Elizabethan building, this museum has a range of artefacts illustrating rural life in south-west Shropshire.

BISHOPS CASTLE RAILWAY AND TRANSPORT MUSEUM
This museum was opened in 1999 with the intention of recording and preserving the remaining memorabilia and records of the local railway.

Visit Hubble and Hattie on the web:
www.hubbleandhattie.com • www.hubbleandhattie.blogspot.co.uk • Details of all books
• Special offers • Newsletter • New book news

Walks in North East England
(Durham, Lincolnshire, Norfolk, West Yorkshire)

Durham – dales of Durham

OS MAPS EXPLORER OL31 NORTH PENNINES

County Durham tends to be overlooked as it is encircled by three prominent counties: Northumberland, with Hadrian's Wall to the north; Cumbria, with the Lake District to the west, and 'God's own county,' Yorkshire, on the southern border. This, despite the fact that several main roads cross Durham north to south, and the county has a long and intriguing history.

The capital city Durham is fundamental to the county with its cathedral and castle soaring over the River Wear, creating such a magnificent historical spectacle that, in 1986, Durham was designated a UNESCO World Heritage Site. University students are fortunate that, since 1832, the castle has been the home of Durham University, thanks to Cuthbert, Bishop of Lindisfarne, an island off the coast of Northumberland.

After Cuthbert's death in 687, miracles were reported to have occurred at his grave, and it became a place of pilgrimage. Fear of Viking raids prompted the monks, some 200 years later, to exhume his bones, trekking around the region for ten years before finding what they considered to be the safest place for them: Dunholm, a hill on an island; an easy place to defend. Cuthbert's new resting place also drew lots of visitors, and, to accommodate them, a town, now called Durham, grew up around the hill: a city founded on faith and fervour.

In order to control the people, in 1072 the Normans built a castle, and then, in 1083, the community of monks, who had looked after Cuthbert's body, was replaced by a Benedictine Priory. Ten years later in 1093 William of Calais, the Norman bishop of Durham, began construction of the cathedral. In 1104, Cuthbert's remains were buried there, even though the cathedral was not finished until 1133.

The county of Durham had special significance as a major barrier to Scottish insurgents. The strong church connection enhanced the importance of the bishopric of Durham to such an extent the king conferred upon its members the status of Bishop-Prince, bestowing the right to mint coins, levy taxes and raise an army, as long as they remained loyal to the king and protected the northern border. The area controlled by the bishops of Durham was referred to as the County Palatine of Durham until 1889. Over time, this mutated into County Durham, and so it is that Durham is the only shire in England with 'county' as a prefix.

For many years farming was the chief industry, although there was some mining of coal. The industrial revolution in the 18th century brought a huge upsurge in mining as it was now possible to reach the deeper, more productive seams. People flocked to the area and villages sprung up all over the county, as coal production grew steadily, peaking in 1913. In 1947, with 234 collieries in the county, the coal industry was nationalized ... by 1994 they had all closed.

The western third of County Durham is the little-known Durham Dales, a designated AONB (Area of Outstanding Natural Beauty), where the Pennines spill into the county with mountains and peaks topping 2000ft (610m) and more in places. The rivers rising high in the hills carve their way to the sea, slashing through the soaring Pennine peaks and creating these amazing 'dales': old English for 'valley.' They are sparsely populated with few settlements.

The Tees and Wear, two well known rivers, fashioned Teesdale and Weardale that stretch from the North Pennines' craggy and sprawling moors to the gentle farmlands in the east. Teesdale winds its way through the southern part of County Durham, beginning at the historic Barnard Castle. From here settlements are smaller and the river gradually narrows as the peaks steadily rise. Here, in Teesdale, is the charming village of Middleton-in-Teesdale, and further up the river are the spectacular falls of High Force, Low Force and Cauldron Snout. An amazing hidden corner of England with plenty to explore.

The Durham Dales are an AONB.

Campsite – Daleview Holiday Park

This family-run campsite uniquely occupies the old Middleton-in-Teesdale railway station, with the modern amenities block, dishwashing and laundry housed in the converted toilets and ticket office. The platform and tracks have been transformed: there is a delightful children's play area, and behind the station is a field for tents and several static caravans. The main area for 40 touring vans is some way from the station, along each side of what were the rail tracks. This is a most intriguing campsite that has the added benefit of being convenient to Middleton-in-Teesdale village.

Pub – The Station Pub

The old waiting room is now The Station Pub, serving a wide selection of drinks, including real ales, and a currently modified menu. This used to be the campsite clubhouse, so is rather humdrum, but the new owners are gradually modernizing it. The pub is open to the general public, and the garden is a very enjoyable place to spend time, especially as the patrons are very friendly and welcoming.

Several places serve refreshments in Middleton-in-Teesdale, just ten minutes away.

The old railway has been converted into Daleview Campsite and the Station Pub.

Pearls of Wisdom 🐾

I didn't expect to be practicing agility here, weaving between these large, brightly-coloured sticks (play pencils for children, whatever they are). Okay, but where's the tunnel? I love racing through tunnels; the best part of my agility classes. This was typical of the campsite: strange! Long and thin with funny little spaces tucked away. The frisbee-playing green was odd-shaped: round with a flattish top. The wooded path down to the road was wonderful, though, and my owner thought it was an access route to the old train station. Whatever, it was a really exciting place that led to the river where – hooray! – I could swim. The walks were alright, if a bit too much tarmac. I did not have to go on the lead as it was very quiet, and although the sheep were not a problem there were cows ... and a bull. He was BIG!

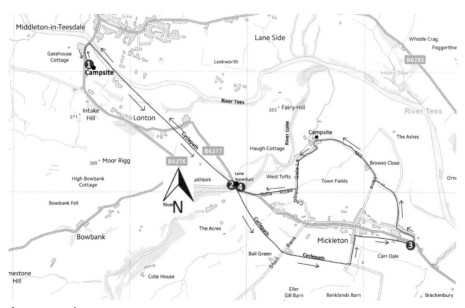

A TRAIN RIDE! ROUTE

SHORT WALK – A TRAIN RIDE!
Distance: 5.5mi (8.8km)
Duration: 2.5hr (Easy)
Terrain: Footpaths, some very quiet roads, cyclepath, tracks, gates, stiles, ladder stile, fields

Section 1: 1.25mi (2km)

- Exit campsite via dog walking access at back
- Turn left into dog walk, going downhill through gate to road
- Turn right along road towards bridge
- Turn right before bridge through gate and down steps into field
- With river on left follow the path out to driveway
- Continue along driveway through farmyard onto wide track, and through gate into field
- Straight ahead across field and up slope into trees; cross stile into next field
- Bear left over stile ahead into next field
- Cross field and over stile opposite onto road
- Turn left along road, then right over stile in wall to left of big black gates: through gate into field
- Follow path across field, passing gate on right; over ladder stile onto railtrack, turning left
- Continue along path passing small campsite; farm on left
- Follow clearly defined path through gates and over tracks as necessary, crossing viaduct over River Lune, through gate to road (walk along road both ways for a few paces to see the magnificence of the structure)

The viaduct across the River Lune.

Section 2: 1.5mi (2.4km)

- Cross road, then through gate opposite back onto track
- Continue along track, then through gate into small car park
- Cross car park and through gate, following track through gates as necessary
- Bear left up slope to road, turning left
- Straight on at corner; through gate into field
- Cross field, bearing right to wall, through gate in right corner into next field
- Cross field then through gate opposite into third field
- Bear right to top right corner and through gap in wall into chicken run
- Cross run, through gate into field and over stile opposite into next field
- Cross field, over stone stile with heavy log into third field
- Straight ahead along edge of field, keeping close to wall on left, then over stile with log on top in middle of wall; between two trees onto path
- Follow path out to road
- Turn left along road, and round bend on right down minor road 'Low Side'
- Continue along road and round left bend
- Turn right along minor road signposted 'Wath Bridge'

Section 3: 1.5mi (2.4km)

- Follow road round left-hand bend, passing sewage works, and path to bridge with bull in field!
- Continue along road, ignoring all roads off to left and right, and passing through farm with caravan park entrance on right corner
- Follow road round left-hand bend, and uphill (steep) as it winds upward
- Turn right at next junction, passing gate and dog bin on right corner
- Continue along road, crossing busier road to minor road on left
- Follow road to viaduct
- Turn right through gate onto viaduct

Section 4: 1.25mi (2km)

- Follow track to small campsite on right, then go right over ladder stile into a small field
- Bear left, passing gate on left, and through small gate and stile onto road
- Turn left along road then right at bend over stile, signposted, into field
- Cross field through gate into next field
- Bear right down slope and over stile
- Follow path down through trees across field to wide track
- Continue along track and over stile in right corner
- Follow track through farmyard onto driveway with river on right
- Bear right onto grass path, keeping close to river on right, then up steps and through gate onto road
- Turn left along road to campsite entrance

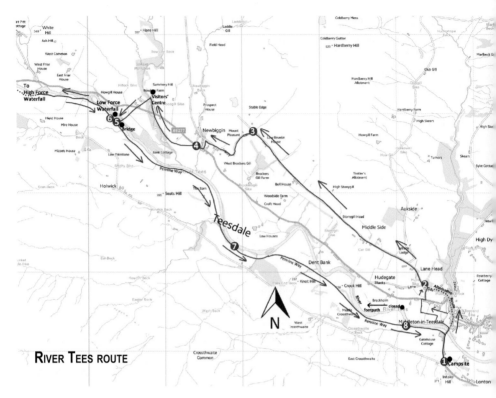

RIVER TEES ROUTE

LONG WALK – RIVER TEES
Distance: 9.5/12.5ml (15.2/20km)
Duration: 5-7hr (Moderate)
Terrain: Footpaths (some very narrow), many quiet roads, fields, footbridges tracks, gates, stiles – many stone (easy for agile, thin dogs); some steep, rocky climbs

Section 1: 1mi (1.6km)
- Exit campsite via dog walking access at rear
- Turn left into dog walk, going downhill and through gate to road
- Turn right along road, crossing bridge
- Turn left immediately after bridge onto riverside footpath, signposted
- With river on left follow path over footbridge, turning right immediately after bridge and going uphill with wall on left
- Follow path round to left then right, passing house on left
- Turn left after house along access road between houses
- Take right fork onto wide track between walls
- Follow track, bearing left around field onto narrow footpath between walls
- Turn right over stone stile with gate in wall by large tree (easy to miss) into field
- Cross field to gate opposite out to B6277 (busy as only route along Teesdale)
- Turn right along road, then left into minor road flanked by two huge upright stones

- Continue uphill to junction
- Cross road to pavement opposite by wall postbox
- Turn left along pavement, taking right fork
- Straight ahead at junction

Section 2: 2.5mi (4km)
- Follow road, climbing steadily to junction (amazing views)

Section 3: 1mi (1.6km)
- Turn left at cul-de-sac junction, and down to Newbiggin village
- Follow road round to right into village
- Turn left down lane immediately after the chapel (noticeboard on rear wall) to B6277 again
- Turn right along B6277, passing village hall on left
- Turn left into field through small gap beside gate, signposted
- Cross field towards trees and through gap in right corner under a tree onto path between wall on right and fence on left, crossing footbridge into field

Section 4: 1mi (1.6km)
- Turn along edge of field, keeping close to wall and stream on right, and through gate into next field
- Continue along wide track beside wood on right, then though gate marked 'footpath' and into farmyard
- Cross farmyard onto driveway out to B6277 again
- Cross B6277, bearing right through gate into wood
- Follow path, bearing left through gap onto road
- Turn right, cross bridge, turning left onto access road to Bowlees Visitor Centre
- Continue along road to information board on right (this is the best time to visit Gibson's Cave
- Straight on to the Visitor Centre (ideal place for refreshments)
- Exit Visitor Centre via front by wheelchair ramp
- Go straight ahead along road to B6277
- Bear right across road and through gate into field, signposted
- Cross two fields through two gates
- Cross stone stile, then down steps along wide path to bridge (to right of bridge are various paths leading to a better view of Low Force waterfall)
- Cross Wynch Bridge (one person at a time)

Section 5: (optional) 3mi (4.8km) – it seemed longer to me
- Turn right up steps with river on right for waterfalls at High Force, signposted (the 1.5 mile path is well defined and clearly signposted. The restaurant is accessed via the bridge with gates at both ends)
- Retrace steps, with river to Low Force now on left, then bearing left at house on right

Swimmers enjoying Low Force on the River Tees.

and descend boulder stepping stone path to bridge

Section 6: 1.5mi (2.4km)

- At junction at Wynch Bridge turn left after section 4 or straight on from section 5 up stone steps onto Pennine Way with river on left
- Continue along path, keeping close to fence on left, then onto grass path with fence now on right and over footbridge and stone stile
- Follow path through gap over stepping stones, passing footbridge on left, and through kissing gate into field
- Continue along the clearly signposted Pennine Way, keeping close to river on left as the path crosses fields with connecting stiles and gates

Section 7: 1.5mi (2.4km)

- Turn right over stile in fence (unusual), cross stream via large stepping stones and into small field
- Cross field and over stile opposite (difficult) onto path
- Follow narrow path over footbridge, up stony slope away from river as it winds across the hillside, still with river on left below, and over stile into field
- Continue along path across fields and over stiles to junction with wide track, and gate on left
- Keeping gate on left, cross track, bearing slightly left round small mound, then right onto path beside wall on right, crossing stile ahead
- Follow clearly-defined path as it continues to track the river on the left (often beside fences and walls)

Section 8: 1mi (1.6km)

- Cross field close to fence on left, and over footbridge through gate into next field
- Cross field with wall now on left (auction sheds in view ahead on left), and through gate into field
- Follow path, passing buildings on left, and through gate with building on right out to road
- Turn right along road to campsite entrance

IN THE VICINITY
FISHING
The River Tees has a revered reputation among the angling community, especially its

upper reaches from Middleton-in-Teesdale towards the waterfalls of Low and High Force. This, despite the fact that some places are difficult to reach. The fishing is so good it is explained locally that "there is just something about the way Tees water flows." Permits are available online from High Force Hotel or Middleton-in-Teesdale village newsagent. However, if you stay at Leekworth campsite on the banks of the river, a mile (1.6km) from the village, fishing is free as long as you have a rod licence. Grassholme Reservoir is another popular location for anglers, catering specifically for the disabled. Besides a visitor centre there is a shop stocked with all-things 'fishy' as well as drinks.

BIRDWATCHING

This is a popular, all-year-round activity in the area. Besides the many online suggestions of ideal places to birdwatch, there are also guided walks, with some even offering photographic opportunities.

CYCLING

For those who are fit enough to tackle some of the hills this is an ideal area for cyclists, with lots of interesting places to see. Routes for differing abilities can be found online.

WILD SWIMMING

There are places to wild swim in the river Tees, though it is vital to check online where it is safe to do so.

BOWLEES VISITOR CENTRE

The centre houses a wealth of information about the area, as well as a café, shop and displays and exhibition about the region. An ideal base from which to begin exploration of the area.

HIGH FORCE; LOW FORCE

The River Tees rises high in the Pennines and, as it makes its way to the sea, it slowly increases in size and speed. Then, at Whin Sill Rock, it plunges 70ft (21m) into the gorge below, creating a spectacular sight – High Force. A charming walk allows visitors to view what the artist J W Turner sketched. 1.5 miles (2.4km) downstream, this spectacle is repeated at Low Force, though, as its name suggests, rather less dramatically. The drop may be only 18ft (5.5m) but this and the surrounding pools and rocks make an impressively stunning sight, nevertheless.

In addition, close by is the famous Wynch Bridge, built in 1830 to reduce miners' journeys to the lead mines at Middleton. It is listed and, although still in use, it is advised it be crossed one person at a time. In June 2019 the area was used in the film *1917*. Signs were erected to reassure visitors that the various body parts lying about were prosthetics!

MIDDLETON-IN-TEESDALE

Nestling on the banks of the River Tees is this delightful market village; gateway to Upper Teasdale. When the London Lead Company relocated its headquarters here in the early

19th century, it grew significantly, and, in memory of the superintendent of that company, Robert Walton Bainbridge, a fountain was erected in the centre of the village in 1877. The village was important enough during this time that the rail branch line from Barnard Castle terminated here. However, this closed in 1962 and is now a cyclepath.

There are a variety of small independent shops, cafés and hotels, etc, and a tourist information office that is well worth a visit in order to truly appreciate the significance of this lovely place. The hub of the village is on the north bank of the River Tees. The cattle market, recycling centre, and what used to be the rail terminus, are on the south bank. One of the few bridges in the dale, for vehicles or pedestrians, connects the two parts.

Barnard Castle
This market town has a long and interesting history, and there is plenty to see and do. Although it is more than 11 miles (17.7km) from the campsite, there is a regular bus service from Middleton-in-Teesdale.

Eggleston Hall Gardens
Though there have been gardens at Eggleston Hall since the 16th century, the building itself is Georgian, dating back to the 19th century. It is privately owned, and is open to the public on rare occasions only. The gardens, however, can be visited all year and specialize in rare plants, especially those which will be able to cope with the dales climate. Dogs are welcome to accompany their owners.

Lincolnshire – a hidden gem
OS Maps Explorer 282 Kincilsnhire Wolds North

On the east coast, butting up against 50 miles (80.4km) of the North Sea, is Lincolnshire: a long, fairly thin county that borders eight others. Despite being the second largest county in England, nowadays, it is somewhat overlooked, though it was not always so. In the Roman era it had real significance: Lincoln itself, known as 'Lindum Colonia,' was the second most important settlement after York, and became a centre of political and cultural activity during the three centuries of Roman influence. To connect the towns and cities they had established, the Romans built a network of roads and canals, and three of the most important of these – perhaps the busiest – passed through Lincolnshire via Fossway, Ermina Street, and the Saltway.

The Normans also considered the area strategic, especially William I when he invaded England. The first Norman castle was built at Lincoln in 1068 and, interestingly, in 1367, Henry VI was born there. Then there's the legend of King John's misadventures ... an extremely unlucky king he was the villain in the story of Robin Hood, and then, in 1215, he was forced by the barons to sign the Magna Carta, which limited his powers. A copy of this is in Lincoln Cathedral, also built by the Normans. Finally, whilst retreating from London in 1216 with all his treasure, King John misjudged the tides in The Wash and it is thought that all of his treasure was swept away and he ended up with nothing, but as he died just a few months later what actually happened remains a mystery.

Agriculture is extremely important to the economy of Lincolnshire, and has been for many centuries. Sheep with particularly long coats – the 'Lincoln Longwool' – were commonplace 500 years ago, though now are very rare. However, the 'Lincoln Red' cattle are still seen in fields thereabouts. These days many farms are arable only and a range of crops are grown in the county, with vegetables mostly in the south and grain in more northern areas. There are, however, still a few livestock farms dotted about.

Although Lincolnshire is very rural, the landscape is, in fact, surprisingly varied, with four discernible regions. The 'fens' in the south east of the county used to be peat marshland but, having been drained over the centuries, these are now flat, fertile farmland. Then there are the 'marshes' along the coastal area where there are various ongoing environmental projects. On the western side of the county is the 'Lincoln Edge' (cliffs), a north to south stretch of high ground.

The fourth region is the 'Lincolnshire Wolds,' a range of gentle hills in the north east of the county. Not especially high, reaching only 551 feet (168 metres), they are, nonetheless, the highest point between Kent in the south and Yorkshire in the north. The landscape, with its woodland, grassland, hidden valleys and charming hamlets, is so exceptional that 216 square miles (558 sq km) of the Wolds were designated an AONB (Area of Outstanding Natural Beauty) in 1973. The poet John Betjeman was so impressed during visits to friends that he was inspired to pen poems about the county, such as *A Lincolnshire Tale, A Lincoln Church*, and *House of Rest*.

With many footpaths, some through farmyards and, somewhat unusually, the back gardens of houses, this is an ideal area to explore with your dog. The Wold experience was immersive from the start as the pub and campsite are located in the AONB.

CAMPSITE – THREE HORSESHOES

The campsite lies in the heart of the Lincolnshire Wolds at the rear of the pub, and is overlooked by fields on three sides, with cows in one and farming work in another: a delightful, quiet, rural setting. Besides pitches for caravans and motorhomes, 16 of which have electric hook-up, there are pods and bell tents.

The site is spacious enough to accommodate several tents, with outdoor space for games. There are two small amenity blocks and an outside dishwashing area. It's a well organized, efficiently-run site; an incredible achievement considering the owners acquired the campsite and pub in a derelict state in 2012. They have worked very hard to create such a pleasant experience for visitors.

PUB – THREE HORSESHOES

Rather hidden away, the pub is a short walk along a cul-de-sac, and is an attractive building, considering the state it must have been in just a few years ago. It's a welcoming venue with helpful, friendly staff (they loved Pearl), serving delicious food. At the side of the pub, stretching out into the garden, is the outdoor section called 'Jam Jar Bistro,' which has a small bar and serves lighter meals throughout the day, including a delicious breakfast. Takeaway is also available, and meals – including pizzas and burgers – can be collected or delivered to your pitch. The pub has an excellent reputation and has lot to offer visitors.

The campsite is surrounded by fields; note the tractor in the background.
The Three Horseshoes 'Jam Jar Bistro' outdoor section.

PEARLS OF WISDOM

This was a nice place because so many people made a fuss of me and gave me yummy treats. It was a shame there was no special place for me to play chase my frisbee, although I was able to run about when there was more space. We also found a small piece of grass outside.

The longer walks were good; I even had a ride on a rattling, van-type thing with seats! A bus, I think it was called. Sometimes we even walked very close to houses, passing people sitting outside enjoying the sun; I had to go on the lead here when my owner mentioned the word 'garden.' There was rather a lot of hard tarmac but it was very quiet so I did not have to go on the lead. An okay place.

SHORT WALK – ROUND AND ABOUT
Distance: 4mi (6.4km)
Duration: 1.5hr (Easy)
Terrain: Footpaths, quiet roads, lanes, stony tracks, fields, kissing gates, stiles; some steady climbs

Section 1: 1mi (1.6km)
- Exit campsite via pub, turning left to road
- Turn right along road
- Straight on at junction, passing bus shelter on right
- Turn left by tree between houses onto lane, signposted
- Follow lane out to road, continuing straight ahead
- Turn left at junction along road: Top Lane
- Turn right through kissing gate onto footpath, passing house and garden on left; through kissing gate into field
- Follow path along edge of two fields with hedge on left, then through another kissing gate into large field
- Straight ahead, crossing wide track with temporary fence on left

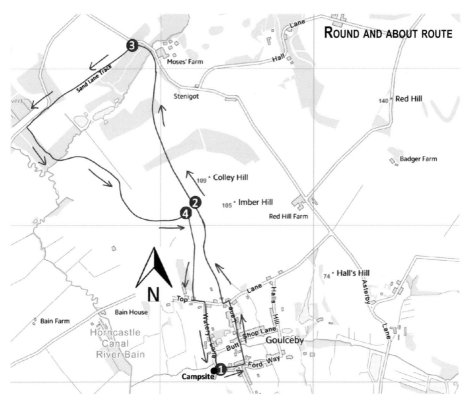

Section 2: 1mi (1.6km)

- Bear right onto parallel footpaths that snake up over the hill ahead
- Continue along path over hill and through kissing gate in hedge ahead into small field
- Cross field, then through kissing gate opposite, and down steps into woods
- Straight on along path, through wood and out to field
- Follow path across field through wood opposite, then through another kissing gate out to field
- Bear right across field towards buildings; through kissing gate out to road, turning left along road

Section 3: 1mi (1.6km)

- Turn left at left-hand bend onto wide track
- Continue along track to road, turning left along road
- Turn left onto path between fences with wood on right
- Follow path, taking clearly defined detour to avoid muddy patch over footbridge, then through kissing gate out to field
- Bear right across field to signpost in middle; bear left up slope (look out for muddy patch)
- At top of slope head towards left corner to cross stile beside second gate to right of corner, onto wide, stony track

Section 4: 1mi (1.6km)

- Continue downhill along track to road
- Turn left along road and right at junction
- Follow road past bench on green patch, tuning right to pub and campsite

LONG WALK – IN VIKING FOOTSTEPS!

Distance: 10.5mi (16.9km)
Duration: 5hr (Easy)
Terrain: Footpaths, fields,
tracks, many very quiet roads,
lanes, stiles, kissing gates,
a few short hills; plenty of
signposts

Section 1: 1.25mi (2km)

Phone to arrange a pick up
by bus to Horncastle from bus
stop at junction of Main Road
and Horncastle Road (see 'In
the vicinity: Buses'). Alight at
the Market Place in centre of
Horncastle

- Turn left along road towards Co-op Funeral Services on Bridge Street
- Turn right along Bridge Street to Sir Joseph Banks Centre and Information Centre (very interesting. Adjacent is a café; a good place for a breather
- Exit Sir Joseph Banks Centre, turning right along road and passing Market Place
- Continue along High Street to junction, with Red Lion on left corner
- Cross road to minor 'no entry' road opposite: Banks Street
- Follow road, bearing right to river

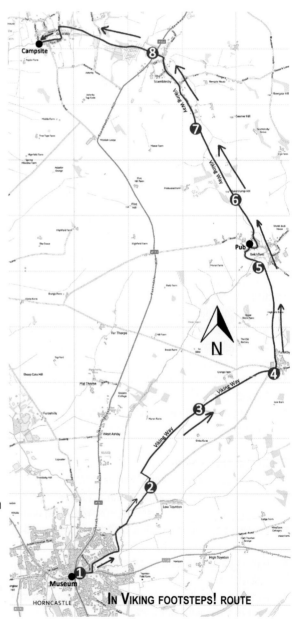

IN VIKING FOOTSTEPS! ROUTE

- Continue along road with river on right
- Turn left at T- junction; then right onto Bowl Alley Lane
- Follow road round right-hand bend, past two schools on left and onto footpath at left-hand bend (this is the Viking Trail)
- Continue along footpath, passing houses on left, and round bend, signposted, out to road
- Turn right along road, taking left fork at junction
- Turn left along wide track at next junction

Section 2: 1.5mi (2.4km)
- Follow track between fields and over small concrete bridge; round to right at corner, then round to left, then right again with hedge on left
- Continue along track as it winds between fields
- Turn right at bridleway junction, signposted, still on gravelly track but away from village on left
- Follow track round to left, then right, signposted
- Continue along edge of field, keeping close to hedge on right, round to left at corner
- At next corner turn right then immediately left, following path along edge of field with hedge now on left
- Follow path round to right at next corner, then left onto stony farm track

Section 3: 1.25mi (2km)
- Continue along track, past barns and farm on right, and out to road
- Straight on along road to Fulletby

Section 4: 1.5mi (2.4km)
- Turn left just past garage, following road round to right past church, then round to left passing Chapel Lane and Manor House Lane on left
- Turn right through kissing gate into field just past bench and noticeboard on right
- Bear left across field and through kissing gate opposite, across next field and through another kissing gate at bottom of slope into third field
- Bear right across field to top right-hand corner, then through kissing gate into next field
- Follow path along edge of field with hedge on right, turning left at corner, still along edge of field with hedge on right
- Take right fork at junction, following path round edge of field
- Take right fork at corner onto wide track going down

Section 5: 1.25mi (2km)
- Turn right at bottom, signposted, then left in 100yds (91m) also signposted, onto grass path
- Follow path across field, bearing right over bridge onto narrow path between fences
- Continue along path then through kissing gate out to wide track, turning right to follow out to road

- Follow road round to right then left, bearing left at junction to pub (a good place to stop for refreshments)
- Exit pub, turning right along road
- Turn right through kissing gate into field immediately after bungalow (plant seller)
- Straight on across field through kissing gate in corner into next field
- Continue ahead along edge of field with hedge on right, and over footbridge into next field
- Straight on along edge of field, still with hedge on right

Section 6: 1.25mi (2km)
- Turn right, signposted, and over footbridge in hedge into field
- Turn left along edge of field with hedge now on left, and through gap in hedge in corner
- Straight ahead along wide, grassy path with fence on right
- Bear right across track by ponds on left, through kissing gate beside larger gate
- Continue along footpath between fences and down slope, then through kissing gate in corner and out to field
- Cross field, keeping wooden fence opposite on right; through kissing gate onto wide track
- Follow track out to field, still along edge of field with hedge on left
- Turn right through hedge out to road

Section 7: 1mi (1.6km)
- Turn left along road, passing houses on right and bearing left at junction
- Continue along road, turning right at junction and then right again just past school
- Turn left over footbridge just past lay-by onto narrow footpath with fence on left
- Turn right over footbridge; then left with stream on left
- Follow path out to A153 by crash barrier

Section 8: 1.5mi (2.4km)
- Turn right, then left to cross road; left along pavement, then right back onto footpath
- Continue along footpath, still with stream on left, over footbridge and through wood out to field
- Follow path round edge of field with hedge/fence on left
- Turn left at corner, cross footbridge then go right with stream now on right
- Continue along track out to road
- Turn right; cross bridge; turn left; cross road to path opposite with stream now on left
- Follow path beside stream, across footbridge to footpath opposite into wood
- Take right fork at junction, following wooden walkway onto footpath through wood, then through kissing gate into field
- Follow footpath along edge of field and through kissing gate out to road
- Turn left along road, over ford, following road round to right
- Straight ahead at junction, passing bus shelter on left
- Turn left up Shoe Lane to pub and campsite

IN THE VICINITY

BUSES

There is a bus stop just down the road from the campsite. The bus service in this part of Lincolnshire is 'CallConnect,' and you order a pick-up much as you would call a cab, except you need to make the necessary arrangements the day before. Simply ask in the pub for the phone number; tell the dispatcher where you wish to be picked up, your destination and the time of pick-up. She will inform you when the bus will be at your stop. Arrive five minutes or so before the agreed time and the bus should appear soon after. The fare for a dog is 50p.

CYCLING

An ideal way to explore the landscape of the Wolds is by cycling. There is an extensive network of routes, details of which can be found online.

BIRDWATCHING

There are several nature reserves scattered around the county that are especially suitable for birdwatching. The closest to the campsite is Red Hill Nature Reserve at Asterby Lane, just 1.5 miles (2.4km) away. Note, though, that dogs are rarely allowed into these places.

CADWELL PARK

This is a motor racing circuit in the heart of the Lincolnshire Wolds. In 1934 Mansfield Wilkinson decided to set up a circuit as his sons were already using the area to race their bikes. Initially, the circuit comprised a chalk track laid around the old manor house, but gradually it was surfaced and extended to a length of 1.75 miles (2.8km) in 1952, and 2.25 miles (3.6km) in 1961. The track's first major car race was held in 1962. It was extensively updated when acquired in 2004 by Jonathan Palmer's MotorSport Vision company. It chiefly hosts motorcycle racing, with events in August and May being particularly popular, although there has been a gradual increase in motorcar racing also.

FULLETBY

This small village in the Lincolnshire Wold is the second highest settlement in the county, and on a clear day there are extensive views to Lincoln Cathedral and the coast. It was also home to Henry Winn, a renowned local Victorian writer and poet.

HORNCASTLE

At the south west foot of the Wolds is this delightful market town. Located at the confluence of the River Bain and Waring, it has a long and interesting history stretching back to the Roman era (evident by its name as Horncastle means 'Roman town on horn-shaped piece of land'). In 1230, it was granted market rights, and markets are still regularly held in the Market Square. Though St Mary's church was restored in the 19th century, it originally dates from six centuries earlier.

At huge cost the Horncastle Canal was finally completed in 1802, but competition from railways forced its closure in 1889. Town walks and information are available at the

Tourist Information Centre on Bridge Street. The town is notable for having a number of antique shops.

JOSEPH BANKS CENTRE

Situated in an attractive building that doubles as the Tourist Information Centre, Sir Joseph Banks was a scientist interested in botany and nature, and the promotion of science. He was also an explorer, and sailed with Captain Cook on *The Endeavour* in 1768. Other influential and important people associated with the area include the Victorian poet Alfred Lord Tennyson, who was born in 1809 in Somersby, and spent most of his life in Lincolnshire, drawing inspiration for his work from his surroundings. Captain John Smith was born locally, too: an explorer who spent time in Jamestown in the USA where he met Pocahontas. Sir John Franklin, another explorer born in Lincolnshire, died searching for the North West passage in Canada.

Norfolk – water, water, everywhere

OS MAP EXPLORER OL40 THE BROADS

There is a local saying that the people of Norfolk 'have one foot in the sea and one on land' because water is always nearby. The eastern part of the county bulges out into The North Sea, so there is more than 100 miles (161km) of coastline featuring a hugely diverse landscape, much of which is an Area of Outstanding Natural Beauty (AONB). With sandy beaches galore, hidden coves, nature reserves, dunes, picturesque villages and seaside towns, there is something for everyone.

The Norfolk Coast Path is the best way to experience these wonders. The North Norfolk coast is also unique in that the waters come directly from the Arctic as there is no intervening land. Fortunately, this is not always the case with the weather! Even so, Norfolk is inclined to be cold, dry and bright.

A plethora of rivers meander around the county, flowing out either into the North Sea or The Wash. Some are long rivers with many tributaries, such as the River Yar that flows through Norwich; others are short like the River Burn that flows northward out near The Wash at Holkham Beach. Sometimes the gentle flow of the rivers creates pools and ponds. A network of five rivers – Yare, Ant, Waveney, Chet and Bure – weave about in the east of the county, connecting lakes and wetlands, and creating the distinctive landscape known as the Norfolk Broads. Surprisingly, this unique environment is not a National Park although the Broads Authority manages and protects it in a similar way.

It was always assumed that the Broads were a natural phenomenon, but Dr Joyce Lambert demonstrated in the 1960s that they are, in fact, man-made; the result of human enterprise. It all started in the Middle Ages when local monasteries excavated blocks of peat, selling them to the local community. This was a thriving business, and 320,000 tonnes of peat a year were supplied to Norwich Cathedral alone. Over the centuries, the resultant hollows filled with water, becoming deeper and wider as the sea level rose. To try and combat this effect, windmills and dykes were built, but to no avail. And so it is that, today, the landscape is comprised of grazing marshes, wet woodlands and reedbeds; navigable rivers, and lakes ... or 'broads' as we know them.

The Broads are popular with all aquatic enthusiasts.

The Norfolk Broads are extensive: 117square miles (303sq km), with over 120 miles (193km) of waterways that are navigable and lock-free, with just five bridges. These restrict the passage of larger vessels as only small boats can sail under them. The many lakes and ponds – broads – are mostly located in the northern half of the area, and come in a range of sizes from small ponds to large lakes. Some of them are actually part of the river, whilst others lie adjacent to the river, and are connected by a dyke. Over the years, there have been various attempts to increase the navigable area of the Broads but none has been really successful.

With such an extensive network of accessible lakes and rivers, naturally enough, the area is extremely popular with the boating fraternity, and all manner of boats of all sizes, from canoes to large sailing yachts, and even some electric- and solar-powered craft, can be found there. There are boats everywhere, cruising along and tied up at moorings. A speed limit on all craft ensures their wash does not damage the banks.

Exploring the Broads by boat offers a different perspective of the landscape, and is well worth experiencing. There are numerous hire companies, but best to book in advance to ensure a boat is available when you want it.

The Broads are only a small region of the county, although it is all quite flat and rural, and especially suitable for agriculture: chiefly arable, with the main crops being wheat, oil seed rape, and barley for brewing. Together with attractive villages and intriguing towns dotted about, there is plenty for visitors, whether they be walker, cyclist or birdwatcher: something for everyone.

Campsite – Causeway Cottage Caravan Park

This campsite is conveniently located at one end of Potter Heigham village, just off the A149, on a charming link road that has a very narrow bridge over the river – hence the name 'Bridge Road' – and is ideally situated to explore the Norfolk Broads The campsite is long and thin, with a few static vans in addition to about 20 pitches, all with electric hook-up and water tap. The cottage on the right of the narrow entrance is the reception, next to which is a rather dated toilet block: having to find 50 pence for a shower is inconvenient ...

The owners are very helpful and pleasant; always working to improve the site

Between the dyke and the campsite is a marsh field, often complete with cows.

(apparently, a new toilet block is scheduled to be built at the far end of the site). There are pleasant views over the marsh fields, which are frequently occupied by a herd of cows keen to check out the strange goings on over the hedge.

Pub – Falgate Inn

Just 400 yards along Bridge Road at the end of the village is this attractive pub. A great deal of work has recently been carried out to the outside areas, where there is a delightful patio at the side and a spacious garden at the rear. The menu is limited but the chef has plans to offer a greater choice, using local produce and herbs from the kitchen garden at the rear of the pub.

Pearls of wisdom

Oh how confusing! Water simply everywhere, but so few places where I could actually swim. Then there were all these strange, huge objects whizzing by on the water; I think my owner called them 'boats?' I wouldn't want to tangle with one of those, I can tell you.

I could not even distract myself by chasing my frisbee as there were very few places to do this. Even so, the walks were good, with lots of footpaths, fields, etc, though the busy road seemed to go on forever before we got somewhere interesting. The campsite was okay although the funny animals on the other side of the hedge were a bit scary ...

Short walk – Rivers and dykes
Distance: 6mi (9.6km)
Duration: 2hr (Easy)
Terrain: Flat, riverside paths, track, footpaths, roads quiet lanes, woods, some gates (lots of water to walk around)

Section 1: 1.75mi (2.8km)
- Exit campsite via entrance onto road
- Turn right along road, passing shops, etc, to narrow bridge
- Turn left onto wide riverside path immediately before bridge

The pub has an inviting patio at the side and a lovely garden at the back.

Sailing on the River Thurne on the Broads.

- Continue along path under bridge, passing holiday cottages, boats, etc, on right; round left-hand bend and across bridge by windmill on left
- Follow clearly defined path as it winds, with river on right, round huge left-hand bend

Section 2: 1.75mi (2.8km)

- Continue straight ahead along footpath via metal gate on left, moving away from river and passing entrance to 'The Holt' on right, signposted 'Weavers Way' (ignore path on left)
- Follow path round right-hand bend, ignoring path on left, and through gate, then straight on with wood and ponds on left, passing path on left to viewing platform, jetty on right, and bird hide. Through another gate

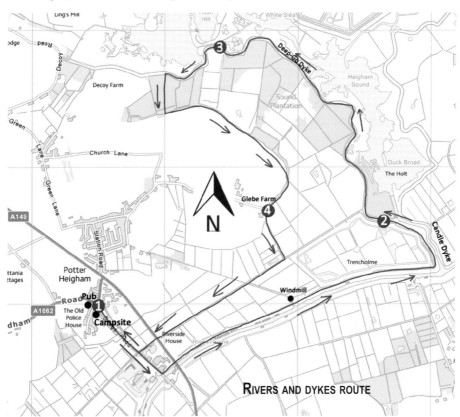

RIVERS AND DYKES ROUTE

Section 3: 1.25mi (2km)
- Continue along path, passing wood on left
- Turn left into wood across footbridge, signposted
- Follow path as it bears right, keeping close to stream on right (very muddy)
- Turn right at junction along footpath
- Continue along path beside stream, keeping close to fence on left, then out to field
- Cross field towards wood, crossing track between gates over footbridge
- Bearing slightly left follow path through wood, ignoring all adjoining tracks

Section 4: 1.25mi (2km)
- Continue straight on at junction, passing house on right
- At next junction turn right onto wide track
- Follow track over A149 to minor road
- Turn right along road to campsite entrance

LONG WALK – FIELDS AND RIVER
Distance: 9.25mi (14.8km)
Duration: 4.5hr (Easy)
Terrain: Flat but some rutted areas, footpaths, tracks – stony and grassy, fields, woods, roads (minor) gates and a couple of stiles (lots of water to walk around)

Section 1: 1.25mi (2km)
- Exit campsite to road via entrance
- Turn right along road and over narrow bridge, passing small car park on right
- Turn right along tarmac lane signposted 'Repps Riverbank'
- Bear left onto footpath, keeping close to wooden fence on right
- Follow path with dyke on left, river (lots of boats), and holiday homes on right, passing an amazingly restored windmill on left and out to access road

Section 2: 1.25mi (2km)
- Turn left along road (turning right leads to a slipway where dogs can swim, relatively safe from passing boats), passing car park on left. Round bend with Wind Energy Museum on right and caravan park on left
- Turn right along footpath into field, signposted
- Straight across field over wide farm track

A windmill on the River Thurne: one of the very few with sails.

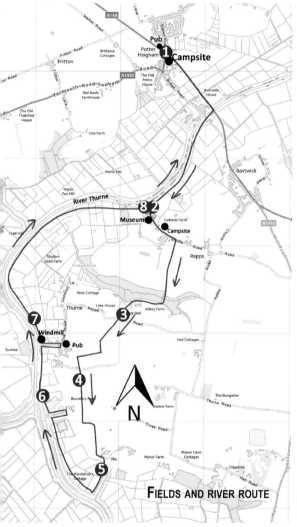

FIELDS AND RIVER ROUTE

- Bear very slightly right onto wide, grassy track, heading towards trees
- Bear left around trees, then right into wood
- Follow path through wood, passing footbridge on left
- Turn left at junction through gap in hedge onto wide, grassy track; round bend onto narrow path with fence on left and out to road
- Cross road to footpath opposite

Section 3: 1mi (1.6km)
- Bear right, following path across field and out to wide track
- Turn left along track, then right at junction towards buildings
- Turn left into field through kissing gate
- Cross field and through kissing gate opposite into next field
- Straight ahead, keeping close to hedge on right and passing church on left, out to road

Section 4: 1mi (1.6km)
- Bear left onto footpath opposite
- Follow path along edge of field with hedge on right, then left along next field edge to corner
- Turn right, following path between hedge on right and fence on left out to access road
- Turn left along road, passing small car park
- Turn immediately right onto footpath, passing car park on right
- Continue on path, keeping close to hedge on right, passing first left then right around building onto concrete area to access road
- Turn left along road, passing buildings (including cowshed on right)
- Turn right at junction, following concrete track over stile into car park

Section 5: 1mi (1.6km)
- Bear left across car park, following grass path left and then right to mooring inlet
- Continue ahead, passing inlet on left
- Turn left along grass track with inlet still on left
- Follow path, keeping close to water on left, and through gate
- Continue on path to right round another mooring inlet, then left across access road
- Turn left again onto stony track by campsite reception area, with water still on left and field on right

Section 6: 0.75mi (1.2km)
- Follow riverside path round to right, keeping river on left, and through gate to next mooring inlet
- Continue on path round right-hand bend along inlet and through gate out to road
- Turn left to pub on right (The Lion at Thurne: a good place to stop for refreshments)
- From pub continue straight ahead along road with houses on right and water on left onto grass path

Section 7: 1.75mi (2.8km)
- Follow path beside river past windmill and through gate, then over stile and through another gate, passing holiday cottages out to access road

Section 8: 1.25mi (2km)
- Cross tarmac road
- Follow path with dyke on right, and river (lots of boats) and holiday homes on left, past windmill and out to road
- Turn left along road over narrow bridge, passing shop,s etc, to campsite entrance on right

IN THE VICINITY

FISHING

With so many rivers and waterways the Norfolk Broads is ideal for all kinds of fishing, and there are all kinds of fish, although it is essential that a fishing permit is obtained via the Environmental Agency, a Post Office or online. Also care needs to be taken not to fish on private land. The Broads Angling Strategy Group (BASG) offers advice about fishing and coaching sessions.

BIRDWATCHING

With a constantly-changing environment, the variety of birds passing through the area is astonishing. For the more serious bird enthusiast there is a nature reserve at Hickling Broad, adjacent to the River Thurne, which has bird hides, as well as several trails around the reserve and, in summer, boat tours. There is a charge to enter although it's free to members. More importantly, dogs are not allowed.

BOATING

Numerous boatyards in and around Potter Heigham offer boat hire: the largest is Herbert Woods (difficult to miss). Claiming to be the second largest outfit in the Broads, Woods has been operating since 1929, and offers an eclectic range of hire craft/options.

NORFOLK OUTDOOR ADVENTURES

Here it is possible to experience a different kind of boating adventure – kayaking and paddle-boarding. A range of activity options is available.

LATHAMS

This large store in Potter Heigham sells just about anything and everything, and is a well-known local landmark (see below).

POTTER HEIGHAM

This village on the River Thurne is something of a contradiction. A major boating centre with several boatyards that hire out boats, including Herbert Woods, it is also home to discount superstore Lathams (see above), famous throughout Norfolk, and numerous holiday homes that line the banks of the river.

Potter Heigham also has a long and fascinating history typical of rural villages, and, besides St Nicholas church with its 12th century tower, there is the medieval bridge that dates from 1385, and is so low that only small boats can sail under it, and even then only at low tide. As a consequence the bridge does divide the boating experience to either upper or lower River Thurle. Sailing under the bridge is one of the challenges facing yachts that enter the 'Three Rivers Race,' which takes place during the first weekend in June. Competitors have 24 hours to cover as much as possible of the rivers Bure, Acle and Thurne that comprise the 50 mile (80km) course.

WIND ENERGY MUSEUM

Just over a mile (1.6km) from the campsite next to the River Thurne is this unique museum, affiliated to the East Anglian Mills Society. In 1949 when the majority of disused mills were being dismantled, Ronald Morse bought a dilapidated mill in Thurne. The present museum opened in 2014 and has an extensive collection of exhibits, including full-size wind pumps, plus contemporary photographs and drawings, all set in 2.75 acres.

THURNE MILL DRAINAGE PUMP

This is the mill that Ronald Morse also bought and restored to its present condition. Located on the River Thurne, it is often used by the media because it is such an iconic landmark. In 2020 it was 200 years old

West Yorkshire – in the footsteps of Heathcliff

OS MAPS EXPLORER OL21 SOUTH PENNINES

Yorkshire is a unique county in that it was so large it was sub-divided into three regions called 'Ridings.' As a child I always wondered why only three – North Riding, West Riding

Charming villages nestle in steep valleys between the foothills of the Pennines.

and East Riding – as it seems there should have been four. They are very ancient divisions derived from an old Norse word meaning thirds, and are even mentioned in the Domesday Book of 1086. This all changed in 1974 as a result of the Local Government Act of 1972, although the new West Yorkshire is roughly equivalent in size to the old West Riding of Yorkshire.

West Yorkshire is a diverse county with, in the north, large urban conurbations such as Bradford, and ribbons of settlements stretched out along the network of roads, canals and railways. The south and west are more rural, with charming villages, steep valleys between the foothills of the Pennines, and hills capped with the quintessential 'moors' that epitomize the celebrated, spectacular landscape.

These moors are actually the result of many centuries of over-grazing and tree felling, and, usually, the soil is poor – sometimes with large areas of peat – and often marshy. The combination of altitude, poor soil and water impacts hugely on the flora, the covering of low-growing shrubs such as gorse or bracken and bog mosses and grasses portraying a harsh landscape: unforgiving, stark; bleak.

The parcels of moor near the campsite may only be the leftover fragments of the huge expanse to the south and west, but the essence is the same. As the moor is approached, the horizon is filled with an undulating brown carpet stretching off into the distance, with grey threads snaking through it. Slowly, the maze of tracks reveal themselves: some wide; some mere indentations in the gorse mat. The sleek appearance of the trails is an illusion, however, as the wide, rutted paths are hazardous for the unwary, and the narrow ones pluck at clothing and whip ankles as you pass. Apart from the periodic sudden marshy patch underfoot, or occasional rise and fall of ground, the landscape is relentlessly unvarying.

The moor reflects the weather's tone. A blue sky contrasts with the brown moor, creating a golden colour that casts a benign gentleness, masking the hazards. Menacing grey clouds obscure the moor's splendour, emphasizing the bleakness of this place.

The changing moods of the moor are imaginatively captured in the Brontë sisters' novels, evocative of Cathy running across the moor, her voluminous skirts sweeping over the low shrubs, calling, calling for Heathcliff. The sisters' stories chime perfectly with the landscape, and only Pearl's presence reminds me that this is *not* the 19th century.

The Brontë sisters lived in Haworth Vicarage, where their father was the parson of the Church of St Michael and All Angels. The five girls had one brother, Branwell, who found the family's expectations of him too great and so resorted to drink and drugs in order to cope. He died at 31, a broken man.

Of the five sisters, two died just before reaching their teens, whilst the remaining three girls spent their time in the parsonage writing and walking the moors, because the village was smelly and filthy. Despite many difficulties, they managed to get their work published using assumed names, and, in 1847, Charlotte, the eldest, published *Jane Eyre*; Emily, the middle sister, published *Wuthering Heights*, and Anne, the youngest, published *Agnes Grey.*

Unfortunately, they did not live to enjoy their new-found wealth: Emily died aged 30 in December 1848; Anne died aged 29 in May 1849, and, though she did live for a further six years, Charlotte died in 1855, whilst pregnant, aged 39.

Their novels were all the rage then, and have since become classics, of course. Still popular, several TV and film adaptations have been produced from them.

CAMPSITE – UPWOOD HOLIDAY PARK

Situated high on the edge of Black Moor, overlooking the villages of Oxenhope and Haworth, Upwood Holiday Park – a very large campsite with three distinct sections – has spectacular views.

Turning into the access road the first entrance is restricted to full-time residents, the second to holiday lets, and the third to tourers, although even here it seems many of the large number of pitches are occupied by static caravans as well as yurts and camping pods. Though there are many clearly identified hardstanding pitches, the grass ones seem more randomly arranged.

Being such a large site the amenities block is quite a distance from some pitches, though it does have modern amenities that include dishwashing and laundry facilities. Unusually (and inconveniently), the showers are coin-operated. In the far corner is a gate leading directly onto the moor.

PUB – ON-SITE BAR

Perhaps because of the reduced opening hours, the busy bar is popular with all sections of the campsite, which, together with TV screens at each end of the big room, means it is very noisy. The room is expertly divided into sections of various sizes, so creating a more intimate atmosphere. Ordering seems convoluted but this may be due to Covid restrictions. The tasty food is normal pub fare. Wifi is accessible here only.

Despite the foregoing, the bar is a pleasant place to have a drink during quieter times, or meet up with friends, especially as dogs are welcome.

PEARLS OF WISDOM 🐾

What is this strange ground, with funny, short, spiky bushes? It's difficult to explore as there is so little room; just as well there are lots of paths of all sizes criss-crossing the ground. This seemed to go on and on but then suddenly there would be wet, squidgy places, some huge stones – even a wall! All very interesting and exciting, especially when I met friends.

I heard my owner mention 'moor,' but more of what? I do know it was not suitable for chasing my frisbee: the only available space was next to our van but I was not allowed to run around there. Walks were on lots of up and down stony tracks and tarmac, though not too many vehicles whizzing past.

I did find places to swim, though, and even managed a frisbee game. Yipee!

SHORT WALK – THE MOOR EXPERIENCE
Distance: 5mi (8km)
Duration: 2hr (Moderate)
Terrain: Moorland paths, tracks; footpaths, grass tracks, fields, roads, footpaths, gates, stiles (mostly sheep-proof). Up and down hills (short and not too steep). Amazing views

Section 1: 1.75mi (2.8km)
- Exit campsite via dog walking access
- Turn right along track and through gate onto moor
- Turn immediately right along narrow path going up, keeping close to wall on right
- Bear left at top of slope onto very narrow but clearly defined path between bracken, and head towards boulders
- Continue along path, passing boulders and pond on right as it winds across the moor towards wall, taking left path to skirt bog
- On reaching the wall follow path with wall on right to cross by another group of boulders
- Turn left and continue along path, going slightly downhill with wall now on left
- Keeping left at junction join wide track junction beside broken wall
- Turn right along wide grass track, passing junction on left to way-marker ahead
- Take right fork along wide, clearly defined path, going down to road
- Turn left along narrow path just before gate, keeping close to wall with road on left
- Several paths wind across the moor skirting boulders and bracken patches: follow the most obvious one running parallel to road that eventually reach a junction with wide track
- Turn left along track and through gate out to road

Section 2: 1mi (1.6km)
- Turn left along road, passing buildings on right
- Turn right at bend onto stony access road
- Follow driveway through gate (Bank House Farm) onto wide track
- Continue uphill along track

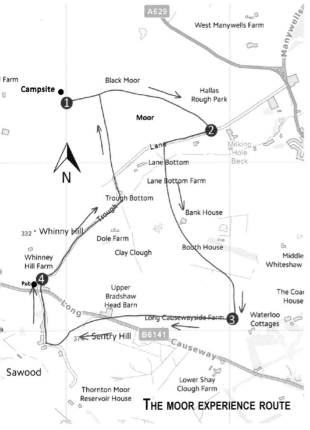

THE MOOR EXPERIENCE ROUTE

- Turn left through gate; cross farmyard and through another gate into field
- Straight on along edge of field with wall on left, and through gate
- Continue along path with fence on left
- Bear right uphill, taking right fork and still climbing: over stile (sheep-proof)
- Bearing slightly right across field, cross stepping stones (dry bed in summer)
- Bearing right, continue across field, keeping mound on left, and onto wide track
- Turn right along track and over stone pipe, continuing along track to wide, grassy track beside wall

Section 3: 1mi (1.6km)
Some amazing views on this part of the walk

- Turn right along grass path, keeping close to wall on left, then over stile in wall (sheep-proof)
- Turn right along track between wall and fence; over stile (sheep-proof) back into field
- Straight ahead along edge of field with wall still on left, and over another sheep-proof stile; across field, then through gate in left corner and into next field
- Cross field, keeping close to wall on left, then through a gap where a gate used to be
- Bear right downhill with wall now on right, and through gate out to road
- Turn right along road to pub (not dog-friendly, despite being called The Dog and Gun Inn)

Section 4: 1.25mi (2km)
- Turn right after pub and along Trough Lane through pub car park
- Follow road round to right at car park, then round to left, then right (take care: narrow road; traffic very light but fast)
- Turn left through gate at bend onto Black Moor
- Follow clearly-defined track, wide in places, uphill to junction with another wide track beside wall
- Turn left, crossing wall (broken)

- Take left fork, continuing along track and through gate onto path
- Follow path to campsite dog entrance

LONG WALK – CATCHING UP WITH THE BRONTËS

Distance: 7.25mi (11.6km)
Duration: 5hr (Challenging in places)
Terrain: Moorland paths and tracks – many very stony and uneven, riverside path, footbridges, quiet roads, footpaths, uneven stone steps, gates and narrow gaps. Long hills (up and down); some very steep. Exacting walk in places

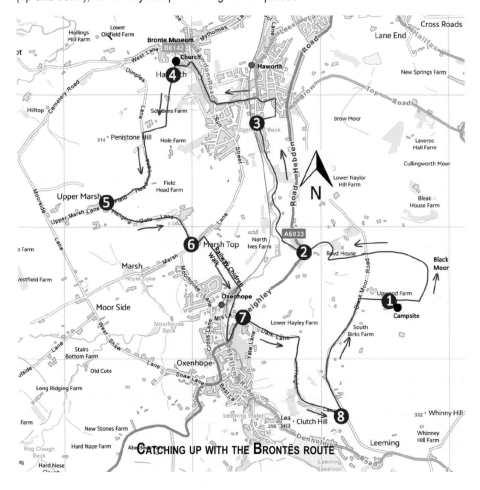

CATCHING UP WITH THE BRONTËS ROUTE

Section 1: 1.25mi (2km)
- Exit campsite via dog walking access
- Turn right along track and through gate onto moor

- Turn immediately left along narrow path going down (very steep and narrow in places) to wide stony track by gate, keeping close to fence on left
- Turn left though gate, continuing along track to road
- Cross road, bearing slightly right onto Delf Hill Farm driveway
- Continue along track round right-hand bend signposted 'Hebden Road,' and through gate onto wide, grass track
- Follow track as it winds downhill, through second metal gate next to small wooden one, passing house on right to road (take care – busy)
- Cross road to footpath opposite, signposted, and through gate

Section 2: 1mi (1.6km)
- Continue down steps and through wood, still descending
- Turn left through narrow gap between stone wall and wooden fence across path and into field
- Straight ahead, passing footbridge on left (a good place for dog swimming on the other side of footbridge) onto clearly-defined path (Millennium Way)
- Turn right to follow riverside footpath, with river on left, passing tunnel under stone railway bridge. Up a slope, passing gate on left, and through gap ahead out to driveway
- Turn left, passing house on right
- Keep left onto very narrow path by low stone wall
- Follow path through gate and down narrow stone steps into field
- Straight ahead, keeping close to fence on left and passing footbridge; then through kissing gate
- Follow path towards new houses, keeping river on left still

Section 3: 0.75mi (1.2km)
- Turn right along tarmac path with houses on left
- Follow path up slope and round right-hand bend, then left over footbridge into field
- Turn left along path with new houses on left, through three gates (two kissing) and down steps out to road
- Turn left along road round right-hand bend; left at roundabout onto Bridgehouse Lane
- Continue uphill over railway bridge, turning right into park (toilets here)
- Bear left to exit at top left corner onto Butt Lane junction
- Cross road to cul-de sac opposite, heading towards Fleece Inn
- Follow road uphill round to right and out onto pedestrianised cobbled road (Main Street)

Section 4: 0.5mi (0.8km)
Along Main Street are many mostly small independent shops and a variety of eateries: an ideal place to stop for refreshments as most welcome dogs. The Brontë Museum housed in the parsonage is on Church Street: a turning on the left at the top of the hill. When I visited the Museum and Church Street were closed to the public. Dogs are not allowed in

the museum. As the street was closed off, too, I do not know if it is possible to walk along Church Street and past the museum.

Section 5: 1mi (1.6km)
- Up steps through church entrance, then left along footpath signposted Penistone Hill
- Straight ahead at junction onto narrow path signposted Oxendale. If, after refreshments, additional walking across the moor is appealing, the route to the Brontë Waterfalls (2.5ml (4km)) is off to the right. As it is a popular tourist attraction the way is clearly signposted
- Follow path as it winds across hillside, turning left as indicated at gate, passing house on right, and round corner out to field
- Continue ahead through gate into side garden
- Turn right, passing houses on left
- Turn right up drive to road
- Turn left to junction, passing a farm on left
- Turn left along Hanging Gate Lane to main road (rejoin here from Brontë Waterfalls excursion)

Section 6: 1.25mi (2km)
- Turn left along road with no pavement, then right just past house onto wide, stony track, signposted
- Follow track round to left, then right into field through small wooden gate
- Downhill across field and through gate; over railway line; down steps; turn right; over footbridge, then right again
- Keeping close to river on right, follow path out to car park to Mill Lane, passing Wilton House on left
- Turn right along Mill Lane; then left into park
- Take middle path through park, turning right past trees and out to Station Road
- Turn left along Station Road to roundabout (along Station Road 100 yards (91km) is a Co-op with an ATM and Post Office)

- Turn left along A6033, then right into Dark Lane adjacent to Sue Ryder Hospice

Section 7: 1mi (1.6km)
- Follow Dark Lane up a steep hill, and straight ahead at junction
- Continue along road, which becomes a track and then a road again as it winds uphill (very steep in places with amazing view)

The path to the centre of Haworth passes through the village outskirts.

Section 8: 0.5mi (0.8km)
- Turn left at junction (road now Height Lane) onto Black Moor Road
- Follow road to campsite entrance on right

IN THE VICINITY
HAWORTH
Because the books written by the Brontë sisters are still so popular, the village of Haworth is a major tourist attraction. The campsite is a good base from which to visit the village, even if it is a steep climb (in this part of Yorkshire, wherever you go is a steep climb). There is extensive information online suggesting places to visit connected to the Brontës, so I have highlighted those that are conveniently close.

THE BRONTË PARSONAGE
This was closed when I visited, but note that dogs are not allowed inside.

ST MICHAELS AND ALL ANGELS CHURCH
An imposing building next to the parsonage that houses the Brontë tomb. Again, no dogs allowed inside.

MAIN STREET
Leads up to the church and parsonage, and is a charming, cobbled street with many independent shops on each side, including pubs, restaurants and cafés. At the top is the Black Bull where Branwell Brontë went to drown his sorrows.

BRONTË WATERFALL
On the Brontë Way, 3 miles (4.8km) west of Haworth on the edge of Haworth Moor, is this waterfall, which was the sisters' favourite place to go to escape from the village.

TOP WITHENS
Above the waterfall is a derelict farmhouse, thought to be the inspiration for *Wuthering Heights.*

PENISTONE HILL COUNTRY PARK
The Brontë sisters used to cross this park to gain access to the moor. Nowadays, with a small car park, it is an ideal base from which to explore Haworth Moor.

CYCLING
With moorlands, quiet country lanes and steep hills, there is something for every cyclist, but especially those who like a challenge. Route suggestions can be found online.

BIRDWATCHING
With the wide, open skies of the moors, spotting birds is easy, so remember your binoculars.

More wonderful walks from dog-friendly campsites

Oxenhope

This village, nestling in the valley between Black Moor and Haworth Moor, is not a tourist hotspot, and is much quieter as a result. At one time, though, it was a hive of industry with 20 mills operating in the locality. In 1872, the nearby Leeming Reservoir was constructed to supply water to many of these mills. The mills have now gone, but a 'working village' atmosphere remains.

The old railway station has been enlarged and upgraded, and now has a workshop where rail stock is maintained, and an Exhibition Shed that houses historic engines and carriages. There are plans for further improvements.

Oxenhope is probably best known for its Straw Race, in which competitors have to carry a bale of straw around the village, stopping at each pub en-route, and ending up at the pub at the top of the hill ... a very steep hill!

Keighley and Worth Valley Railway

This heritage railway may only be 5 miles (8km) long but is unusual in that it connects to the mainline at Keighley station. So, although this delightful railway meanders through the stunning moors from Oxenhope to Keighley, discussion continues as to the viability of it carrying commuters. Despite this, some 100,000 passengers a year travel on the line.

The railway and various stations have appeared in numerous films and TV programmes, most notably the 1970 classic *The Railway Children*.

Cliffe Castle Museum

Situated on the north west edge of Keighley, this museum houses many interesting local artefacts.

East Riddlesden Hall

This was once a prosperous farming estate, and now, under the auspices of the National Trust, it reflects the times of those who once lived and worked on the property. The gardens are open all year and dogs are welcome in the lower fields, riverside walks and café outside seating area.

Walks in North West England
(Cheshire, Cumbria, Lancashire)

Cheshire – gongoozling

OS MAPS EXPLORER 257 CREWE AND NANTWICH

Without knowing it I am unquestionably a 'gongoozler' – someone who enjoys watching the activity on the many canals that weave their way around the country. I am intrigued by the whole process of cruising these verdant waterways, though not especially eager to participate. It is thought that the slang term 'gongoozler' was coined by canal workers for those standing idly on the towpath, casually watching them graft. These days it is used by canal enthusiasts, perhaps ironically, to explain their hobby and their interest. A gongoozler is comparable to a train-spotter or a twitcher, and is most frequently to be found at canal locks as the operation of these provides an opportunity to watch the endeavours of others. Although some gongoozlers are critical of efforts here, others are helpful, actually assisting with the complex manoeuvre.

The Cotton Arms campsite has direct access to Llangollen Canal via a small wooden gate at the rear of the site. It is because of the Llangollen Canal that, today, there are over 5000 miles (8046km) of navigable waterways, 2700 miles (4345km) of which are interconnected.

Narrowboats have many thousands of miles of navigable waterways to cruise.

Throughout history, commerce and the exchange of goods have utilised canals as efficient transportation; paramount to a successful enterprise. There are canals all over the world, some of which were constructed as long ago as a thousand years. England's canals enjoyed a heyday during the Industrial Revolution as a result of two periods of intense canal-building. The first, in 1759, was started by the Duke of Bridgewater, who wanted a quicker route from his coal mines in Worsley to Manchester. With the help of engineer James Brindley, the Bridgewater Canal was completed in 1776. So began the first phase of canal building, which gradually ceased during the 1780s due to national fiscal problems, though with an upturn in the economy, in 1789, canal building resumed until 1800 at which time there were 7000 miles (11,265km) of navigable waterways. However, the glory days were over: the new 'railway' was attracting the smart money.

Initially, the canals and railways operated side-by-side, but the writing was on the wall for the latter, and so began the slow but inevitable decline of the canals. The death knell was the downturn in traditional heavy industries after the two World Wars, and most of the canals were abandoned, unused, derelict and forgotten.

The Ellesmere Canal (now known as the Llangollen Canal) was closed by a 1944 Act of Parliament. However, the act also stipulated that, for ten years, it should be maintained and kept full of water for the various industries on its banks, and for the bigger, more important Shropshire Union Canal into which it fed.

This ribbon of water winding through the countryside was a magnet for boating enthusiasts, who took advantage of it to indulge their hobby. One such individual, Tom Roth, wrote a book about his experiences on the Ellesmere Canal, entitled simply *Narrow Boat*. The book, published in 1944, brought the plight of the canals and their potential to a wider audience and, together with rising demand for boating holidays, changed attitudes. When the future of the Ellesmere/Llangollen Canal was reconsidered, it was found to be so popular with holidaymakers that the 1944 Act closing it was rescinded, and so began a re-evaluation of all canals, which has resulted in the amazing amenity we have today.

The canals have been a valuable asset for hundreds of years – now more than ever. As they criss-cross the country through towns and villages, they bring an extra dimension to life: motorhoming on water. Happy gongoozling!

CAMPSITE – COTTON ARMS

This is a large campsite spread over two fields: one behind the pub and the other to the side of it. Having parked in the car park, it is necessary to register with staff in the pub, whereupon someone will then open the height barrier (this process is repeated when leaving, which is not always convenient). Access is then gained firstly to the rear and a small field that has all the electric hook-up pitches and canal views, and then round

to the side and a much larger field. Care needs to be taken in this field as the long grass hides the many ruts it contains.

Being so large it is some distance to the facilities. The two water taps, showers and toilets, though clean, are dated and insufficient for the size of the campsite. It looks as if most of the pitches with electric hook-up are occupied by static caravans: every time I tried to book a pitch there was none available; only spaces in the larger field. Another inconvenience was the

Pearl at the campsite gate leading to the towpath. booking process, which could only be

The front entrance of the Cotton Arms pub.

done via email, and was a long, drawn-out process.

However, the campsite is in a great location on the edge of the charming Wrenbury village, complete with imposing church, village shop and Post Office. Within shouting distance are other eateries. Then there is the impressive canal – the Llangollen branch of the Shropshire Union Canal. Access to the towpath was directly from the back of the campsite via a private gate.

PUB – COTTON ARMS

A large pub that has several entrances, which can be a little confusing at first. In addition to the main entrance off the road (best to use for registering), there is the games room entrance at the side off the car park, and the rear entrance to a large, well-designed outside garden with delightful wooden booths complete with colourful lighting.

This is a busy, lively pub, hosting a variety of events for locals and visitors, and the young staff are friendly and helpful. Offering a range of beers and real ales, and the usual pub menu, the gluten-free cod and chips was the best I've ever eaten – delicious!

PEARLS OF WISDOM

Another place where there were paths beside water but I was not allowed to swim; something about me not being able to get out? Lots of long wooden things glided past – my owner called them narrow boats. I got to go on one this time; it was very long and very narrow. Oh so exciting but in places I had difficulty turning round. Not sure I would want to spend time on one.

There was no special place for me to play on the campsite, but the field was so big it was possible to occasionally chase my frisbee. On walks it seemed that except for the path next to the water, either I was weaving my way through long grass and nasty nettles on stiles, or plodding along tarmac roads and lanes. I think this was because in so many places there were big, smelly animals – cows. They may have only wanted to say hello but they were so big, there were so many of them, and they came too close. There were some pleasing fields near the campsite for me to explore, however.

SHORT WALK – A CANAL
Distance: 5mi (8km)
Duration: 1.75hr (Easy)
Terrain: Footpaths, tracks towpath, roads, fields, stiles (three sheep-proof), gates, kissing gates, lock bridge

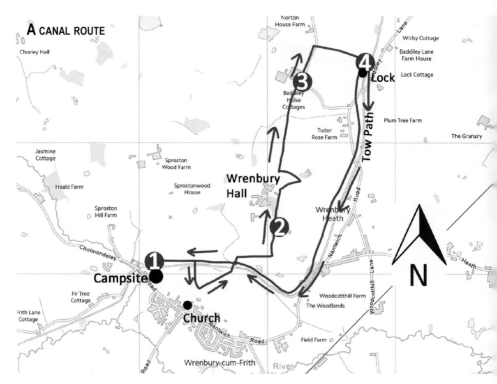

A CANAL ROUTE

Section 1: 1mi (1.6km)

- Exit campsite onto towpath via gate at rear
- Turn left out to road towards grey building
- Turn left along road
- Continue along road to church gates on left
- Turn left through gates, cross graveyard and over stile into field
- Continue straight ahead across field, turning right at junction in middle of field, then through gate ahead into next field
- Follow track along edge of field and over gate ahead
- Turn left and cross canal bridge, ignoring stiles on left
- Bear right towards three trees in hedge and over stile under third tree on left
- Bear left to follow path out to field, turning right along edge of field with bushes on right
- Turn left at corner of field, signposted
- Cross field, bearing slightly left towards buildings and telegraph pole on left
- Turn right along grass track, signposted, between houses and out to road

Section 2: 1.25mi (2km)

- Bearing slightly left, cross road to minor road, passing gates of Wrenbury Hall on left
- Continue along road, turning right along wide track at corner, signposted
- Follow track along edge of field with hedge on left
- Turn left at corner and over stile (sheep-proof) into field with stable and way-marker

- Continue straight ahead along edge of field close to hedge on right and over stile (sheep-proof) into next field
- Straight on along edge of field with hedge still on right, and over third stile (sheep-proof) into another field
- Continue along edge of field with hedge on right and through gate (overgrown stile on left)

Cows drop by for a drink and a paddle in the canal.

- Turn sharp left through another gate, turning right to continue along edge of field, with hedge on right, and through gate towards buildings
- Follow path across small field and through gate opposite out to road

Section 3: 0.75mi (1.2km)
- Bear left along road, passing close to house and other buildings on left
- Turn right at gate and over stile into field
- Cross field, keeping close to fence on left, then over stile in left corner into small field
- Bear right over stile opposite, then cross bridge and lock to towpath

Section 4: 2mi (3.2km)
- Turn right along towpath with canal on right
- Continue along towpath, past locks and under bridges, to campsite gate

LONG WALK – GONGOOZLING
Distance: 9.5ml (15.2km)
Duration: 5hr (Moderate)
Terrain: Footpaths, tracks towpath, roads, bridges, stiles, gates, kissing gates, some steady climbs (some of the paths and stiles are very overgrown; a walking stick would be useful)

Section 1: 1.25mi (2km)
- Exit campsite onto towpath via gate at rear
- Turn left along towpath towards grey building
- Turn right and cross canal bridge
- Straight ahead along road, turning right in 50yd (46m) along minor road, going uphill
- Continue straight ahead at left bend and through kissing gate into field
- Go along edge of field, keeping close to hedge on right, and over stile into next field
- Continue ahead along edge of field with hedge on right

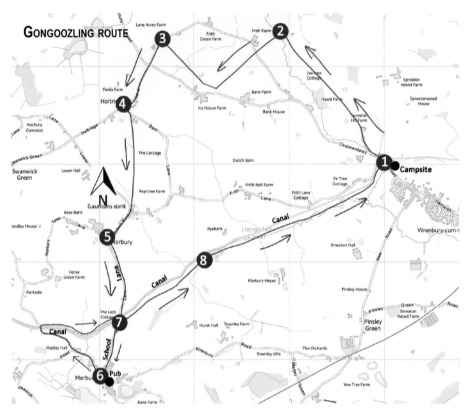

- Follow hedge, bearing right down into wood (slight path)
- Continue along path and through wood and around fallen branch to fence on left.
- Follow path close to fence on left (caution needed as very muddy)
- Continue straight ahead at junction with stiles on both left and right
- Turn right in 20 paces and through small gate out to field
- Turn left along edge of field with wood now on left
- Turn left just before corner and over fallen branch back into wood (huge fallen tree trunk on left)
- Turn right through gate out to field, way-marker
- Bear right along edge of field, keeping close to hedge, then through gate in right corner (concealed stile beside it)
- Continue straight ahead along edge of field with hedge on right to gate in right corner

Section 2: 1.25mi (2km)
- Turn left before gate down to track and cross bridge
- Continue uphill along track through farmyard, watching for gate and way-markers on left
- Turn left opposite large green storage container, keeping close to fence on right whilst heading for yellow way-marker on gate

- Turn right; over temporary fence and through gate; straight on with fence on right and farm building on left (narrow; muddy) out to road
- Turn right then immediately left through gate into field
- Bear right towards hedge, continuing along edge of field with hedge on right, then turn right to cross stile, footbridge and second stile in hedge (overgrown; care needed) into field

A lock keeper's cottage beside a lock on Llangollan Canal is now a private residence.

- Straight ahead to stile opposite (too overgrown to use), turning right and over gate/ dogs under (does not open) in corner out to road

Section 3: 1mi (1.6km)
- Turn left along road to crossroads, passing Long Acres Farm on right
- Straight across along minor road opposite
- Turn left along Back Lane, turning right before house, signposted,

Section 4: 1.25mi (2km)
- Cross bridge and through trees along lane at back of building, and over stile into garden
- Straight across over fence (care: may be electric) into field
- Continue along edge of field with hedge on left, ignoring stile on left, to gate at top left corner
- Bear left onto rough path, keeping gate and fence on left
- Straight on between hedge on right and fence on left, passing stile in fence out to field
- Turn right along edge of field with hedge on right, and over stile in right corner into next field
- Straight ahead, keeping close to hedge on right, and over stile into third field
- Bear right across field and through gate opposite
- Bear left to gate beside building in left corner (stile is 50 yards (46m) to right of gate, but too overgrown to cross)
- Through two gates into farmyard. Third gate is padlocked with no space for a dog to go underneath. Passage between house and building leads to front door and gate to road
- From farm, continue along Gauntons Bank opposite, signposted Norbury, to junction

Section 5: 1.25mi (2km)
- Turn left along School Lane and over canal bridge to junction

- Turn left up steps just before junction into car park
- Cross car park and descend steps to pub, The Swan (ideal stop for refreshments)

Section 6: 1mi (1.6km)
- Exit pub onto Wirswall Road
- Turn right towards School Lane
- Continue along Wirswall Road to canal, passing School Lane on right and Marbury Road on left
- Cross canal bridge, turning immediately left down steps to towpath
- Turn left along towpath under bridge.
- Continue along towpath with canal on right to lock at Church Bridge
- Cross to towpath on other side

Section 7: 1.25mi (2km)
- Continue along towpath with canal now on left
- Pass Ryebank Farm on opposite bank under bridge

Section 8: 1.25mi (2km)
- Continue along towpath with canal still on left to swing bridge at Wembury
- Turn right along road to campsite.

IN THE VICINITY
CYCLING
The many miles of canal towpaths and river walkways are suitable for cyclists, and the Canal and River Trust, which manages the canals and waterways of England and Wales, expects these to increase in the future. Available online are various cycle routes around Wrenbury.

FISHING
Fishing is allowed along sections of the Llangollen and the Shropshire Union canals. Details and permits can be obtained from the Lymm Angling Club.

BIRDWATCHING
Cruising gently along a canal, with binoculars to hand and reference books, is the ideal way to spot birds.

SECRET NUCLEAR BUNKER
Hack Green, situated deep in the Cheshire countryside, surrounded by cattle and arable fields, is the most unlikely place for a military base, yet, first used by the military in WWII, when radar was added so that incoming German aircraft could be more accurately tracked, it has been protecting the UK for more than sixty years.

   After the war, the bunker was used for military air traffic control. It was then abandoned but, with the escalation of the Cold War, it was re-purposed; now it was tracking the skies for nuclear missiles from the Soviet bloc. It was also one of 17 sites designed so that the UK would still be able to function after a nuclear attack. Decommissioned in 1993, it was re-opened as a museum in 1998. It is a unique experience, albeit a rather chilling one. It's also dog-friendly at no charge.

MARBURY

This attractive village, just a few minutes' walk from Llangollen Canal, has a long history, including a mention in the 1086 Domesday Book. Nowadays, it is a relaxing, peaceful place with an amazing pub, The White Swan, which is home to a huge collection of books arranged in functional but attractive bookcases dotted about the place: I could have spent all day browsing. There is also a most spectacular oak tree in the middle of the village green, planted to commemorate the Battle of Waterloo.

NANTWICH

Situated just 5 miles (8km) from the campsite is this interesting town, comprising a large number of both Tudor and Georgian listed buildings. The riverside walks extend to the centre of the town and are wonderful. Wandering around the shops admiring the buildings, and strolling beside the river with your dog is a most pleasant way to spend a day.

Cumbria – Lake District minus the lakes

OS MAPS EXPLORER OL7 THE ENGLISH LAKES SE AREA
OS MAPS EXPLORER OL8 THE ENGLISH LAKES SW AREA
DORRIGO DINKY MAP+ CENTRAL LAKE DISTRICT (AVAILABLE FROM CAMPSITE SHOP)

In terms of physical size, Cumbria is a large county in the north of England on the Scottish border. Situated within its borders is the Lake District; a large area of 912sq ml (2362sq km) comprising many lakes of all sizes – hence its name. Surrounding the lakes are many hills and mountains. The landscape is spectacular, which is probably why the Lake District is one of the most well-known and popular regions in the UK.

Some parts of the Lake District don't actually have lakes, just hills, mountains and valleys, and one such place is the Langdale Valley. However, with an abundance of rivers, streams, ponds and waterfalls, there is still lots of water in the area.

The name Langdale comes from Old Norse,

The hills, mountains and valleys of the Lake District, including the ubiquitous sheep.

meaning 'long valley,' and the valley is appropriately named. This glacially U-shaped valley has two sections; the smaller of which, Little Langdale, is a classic 'hanging valley' (a valley that is cut across by a deeper valley or a cliff) that lies above the larger, wider Great Langdale valley, meaning that water cascades in numerous waterfalls.

Lying within the Great Langdale valley close to the mouth are two delightful villages: Elterwater and Chapel Stickle. There are also ten farms in the area – primarily sheep, as the valley is ideal for the local breed of Herdwick sheep. During my visit I spoke with an elderly farmer still helping his family around the farmyard, even though hobbling on a walking stick, and watched a woman and two children rounding up sheep, using not only a dog but also a quad bike; it was nothing like *One Man and his Dog*. Most astounding of all I watched a woman deliver a lamb; a very difficult birth that, despite her strenuous efforts, resulted in a stillborn lamb, sadly. She did this with a baby tightly strapped to her back – incredible – and afterward simply rose and went to get on with something else. Farming here is obviously not the easiest of occupations, and seeing it a first-hand like this certainly gave me much to think about.

Because slate is so common in the region, and is a functional building material, it was used not only for local buildings such as farmhouses, packhorse bridges, and dry stone walls, but was also quarried. By the 18th century, quarrying was a proficient enterprise, and, at the height of production, there were as many as 30 quarries. Now, there is just the one active quarry at Elterwater. The residue of old quarries can be seen on the southern slopes of Little Langdale.

The National Trust manages the entire area of the Great Langdale valley, comprising approximately 12,170 acres, including the farms. NT is also responsible for the campsite, the Sticklebarn pub, The Old Dungeon Ghyll Hotel, and a youth hostel at High Close.

Great Langdale valley is dominated by fells and pikes – old Norse terms for hills and mountains – especially on the north flank of the valley. Slicing their way through these are ghylls (ravines), down which water gushes. From the valley floor the hills and mountains offer a tantalizing glimpse of jagged tops stretching skyward, beckoning walkers to discover the delights on offer. Routes along the valley floor are relatively straightforward, but strike off up the slopes of the surrounding hills and it quickly becomes hill walking. The higher you walk the more demanding it becomes, until, close to the top, it is mountain walking, and scrambling with some climbing. I found the use of a walking pole essential, as did many of the walkers I met.

Despite there being no lakes in the area the scenery is stunning, the villages enchanting, and the hills and mountains ideal for walking.

Campsite – Great Langdale NT

Situated in the heart of the Southern Lakes of the Lake District at the foot of Scafell Pike, and surrounded by numerous impressive hills, views from the campsite are spectacular. This is a walker's campsite, as access to fells walking routes is easy. The majority of pitches are for tents, and there are just 13 pitches with electric hook-up for motorhomes and campervans, plus a few additional spots around the perimeter when it's quieter. Approach roads to the site are not particularly suitable for caravans and really large

Great Langdale NT Campsite nestling in the valley.

motorhomes. This large, spacious site sprawls along Mickleden Valley, and is divided into five irregular sections with tents dotted about: all vehicles having to park on hard standing beside access routes, with campervans and motorhomes around the edge in an orderly rank. Only the centre of each section is mowed so the long grass suggests wildness and adventure.

There are two toilet blocks with comprehensive amenities, and four different starting points for walks, two of which are footpaths leading directly from the back of the campsite. There's not just one but two pubs within walking distance.

There is an orienteering course around the campsite, and maps can be purchased from reception. Also on the wall of the biomass boiler room is a 'bouldering wall' (a wall fitted with attachments to simulate a rock face for climbing practice), where it is possible to practice climbing for free.

Pubs
• Sticklebarn

This is an unusual pub, being a National Trust establishment. As such, its environmental impact is important, and as many as possible of its resources are locally sourced.

In addition to the usual services a pub provides, Sticklebarn also shows films once a week, and has a selection of games, etc, for wet days when it's not possible to get outside. Being a little way from the campsite (0.7ml/1.1km), getting to it is irksome in bad weather.

• Old Dungeon Ghyll Hotel

Once a farm and inn, in 1900 the hotel was bought by historian and author Professor G M Trevelyan, who then gifted it to the National Trust. Because of its location among the fells in the Great Langdale valley, the building was refurbished as a bar, and many climbers, including some famous ones, have stopped by over the years. Another factor in its favour

The Old Dungeon Ghyll Hotel is the nearest bar to the campsite.

is that it is closer to the campsite (0.3mi (0.48km)).

PEARLS OF WISDOM 🐕

What is going on? I am sooo confused! There are heaps of green spaces, some with short, stubby green growth, and others with long, wavy grasses, but all with many exciting smells. None of the areas we explored seemed to be specifically for me, as I was always on the lead, though I did not mind this.

Most evenings we managed to find room for my daily frisbee game, as there was so much space, even though there were lots of odd structures dotted all over the place. The walks were okay, although some places were very stony. I was forever on the lead, then off; on again, then off, as those flaming sheep kept popping up all over the place. Also, I was not allowed to wander too far to explore, although – hooray! – there was swimming close by and we went several times.

SHORT WALK – ROAMING THE VALLEY
Distance: 5mi (8km)
Duration: 2.5hr (Moderate; one steep, rocky climb)
Terrain: Fields, uplands, valleys, fell paths, stones and boulders, footpaths, tracks (stony and tarmac), minor roads, many gates, some stiles and lots of climbing up and down; one short, very steep climb

Section 1: 1mi (1.6km)
- Exit campsite opposite side to reception (labelled on campsite map 'To Old Dungeon Ghyll' and through kissing gate onto minor road
- Turn right along road
- Straight on at bend, over stone bridge and through gate into field
- Cross field and through gate opposite onto access road, then through gate immediately ahead into large field
- Straight across field and through gate onto narrow, stony footpath close to fence on right
- Follow path across field with beck on right and through gate into next field
- Cross this field and over stile opposite into third field
- Straight ahead over stone slab footbridge, then bear right towards fence
- Follow path beside fence

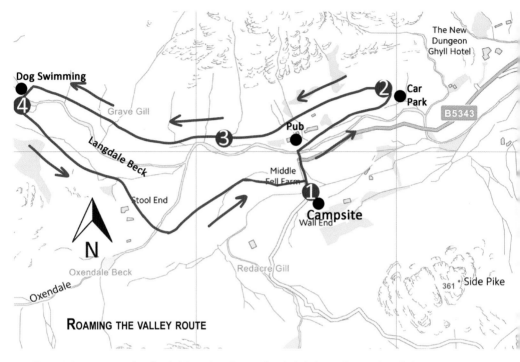

ROAMING THE VALLEY ROUTE

- Turn right over wooden footbridge, then immediately left through gate into field
- Continue along footpath and through gate into car park

Section 2: 1.25mi (2km)
- Bear left across car park and through gate in top right corner onto stony path
- Follow path round corner and through gate (on right is large bird feeding station), round another corner and up slope past stone NT sign on right, then through gap in trees
- Turn left along wide, very stony track and through gate at top (path is not obvious, and is very steep with many stones and big boulders)
- Keep left along path beside wall on left, going down and over footbridge (Cumbria Way)
- Follow stony path, keeping close to stone wall on left as it meanders up and down, then through gate passing pub on left

Section 3: 1mi (1.6km)
- Continue straight ahead over mound to path beside wall
- With wall still on left, follow Cumbria Way through various gates as it snakes along the valley until wall veers off left
- Continue along path for 50yd (46m): first round left-hand bend, then at right-hand bend turn left onto grass track, heading towards fir trees (easy to miss; if you have to cross a stream you've gone too far)

The Langdale Valley leading to the foot of Scafell Pike.

- Continue straight ahead parallel to stream on right to large, wooden footbridge by weir (fabulous place for a dog to swim)

Section 4: 1.75mi (2.8km)
- Turn right along stony track onto narrow path that soon joins wide, stony track
- Continue along track round right-hand bend, then left-hand bend and through gate into field
- Follow track, keeping close to wall on left
- Turn left through gate into farmyard, then turning first right then left, signposted, onto concrete track
- Keeping close to wall on left, continue along track and through gates across fields to minor road
- Turn right along road to campsite entrance on left

LONG WALK – COUNTRY PUB CRAWL
- Eltermere Hotel
- Britannia Inn
- Wainwright's Inn
- Dungeon Ghyll Hotel
- Sticklebarn
- Old Dungeon Ghyll Hotel

Distance: 8.5mi (13.7km)
Duration: 5hr (longer if stopping at pubs) (Challenging)
Terrain: Fields, uplands, valleys, fell paths (stones), footpaths, tracks – stony and tarmac, minor roads, many gates, some stiles (two ladder stiles requiring very agile dogs), and lots of climbing up and down; some quite steep but short stretches

Section 1: 1mi (1.6km)
- Exit campsite via kissing gate in left corner of site behind reception
- Climb slope (steep) through gate onto fell
- Continue up wide, grassy path to narrow footpath (steep)
- Turn left along narrow footpath
- Follow clearly-defined path along contour of hill, and over streams and two ladder stiles (difficult for dogs), passing farm on left
- After crossing stream turn left towards farm going down to footbridge

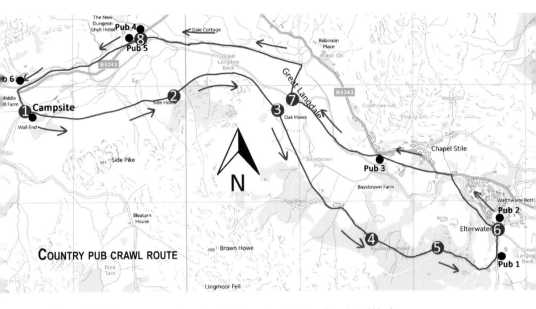

- Turn right along narrow, stony track before footbridge (Cumbria Way)
- Follow path through gate up slope and through another gate at top

Section 2: 1mi (1.6km)
- Continue along Cumbria Way (clearly signposted) along base of hill and through gate on right
- Follow path between two stone walls round right-hand bed to junction by stone barn on left

Section 3: 1mi (1.6km)
- Turn right at junction signposted 'Chapel Stile' and along stony track as it winds up and down through the wood and farmyard onto tarmac path

Section 4: 1mi (1.6km)
- Continue along tarmac track (permissive route) and round bend, steadily climbing in fits and starts through wood, ignoring signpost on left, to big junction by house on left

The views are spectacular, though the paths are often very stony and difficult.

Section 5: 1.5mi (2.4km)
- Continue straight ahead at junction onto wide tarmac lane
- Follow track round left-hand bend at lovely, huge oak tree out to minor road
- Bear left along road signposted Elterwater (just down the road on the right are the entrance gates to the first pub, the Elterwater Hotel, where views from the garden are amazing)
- Exit pub and continue downhill to village
- Turn right across bridge to second pub (Britannia Inn) on left
- From pub, turn right to cross bridge
- Follow road round to right, keeping close to stream on right, climbing
- Bear right along stony track, going down with river still on right
- Continue straight ahead at large stone slab seat, along narrow path and over mound, then across footbridge and through gate out to road
- Turn left to third pub (Wainwright's Inn)

Section 6: 1.25mi (2km)
- Continue along road, passing pub on left
- Turn left along stony footpath, signposted
- Follow path past school on right
- Turn left at junction, then round past houses on left and through gate
- Bearing right, continue along path, passing houses and buildings
- Follow path round left-hand bend and over stone bridge; then round to right onto concrete path
- Follow path, keeping close to stream on right and passing campsite on left, then through gate into field
- Continue along path through three more gates

Section 7: 1.25mi (2km)
- Turn right to cross footbridge, following path ahead through gate
- Bear left through gate, turning left along stony path with stream now on left, and through another gate
- Keeping left, continue along stony track with metal fence on left, through several gates out to car park
- Turn left through car park to B5343
- Cross road to continue along driveway opposite, passing fourth pub (Dungeon Ghyll Hotel) on right

Section 8: 1mi (1.6km)
- Follow driveway round left-hand bend
- Bear left down steps, then round to right to entrance of fifth pub (Sticklebarn)
- Continue through pub garden to car park and picnic area
- Bear left through car park to stony path on right near exit, and through gate into field
- Cross field and through gate opposite

- Turn immediately right, cross footbridge and through gate into next field
- Bearing right, cross field and stone slab footbridge
- Continue straight ahead, keeping close to fence on left, and over stile into next field
- Cross field and through gate opposite into next field
- Cross field to path beside fence
- Continue on path, keeping close to fence and stream on left, then through gate on left into next field
- Bear right across field and through gate to car park of sixth pub (Old Dungeon Ghyll Hotel)
- Turn left along access road to junction, turning left to cross bridge out to B5343
- Turn right along B5343, then left to campsite entrance

IN THE VICINITY
WILD SWIMMING
There is plenty of opportunity for wild swimming in the Lake District due to the large number of lakes and ponds, etc. The water can be deep and is frequently colder than expected, so it's essential the necessary precautions are taken to stay safe in the water.

CYCLING
A cycle trail through Great Langdale Valley also includes a refreshment stop.

SCAFELL PIKE
Of all the 'pikes' surrounding the valley, Scafell Pike is the highest at 3209ft (978m). Not to be confused with Sca Fell, a high peak next to it, this potentially confusing naming of the peaks was possibly due to an OS map error. Scafell Pike is also the highest mountain in England, and a magnet for climbers (many thousands of which have achieved this). There are four routes to the top, one of which starts at Great Langdale valley.

Visitors can freely roam around the mountain due to the generosity of Lord Leconfield, who gifted Scafell Pike and several other peaks in the area to the National Trust in 1919, in remembrance of all the men from the Lake District who died in WWI. It is also an important conservation area so be considerate, especially if taking your dog.

ELTERWATER
This charming village is the gateway to Great Langdale valley, overlooking a small lake of the same name. Elterwater in Old Norse means swan lake.

CHAPEL STILE
A lively village in Great Langdale valley with a school, a church (Holy Trinity) built into the hillside, café and pub, Wainwright's Inn. The village Co-op has been there for over one hundred years.

HIGH CLOSE ESTATE AND ARBORETUM
A mile (1.6km) north of Elterwater village is High Close Estate, with its Youth Hostel and

Arboretum planted in 1866 by Edward Wheatley-Balme, a Yorkshire businessman. It boasts trees from all over the world, and, although rather secluded, it is an interesting place to explore.

GREENBURN MINE

The remains of this mine, which produced copper rather than the usual slate, are in Little Langdale. It's still possible to picture it in operation.

Lancashire – Burrs Country Park: an oasis
OS MAPS EXPLORER 277 MANCHESTER & SALFORD
YELLOW WALK MAPS AROUND & ABOUT BURRS COUNTRY PARK (AVAILABLE AT THE CAMPSITE)

Some names conjure up compelling images, so informing others that the destination of an R&R break is Bury – a suburb of Manchester – results in curious looks.

The approach roads fail to quell feelings of doubt as they meander through an urban jungle, though familiar brown tourist signs to Burrs Country Park and the campsite are hugely reassuring. Still, there are a lot of houses, although these gradually become fewer, with more trees and even green spaces. Suddenly and unexpectedly there is countryside all around, and the road is cobbled as if to underline the total change of landscape. We have arrived at an amazing place: Burrs Country Park in Irwell Valley

In 1986 when Bury Metro Borough Council purchased the site, it looked very different: a derelict industrial area with just a few remaining dilapidated structures, as many of the early mill buildings had been demolished in 1952, and the remainder in 1982. The site was cleared, leaving a few constructions to commemorate its history: the chimney, workers' cottages and water wheel pit. Then it was totally revamped.

The cotton mills in 1792 used the power of the Irwell river to operate the machines, and were built at Burr and Higher Woodhill by a group of local entrepreneurs, who included Robert Peel Snr, father of renowned politician Robert Peel Jr, who would become Prime Minister in 1841.

At one time as many as 400 people were employed in the mills, most of them women and children, about half of whom were under 14 years of age. Only a few men and boys were required to look after the machinery. In order to keep the mills operating 24 hours a day, a 12-hour shift pattern was in operation, requiring night shifts to be lit by candles and oil lamps; health and safety legislation was obviously not a consideration then. On Sundays the mills were silent whilst being cleaned in order to ensure they ran smoothly for the upcoming week.

Worker accommodation was also provided, as evidenced by the remaining cottages, now an activity centre. According to records, these cottages faced a midden (toilet) and comprised 28 'homes,' with 141 people living there. There were no gardens so food and other goods had to be purchased. As the nearest shops were over 2 miles (3.2km) away, the owners set up a mill shop. By the time necessities had been purchased, and money deducted for the 'funeral club,' there was very little pay left for the mill hands.

Some considered this was an inappropriate way to treat employees, especially children, and they campaigned for change. The resultant Factory Act of 1802 stipulated working conditions for apprentices, and the 1819 Factory Act extended regulations, reducing the hours children aged 9-16 should work. This new legislation was due to the efforts of Sir Robert Peel Snr, which seems surprising considering he was a cotton mill owner, and records indicate that conditions for his employees were far from good. Perhaps this conflict of interest was one reason why he sold the mill to his partners.

Mills and factories continued to be profitable enterprises, despite further legislation regulating working conditions, particularly for children. The nail in the coffin for cotton mills was the American Civil War, when cotton supply from the States ended, and it was impossible to find an alternative source at such short notice.

Though the mills continued to be used for various other purposes, the industry experienced a slow, steady decline until 1933 when the entire complex finally closed. Briefly during WWII the site was used to billet Italian prisoners of war.

Interestingly, our campsite pub of choice, the Brown Cow Public House, was not part of the mill complex. Originally a farmhouse built forty years before the mills in 1752, it and the Country Park now have a new lease of life. The Park's 36 hectares contain a variety of environments – woodlands and open green spaces, plus waterways and wetlands – as well as an activity centre, a campsite, and a large, open space for hosting outdoor events. The Park is hugely popular with locals and visitors alike.

CAMPSITE – BURRS COUNTRY PARK CARAVAN AND MOTORHOME CLUB SITE

Like all club sites this large site – there are 119 pitches – is well organized and efficiently run, with spotlessly clean and well-appointed facilities that include an indoor dishwashing area and laundry. Surprisingly, it is only 2 miles (3.2km) from Bury centre, and is part of the Burrs Country Park complex that was created from the old workings of two cotton mills along the River Irwell.

There is much to explore right on the doorstep, with a variety of walks in pleasant countryside. Being so close to Bury, public transport links offer the opportunity to explore further afield: I did not find the trains of the East Lancs Heritage Railway a problem as they passed only a few times for part of the week.

The campsite at Burrs Country Park.

PUB – BROWN COW

Situated at the entrance to the campsite, the pub's large garden and play area for children are clearly visible, though the small entrance is tucked away along a narrow path to the side. Inside, the seating arrangement is rather packed, which does, at least, encourage conversation, especially as it is frequented by many from the campsite. It is a very popular pub serving a range of drinks and the usual pub food, and it's advisable to book (in person is quicker and more certain than by phone). The maxim 'dogs welcome' is perfectly illustrated by this pub, and there are often almost as many dogs as people!

PEARLS OF WISDOM 🐾

I was not sure about this place – lots of buildings and lots of noise – but, surprise, surprise it was fabulous! The special place for dogs on the campsite was very small, though just big enough for a frisbee chase. Over the fence was this huge open space ... plenty of room for frisbee-playing, and there were lots of paths to explore among the trees and down by the water. Hooray! A place to swim very close to the campsite (which I did – a lot!).

Whenever we went there soooo many dogs to greet; all very friendly. I even met other dogs swimming. Walks were good but I am glad the ride in the taxi was short and that my owner was holding me.

SHORT WALK – ROUND AND ABOUT
Distance: 5.5mi (8.8km)
Duration: 3.5hr (Moderate)
Terrain: Footpath, tracks, cyclepath, roads, bridges, stile, gates, kissing gates, lots of steps, up and down climbs (some steep but short). Note: Irwell Sculpture Trail closed due to landslide

Section 1: 1.25mi (2km)
- Exit campsite via two barriers at entrance
- Turn right into park, taking left fork
- Turn left by raised sensory bed; left again through gate
- Turn right to cross bridge ahead
- Turn immediately right along path, taking left fork down to river (a good place for dogs to swim)
- Turn left along river path with river on right
- Follow path up slope beside aqueduct on left
- Turn right up long flight of steep steps
- Turn right at top, following path winding through woods, passing houses on right out to road
- Turn left to B6214, then right along main road to cross at road island ahead
- Continue straight on along road ahead, Garside Hey Road, crossing blocked road
- Turn left in 20 paces through gap into field
- Bear right across field through kissing gate
- Follow path downhill, cross bridge and uphill ahead to cyclepath

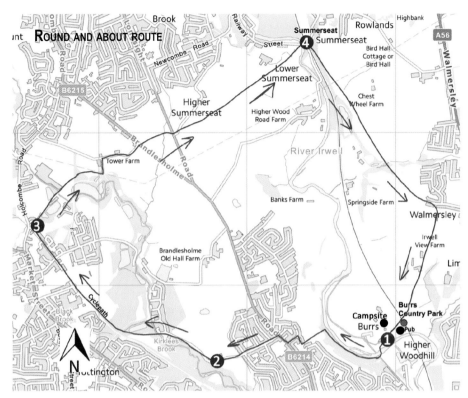

Section 2: 1mi (1.6km)

- Turn right along cyclepath signposted Kirklees Valley LRN
- Continue along cyclepath and round car barrier gate, passing junction with noticeboard (interesting info about Kirklees) and houses
- Follow cyclepath out to cul-de-sac past school on left and playing fields on right
- Keeping right, cross road back onto cyclepath
- Continue ahead under arch, past cricket ground on right, and across long bridge

Section 3: 1.75mi (2.8km)

- Turn right in 50 paces along track going down
- Take left fork down towards water
- Follow path with reservoir on right round left bend, over car barrier and onto tarmac driveway with small field on right (may contain horses)
- Follow driveway uphill past amazing tower on left to garages ahead
- Turn right along lane and follow round left bend past gates out to road
- Turn right along busy B6215 (pavement on opposite side)
- Turn left onto narrow path into field
- Cross field, keeping close to hedge on left; cross footbridge and through gate into field
- Follow path across field to very busy B6214: cross to wide grass track opposite
- Continue along track out to field, keeping close to hedge on left

- Turn left in 100yd (91m), then over stile in hedge into next field
- Follow path across field out to stony track
- Bear left to follow stony track downhill onto tarmac driveway between houses, then round two left-hand bends to cross bridge

Section 4: 1.5mi (2.4km)
- Continue straight ahead up steps opposite to cross rail line (take care), then through gate, up more steps and through kissing gate at top
- Turn right along path through woods with fence on right, then cross bridge and through kissing gate
- Straight on along cobbled footpath and through gate into field
- Keep right; return to narrow footpath in 50 paces
- Follow path down steps and between hedges, then through two kissing gates to road
- Bear left along road towards houses and through gate to another road
- Turn left then first right along Touch Road
- Turn right at junction signposted 'Haystack/Irwell View Farm'
- Straight ahead between buildings and Irwell View Farm over stile (difficult) into field
- Cross field (campsite visible on right), descend stone steps and cross to tree, then up slope and over stile in corner onto footpath
- Follow footpath between green fence on left and wire fence and rail station on right; descend steps to track
- Turn right under arch and bear right onto stony track, passing pub on right
- Cross car park, turning right to campsite entrance

LONG WALK – PEEL TOWER
This is a linear walk from Irwell Vale Station on the East Lancs Railway, which also stops at Burrs Country Park. Information is available online or at reception. The trains do not run on Mondays and Tuesdays, so Pearl and I took a taxi. They were unable to take us to the station, so I got out at Edenfield Storage Park on the B6527 Blackburn Road BL0 0JD and walked to the station
Distance: 11mi (17.7km)
Duration: 5hr (Moderate)
Terrain: Footpath, stony tracks, cyclepath, steps, roads, fields, woods, bridges, stiles, gates, kissing gates, cobbled lanes, some hills (short and steep; also long and steady)

Section 1: 0.75mi (1.2km)
- Turn right along B6527, then first right along Hardsough Lane
- Follow lane past buildings on left round left-hand bend and down to houses
- Turn right under subway to station

Section 2: 1.25mi (2km)
- Exit station via car park, turning left along Aitken Street, and across bridge
- Turn left again along Bowker Street towards chapel

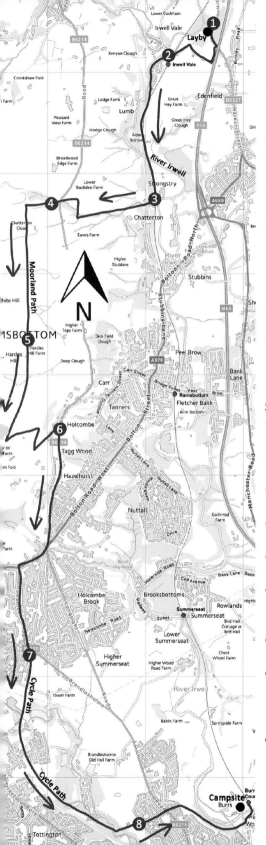

Peel Tower route

- Bear right, keeping close to chapel wall on left, signposted, and passing chapel on left
- Keep right along narrow path between fence and wall and through kissing gate
- Follow path with fence on right over footbridge, then left with river on left
- Continue along narrow path to road with river on left
- Turn left on road and cross bridge, then immediate right onto path with river now on right
- Straight ahead at bend, up concrete track onto cyclepath
- Bear left, following cyclepath to end and turning right out to road through gap in wall

Section 3: 1mi (1.6km)

- Turn sharp right, following road round to left onto track, passing stile on right and house on left, then through gate onto wide track beside wall on left
- Continue along track, now with river and waterfalls on left: through gate
- Follow wide track between fields, then uphill into wood
- Bear right down path to river at way-marker 'RW'
- Continue along path, cross footbridge and up other side under fallen tree, then over stile to small field
- Bear left in field between bushes and over stile into next field
- Continue straight ahead along edge of field with hedges on right, then through gate in right corner out to large junction
- Turn left along grass track out to B6214 (busy)

Section 4: 1.75mi (2.8km)
- Cross road via gate opposite into field
- Continue uphill onto wide track along edge of field with fence on right
- Follow track bearing left towards wall on left , then through gate in corner onto moor
- Turn left along wide track with wall still on left and through gate
- Follow track as it skirts high moors, passing farm on left to three-way junction by bench
- Turn second right onto wide, stony track (not tarmac) by bench

Section 5: 1.25mi (2km)
- Continue along path as it snakes uphill and round to Peel Tower (amazing views)
- Follow stony track downhill as it passes the tower round sweeping left-hand bend at farm and zigzags down, ignoring paths leading off to T-junction

Section 6: 2mi (3.2km)
- Turn left along track towards garages at Moor Bottom Road
- Turn right along cobbled track past houses on left and out to road
- Cross road to cobbled road opposite (Holcombe Old Road)
- Continue downhill to minor road
- Bear left, crossing road and down steps opposite, then along lane, passing pub garden on right
- Follow lane out to large junction of major roads
- Turn right uphill along A676 then left along B6215 Holcombe Road
- Continue along road to Miller and Carter restaurant
- Turn left along B6215 Brandlesholm Road
- Turn right in 50yd (45m) onto cyclepath

Section 7: 2mi (3.2km)
- Follow cyclepath over bridge past cricket ground on left and out to access road
- Cross road, bearing left past school and notice board on left, ignoring paths leading off
- Turn left onto narrow footpath opposite flight of steps and signpost
- Follow footpath downhill, cross bridge and up other side
- Take right fork, still climbing and bearing left: cross stile into field
- Bear right across field towards houses and out to road

Section 8: 1mi (1.6km)
- Turn right up Garside Hey Road to B6214
- Turn right along main road, and second left onto Burrs Close
- Turn right onto narrow lane between houses, signposted
- Follow path as it winds through trees, passing houses on right
- Turn left down steep flight of steps to aqueduct and cross bridge
- Turn left along path with aqueduct on left, passing car park on right

- Turn left over bridge and right over second bridge
- Bear left through gate ahead, passing raised sensory beds
- Turn right along path beside green and through gate
- Turn right to campsite entrance

IN THE VICINITY
FISHING

The Ramsbottom Angling Association is responsible for the fishing in Country Park, which is allowed at specific places along the River Irwell and in ponds. Information and further details are available from the angling club, and permits are available from the water bailiff on the bank, and the activity centre.

BIRDWATCHING/WILDLIFE

With such a diverse habitat in the park there is an abundance of wildlife and birds to see. There are no dedicated bird hides but benches and seats are scattered around so remember the binoculars!

EAST LANCASHIRE RAILWAY

Originally, the railway was an important lifeline for commerce along the Irwell Valley, connecting businesses with local, national and international markets as well as providing passenger services for the area. This all came to an end in the late 20th century and the line was finally closed in 1982.

Just five years later, in 1987 the East Lancashire Railway Trust reopened part of the line between Bury and Ramsbottom, since when the line has been upgraded and expanded, and now operates on a 12 mile (19.3km) stretch between Heywood and Rawstenstall, making an important contribution to local communities. It runs every weekend throughout the year with additional outings during the summer, as well as special themed trips. As with most railways of this type, it is run by volunteers.

PEEL TOWER

Situated high above Bury on Harcles Hill is Peel Tower; a well-known local landmark built in 1852 as a memorial to Sir Robert Peel, the son of a prominent local family that owned a cotton mill in the Irwell Valley.

Sir Robert Peel was born in Bury but, after completing his education at Oxford University, he became a politician, eventually becoming Prime Minister in 1834, and again in 1841. Sir Robert Peel it was who established the Police Force, which is why police constables and officers are sometimes known as 'bobbies' or 'peelers.'

At 128 feet (39m) high the tower dominates the skyline and is visible for miles. Over time, the tower deteriorated and became unsafe to enter and climb the 171 steps to the viewing platforms. It was eventually reopened 30 years after it closed in 1985 when a new staircase was installed. It is now possible, when the volunteers open it, to enter the tower and climb the stairs in safety. Look for a white flag flying from the mast which indicates that the tower is open.

Peel Tower on Harcles Hill.

IRWELL RIVER SCULPTURE TRAIL

All along a 30 mile (48km) stretch of the River Irwell, from Salford Quays through Burrs Country Park, up to the Pennines above Ramsbottom and Bacup, is an outdoor art gallery. Scattered along this route are some 28 pieces of sculpture by artists from all over the world, three of which are in the park. The Waterwheel, situated on the site of a large cotton mill at the entrance to the park, symbolizes constant change; the Stone Cycle illustrates the connection between past and present, and the last piece, at the confluence of a canal and a river, resembles a giant mousetrap: its title is Picnic Area ...

BURY

It was as a result of the mills on the River Irwell that Bury grew rapidly from a village to a Victorian town. Now, as it has been for around fifty years, it is a commuter town or bedroom community for Manchester. During this period there has been extensive residential growth as well as improved transport links to Manchester; especially the renowned Metro Link.

Right in the centre of Bury, just a couple of miles from the campsite, is Bury market, famous throughout the region with visitors from far and wide. The indoor market is open every day, but the outdoor one on Wednesday, Friday and Saturday only. With over 370 stalls, it may even be possible to buy the kitchen sink here.

Bury also has an art museum, a transport museum,and the Fusilier Museum, home to the collections of the XX Lancashire Fusiliers and the Royal Regiment of Fusiliers. Other interesting sights are a castle and the Whitehead Clock Tower.

Walks in Central England
(Leicestershire, Warwickshire, Worcestershire

Leicestershire – making history

OS MAPS EXPLORER 232 NUNEATON & TAMWORTH

An historical footballing moment in 2016 was so momentous that it has spilled over into folklore: Leicester City football club won the premier league after languishing in the lower divisions for more than ten years.

Football pundits did not rate Leicester's chances. The title had oscillated between the same four teams for 21 years, while Leicester had been in the league for only two seasons, fighting to avoid relegation. Football commentator Gary Lineker was so confident about Leicester's failure he declared that if the team *should* win, he would present a BBC Match of the Day episode in his underwear. Well, that was a sight ...

Another historical event – one that occurred over 500 years ago – had far-reaching effects that are still relevant today.

In the heart of the Leicestershire countryside is the site of the Battle of Bosworth, one of the most famous battles that changed the course of English history, and ended the 30-year War of the Roses. In 1485, Richard III fought Henry Tudor, who claimed the English throne was rightfully his, despite very tenuous connections. Henry's mother was a descendant of Edward III, and his father was a minor Welsh prince who provided him with a loyal base from which to challenge Richard.

To complicate things further, one of Richard's key supporters, Lord Stanley, was married to Henry's mother. Stanley waited to see which way the battle was going before joining the fray, and, as Richard led a final desperate charge on Henry's followers, he took Henry's side. Richard, now surrounded by his enemies, was defeated and killed. Henry VII was immediately crowned on the battlefield whilst Richard's body was hastily and unceremoniously buried in Grey Friars Priory in Leicester.

Henry VII was very astute in consolidating

Pearl at the site where King Richard is thought to have been killed.

his position as king. He persuaded 15th century scribes to emphasize his qualities and authority whilst denigrating Richard, and to imply that the Tudor dynasty was the start of a new era. Shakespeare's play *Richard III*, written when Henry VII's granddaughter, Elizabeth I, was queen, reinforces the idea that good triumphed over evil by portraying Richard as a deformed hunchback, and the play has been instrumental in perpetuating this view. The original 'fake news,' perhaps ...?

Richard had been a staunch supporter of his brother, King Edward IV, whose sudden death was untimely. Initially, Richard followed his brother's wishes, ruling as Lord Protector and taking the two princes, his nephews Edward V and Richard Duke of York, under his care, installing them in the royal apartments in the Tower of London. However, very soon Richard proclaimed himself king, although why he did is not clear. And what actually happened to the two princes in the Tower, who simply disappeared? It was a mystery then and is as much a mystery today, although it is generally assumed that they were murdered; a common hypothesis is that they were killed by Richard in an attempt to secure his hold on the throne. Their deaths may have occurred sometime in 1483, but apart from their disappearance, the only evidence is circumstantial.

Richard's body was lost when Grey Friars Priory was demolished in 1538 as a result of the dissolution of monasteries, since when the site has been renovated many times. In 2012 an archaeological exploration unearthed a skeleton: the remains of one of the most significant historical figures in British history was found buried beneath a car park. Modern analysis has shown that whilst Richard did have a spinal deformity, this was easily disguised by his clothes: the Bard's portrayal of this was a gross exaggeration. Even the famous portrait of him was a misrepresentation, as he was actually blonde with blue eyes. Richard's remains were re-interred in Leicester Cathedral in March 2015.

Even 500 years later Richard III is still widely perceived as a wicked, evil king, and there is ongoing discussion as to his character and motives, primarily the result of the work of the Richard III Society that was founded in 1924. Over the years, his detractors' claims have been proved excessive, though there are still many anomalies.

The precise location of the Battle of Bosworth has long been disputed. Originally thought to have taken place at Ambion Hill, extensive investigation carried out in 2005 revealed that the actual site of the battle is about a mile (1.6km) from here, on land at Fen Lane Farm. Research and modern technology have clarified several earlier riddles, although, despite years of study, some details are still shrouded in mystery, and may never be resolved.

CAMPSITE – GLOBE INN

Access to the campsite is via the car park at the back of the pub, into a long, thin field with pitches each side of the access road that bisects the site. A large part of the rear of the site is gated off, seemingly for resident units. There's a small area for tourers, with electric hook-up and water, just inside the entrance. The toilet block, if you can call it that, comprises two outside lean-tos on the car park at the rear of the pub: one is a shower, and the other a toilet; there's no sink. The chemical toilet is in front of the toilet.

The site itself, however, is lovely: neat and tidy with pleasant views, and adjacent to

The campsite is at the back of the pub in a long, thin field.

a canal. The owners have only just taken over the campsite and have plans to modernize it.

Pub – Globe Inn

A large car park at the rear of the pub does not impinge on the charming outside space in a large alcove by the back entrance. Inside, the pub is divided into sections that create a cosy, intimate feel, and it is beautifully decorated. Well organized and efficiently run, the staff are pleasant: really helpful and accommodating. The food is delicious, which probably explains why it is difficult to book a table.

The owners have only recently taken over the pub, and have done a superb job of updating it, which bodes well for the campsite.

A friendly welcome awaits at the delightfully refurbished Globe Inn.

Pearls of Wisdom

Just a few bounds away was yet more water that I am not allowed to swim in: urgh! The path beside it was really exciting, too: lots of curious smells and long wooden things on the water – houseboats, apparently. Some had gaps in their sides, and I loved catching a glimpse of what was inside them. I would have liked to hop up on one and explore but this was not allowed either. Occasionally, delicious foody smells wafted from inside the boats, and I was very tempted to stretch through the gap and have a taste!

Across the road was a field in which to chase my frisbee – fabulous! – and we also went on a train ride: at least I think it was a train. All-in-all, a really thrilling place with lots of fun things to do.

Short walk – Snarestone Wharf
Distance: 5.5mi (8.8km)
Duration: 2.5hr (Easy)
Terrain: Woodland tracks (wide and narrow), footpaths, towpath, gates and kissing gates, stiles, fields, roads – quiet and busy

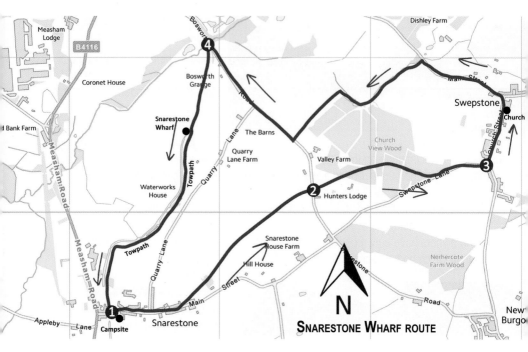

SNARESTONE WHARF ROUTE

Section 1: 1.25mi (2km)

- Exit campsite out to road via pub car park
- Turn right along road, passing school on left, then left along Quarry Lane
- Turn right along footpath immediately after white house on right
- Follow path over stile into field
- Straight on along edge of field to large tree on right, then bear left across field and over stile in top left corner into next field
- Cross field over stile (broken) into third field
- Follow path across field and round to right over stile opposite, cross field number five, then over stile ahead into sixth field
- Cross field, keeping buildings on left and heading towards orange post, then through hedge and over stile out to road

Section 2: 1mi (1.6km)

- Cross road to footpath opposite
- Bear left, following path over stile in hedge on right into field
- Bear left across field and over stile ahead into wood
- Take left fork between trees and along wide, grassy track, bearing right towards way-marker: through gate
- Follow path between trees through gap in hedge on left onto narrow footpath
- Bear left across wide, earth track onto narrow path between trees, then over wide grass track through small gap in hedge by way-marker
- Continue straight ahead over wide track

- Follow path as it winds through trees parallel to road on right, then through gate in hedge into field with big gates on right
- Straight on across field between two trees and through gap in hedge by telegraph pole
- Bear right across field and over stile in hedge by way-marker, then through copse and out to churchyard.

Section 3: 1.75mi (2.8km)
- Bearing slightly right, cross churchyard, keeping church on right, then through gate into field
- Bear slightly right to cross field, heading towards big red house, then through gap in hedge out to road
- Turn left along road (take care: rather busy)
- Turn left onto wide track just after small bridge
- Bear left, passing gate on right, onto grassy track, keeping close to fence on right with hedge on left
- Turn left at way-marker over footbridge
- Continue along track with fence on right, turning left through gap by gate and out to road (very quiet)
- Turn right along road

Section 4: 1.5mi (2.4km)
- Turn left onto wide, stony track and over stile just before bridge
- Follow track round to left and down slope into field after big, posh house with very neat lawn
- Continue along edge of field with hedge on right
- Turn right over bridge then left onto towpath with canal on left, passing foot swing bridge and café information area on right
- Continue along towpath and round to right, left over bridge, then right again back on to towpath with canal now on right
- Follow path away from canal up slope and round to playing fields
- Straight across, passing play area on right
- Turn left through gate following lane to road
- Turn right along road to pub and campsite

LONG WALK – GONGOOZLING AGAIN!
Distance: 7.75mi (12.4km)
Duration: 4hr (Easy)
Terrain: Towpath, fields, woods, footpaths, tracks, quiet roads, gates, gaps, stiles

Section 1: 0.75mi (1.2km)
- Exit campsite out to road via pub car park
- Turn right along road, passing school on left
- Turn right along Occupation Lane, then left into field just past houses

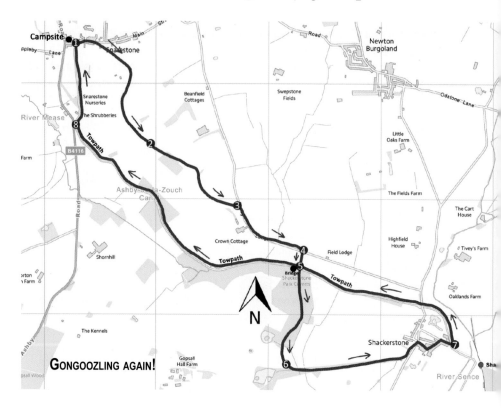

GONGOOZLING AGAIN!

- Cross field and over stile to next field, then through gap in hedge into third field.
- Straight ahead across field towards hedge, passing this on right
- Follow path, keeping close to hedge on right, then round to left at corner
- Turn right through gap in hedge, signposted, onto wide track
- Turn left in 25yd (23m) then right into wood

Section 2: 1mi (1.6km)
- Follow path through wood and over stile to field
- Continue straight ahead along edge of field with hedge on left
- Straight on at wide junction, still with hedge on left
- Turn left over stile in hedge just before corner
- Turn right along edge of field with hedge now on right and through gap in hedge into copse
- Follow path through copse and over stile into field
- Turn right, cross field and over stile ahead beside gate out to road

Section 3: 0.5mi (0.8km)
- Turn right along road (quiet)

Section 4: 0.75mi (1.2km)
- Turn right by road sign onto narrow path with fence on left, then through gap in hedge into wood
- Continue along path with fence still on left and over canal bridge into field
- Follow path along edge of field with trees on right onto wide track
- Turn right along track, then immediate left round hedge, and sharp right around second hedge into field
- Straight ahead along edge of field with hedge on right (no indication of path)
- Turn right at corner onto wide track, then left, crossing another track
- Turn left over footbridge at edge of wood

Section 5: 1mi (1.6km)
- Follow path along edge of field, keeping close to wood on left, round to right at corner
- Turn left in 50yd (465m) over stile and into wood
- Continue through wood out to road
- Turn left along pavement to Shackerstone village
- Turn right at junction and left at next junction to Rising Sun pub(would be a good place to stop for refreshments if it did food at lunchtime)

Section 6: 1.25mi (2km)
- From pub turn right at junction
- Continue along road and over bridge
- Turn left through gate onto towpath with canal on left
- Follow towpath, passing under bridge previously crossed

Section 7: 1.5mi (2.4km)
- Continue along towpath with canal still on right, passing under several bridges to one with small car park on left bank

Section 8: 1mi (1.6km)
- Continue along towpath and up slope by tunnel at bridge into pub car park with campsite on right

In the vicinity
Fishing
The canal offers fishing although permits are required, and can be obtained from the Measham and District Angling Club.

Snarestone
This small village has a linear layout along Main Street surrounded by farmland and countryside (there's even a field of sheep off Main Street). The village is mentioned in the Domesday Book and has several interesting buildings, including two pubs. The proximity of the canal is an added bonus.

More wonderful walks from **dog-friendly campsites**

One of the many narrowboats on the canal.

Ashby de la Zouch Canal

This canal is unusual in two respects. First, even when it was built in 1794 it did not reach Ashby, though it does connect to Coventry Canal at Marston Junction. Second, within its entire length, currently 22 miles (35.4km), there are no locks.
There is, however, a 250yd (228.6m) tunnel as it passes the village of Snarestone. Just half a mile (0.8km) further on the canal terminates at Snarestone Wharfe. Here are a café and charity shop, and the canal widens at this point to allow boats to turn around, though there are plans to extend the canal northwards.

Shackerstone

A small village situated on the River Senc, this is the headquarters of the Battle Line Railway, with a store of rail stock and memorabilia.
    As the Ashby-de-la-Zouch Canal passes through the village it crosses the river and turns sharply, frequently surprising unwary boats.

Battle Line Heritage Railway

This heritage railway line is so called because the station at Shenton is so close to Battle of Bosworth Field that a designated footpath runs from the station to the Visitor Centre, with informative notices along the way. The other end of the line is Shackerstone which connects with the Ashby-de-la-Zouch Canal.

The Battle of Bosworth Visitor Centre

Set up in 1973 at Ambion Hill, it was considered likely that this was where the battle took place. However, research over a five-year period from 2005 established that the actual battle site is about a mile (1.6km) away on land at Fen Lane Farm.
    A trail has been incorporated from the Visitor Centre to the new site, and the exhibition and notices around the site and trails are informative, with guided tours being particularly enlightening. Dogs are allowed on-site but not in the exhibition hall or café.

Alpaca Farm

Just half-a-mile (0.8km) along Main Street is the Alpaca Farm, which actually houses several species, including goats, pigs, donkeys, etc. With a café and wool shop, this is an interesting place to spend some time, although it's not dog-friendly, unfortunately.

1620 House & Gardens at Donington le Heath

This rare and unique place has been renovated to tell the story of the people who lived here. Beautiful as the house and gardens are, the philosophy here is very much hands-on, and visitors are encouraged to sit on furniture and handle objects. The one exception is the bed in which Richard III is said to have slept before the Battle of Bosworth.

Warwickshire – Shakespeare country
OS Maps Explorer 205 Stratford-upon-Avon & Evesham

Though Warwickshire is one of the few landlocked counties in England, water, as in the presence of the River Avon, is an important geographical and cultural feature.

Confusingly, there are eight rivers called Avon in Great Britain: four in England, three in Scotland, and one in Wales. Before the Romans arrived, local tribes referred to nearby rivers as 'Abona,' the Celtic word for river.

The River Avon that runs through Warwickshire from its source at Naseby in Northamptonshire to Tewkesbury in Gloucestershire, where it joins the River Severn, is the longest at 96ml (154m). As it meanders southwest it passes through Leicestershire, Northamptonshire, Worcestershire and Gloucestershire, but is synonymous with Warwickshire because its longest segment is in this county. It is also sometimes referred to as Shakespeare's Avon as his birthplace is a town on the banks of the river. In fact, a great many of the towns and villages in Warwickshire are on or close to the river.

Stratford-upon-Avon is the most well-known town in the county because, in 1564, it was where world-renowned English playwright William Shakespeare was born and died. Scattered around the surrounding countryside of Warwickshire are many places associated with him, his family and friends, and so it is that the road signs at county boundaries inform visitors that Warwickshire is 'Shakespeare's County.'

Shakespeare is buried in Holy Trinity Church in Stratford-upon-Avon, situated on the banks of the River Avon. That we know where he is buried is due to a fortunate set of circumstances. Firstly, as lay rector of the church, a resting place in the chancel was an entitlement. Secondly, it was customary in the 17th century to enable graves to be re-used by exhuming the bones of previous incumbents after 25 years. This obviously did not appeal to Shakespeare who, rather than have his name on his grave slab, inscribed a curse: "Good friend, for Jesus' sake forbear, to dig the dust enclosed here. Blessed be the man that spares these stones, And cursed be he that moves my bones." No-one, it seems, was prepared to test the veracity of this curse ...

In recognition of Shakespeare's significance the town boasts several theatres. On the banks of the River Avon a large theatre complex managed by the Royal Shakespeare Company features an extensive theatrical programme in addition to all the Shakespearean plays regularly performed there. There's also the fringe Attic Theatre at the Lazy Cow on Bridgefoot.

The preponderance of Shakespearean attractions rather overshadows others in the county: the charming county town of Warwick, for example, with its many striking buildings and magnificent Norman castle, which has a long and eventful history.

Near the eastern boundary of the county is the town of Rugby, and many believe that it was here in 1823 that the game of rugby was born when, during a football match, William Webb Ellis, a pupil of Rugby School, picked up the ball and ran with it, thereby creating the new game. The Webb Ellis Rugby Football Museum in the centre of the town and near the school is housed in the premises that have been making rugby balls for generations, and boasts a plethora of rugby memorabilia. In 2016, a state-of-the-art World Rugby Hall of Fame was established in the town.

Then there is the beautiful Regency town of Leamington Spa, so called after the River Leam that flows through it. This was the place to visit in the 18th century for its waters, which were thought to have medicinal benefits.

In addition to all of the foregoing is the varied and pleasing countryside. With the Peak District adjacent, the north of the county is undulating, while the hills of Cotswold nudge into the southern tip. In-between are rolling pastures generally used for wheat, beans, barley and turnips, as well as grazing. At one time much of the county was covered by the ancient Forest of Arden, hence several place names ending with 'in-Arden,' and Shakespeare also featured the forest in some of his plays. Sadly, over the years much of it has been cut down to provide fuel for various industries, and little remains except in name.

Surprisingly, it seems that Warwickshire has much to offer over and above its association with Shakespeare.

CAMPSITE – COTTAGE OF CONTENT

The name of the pub campsite so intrigued me I was delighted a visit was viable because it met my criteria. Being a medium-size campsite with 25 pitches, I was surprised to find it was full on several previous occasions when I tried to book, which intrigued me even more.

The campsite is a field behind the Cottage of Content pub, accessed along a narrow driveway between two buildings, and overlooked by the pub beer garden and a small car park. The hook-ups are situated around the perimeter of the field, with ample space for non-electric units in the middle.

Adjacent to the car park is a play area, and next to the pub's beer garden are two large, modern wet-rooms. There are additional toilets just inside the back door of the

The pitches are arranged around the edge of the field. Access to the other fields for dog exercise is in the corner.

pub; well, there is a ladies, at least, and behind the wet-rooms is a large, useful dishwashing area. There is no designated reception; booking and registration is managed in the pub.

PUB – COTTAGE OF CONTENT

This popular pub is situated in the hamlet of Barton just across the fields from the attractive village of Bidford-on-Avon in Warwickshire. On offer are a variety of beers and ciders, as well as home-cooked food for both lunch and dinner. It is a very lively pub with a schedule of events: Thursday is quiz night; Saturday is live entertainment, and first Tuesdays

The Cottage of Content pub on a rather grey day. Entrance to the campsite is through the passage on the left.

in the month are open mic nights. There are also annual events such as fireworks and a bonfire on November 5 weekend. With fishing possible in the river and a regular car boot sale in Bidford, there is plenty to do right on the doorstep.

Pearls of Wisdom

Whoopee – what a fabulous place! Just a short walk across the campsite to the corner, through a gap in the hedge, and there I was up and over the mound into a large field. So much to search out; so many different ways to go: along the top of the mound this way to a copse; that way to the river. I did find a way down the bank to the water – easy-peasy – but my owner had problems. I love swimming!

And what a lovely lot of fields before the road – even sheep in one of them did not spoil things – and enough space to chase my frisbee. Awesome!

I have to say I did not especially enjoy walking along the road, or travelling on the bus, though when we got off there were a great many fantastic places to check out.

Short walk – Beside the River Avon
Distance: 5.75mi (9.2km)
Duration: 3hr (Easy)
Terrain: Riverside path, footpaths, quiet roads, meadows, fields, mostly kissing gates, some stiles: flat, easy walking

Section 1: 1.5mi (2.4km)
- Exit campsite via right corner of camping field
- Turn right along top of embankment and round to left, then down steps onto footpath
- Continue straight ahead along footpath, through four kissing gates and over three fields out to road by bridge
- Cross road to car park and bear right to riverside path
- Follow riverside path with river on right, past fence and past playing fields on left, and cross footbridge into field
- Continue straight ahead along edge of two fields and through kissing gate into third field
- Cross field and through kissing gate, then across footbridge to stony lane

Section 2: 1.5mi (2.4km)
- Turn left, signposted, along lane

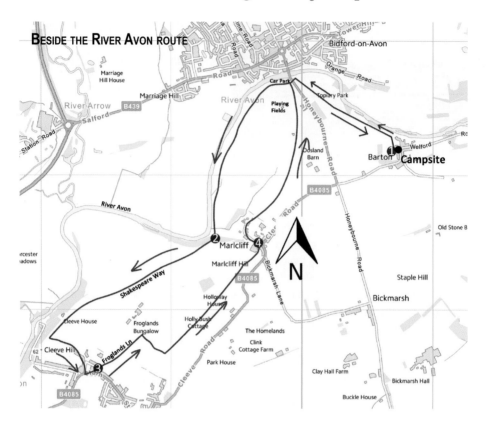

- Turn right onto grass track immediately before black-and-white house with thatched roof and through gate
- Straight ahead towards steps in 25yd (23m)
- Turn right along footpath at bottom of steps
- Follow footpath up slope between copse on right and hedge on left, and through gate at brow of hill
- Continue along footpath (Shakespeare Way) then through another gate and on along brow of hill (lovely views)
- Cross track and follow narrow footpath ahead between hedges and through gate
- Continue straight ahead onto tarmac driveway, passing house on right and through gate
- Turn immediately left into field between two large iron posts
- Straight ahead along edge of field onto tarmac driveway and through gate onto road
- Follow road round to right, then immediately left along Back Lane

Section 3: 1.25mi (2km)
- Turn left at T-junction and continue along road, Froglands Lane, passing farm shop, then through heavy brown gate onto stone drive

The bridge at Bidford-on-Avon from the riverside path.

- Turn right onto grass track, keeping house on left, and in 25yd (23m) through gate on right with blue hose over it onto tarmac footpath between fence and hedge
- Continue along footpath and through kissing gate into field
- Straight ahead along edge of field and through gap in hedge into next field
- Turn left immediately (away from kissing gate), continue along edge of field with hedge on left and through kissing gate in corner
- Bear right and along edge of field with hedge now on right
- Follow hedge round to left at corner
- Turn right into next field through large gap in 50yd (46m)
- Continue straight ahead across three fields, over stile opposite, passing gate on left, and into next field
- Straight ahead down slope towards small gap in trees, down steps and through gate out to road and bench

Section 4: 1.5mi (2.4km)
- Continue straight ahead along road, The Bank, past village green on left
- Keep left onto path between houses
- Follow lane round bend and through kissing gate onto footpath and into field
- Straight ahead along edge of field and through kissing gate in corner
- Continue ahead along edge of field
- In 200yd (183m) turn left through gap in hedge and over footbridge
- Continue ahead through gap in hedge in corner, straight across next field and through kissing gate opposite
- Bear left around playing fields to riverside car park beside bridge
- Through car park, cross road and through kissing gate into field
- Bear right, cross field and through gate
- Cross field and through two kissing gates into next field
- Continue straight on and along edge of field, then up steps to top of embankment
- Turn right along top of embankment and left at corner, then down steps and through trees into campsite field

LONG WALK – IN SHAKESPEARE'S FOOTSTEPS
Distance: 7.75mi (12.4km)

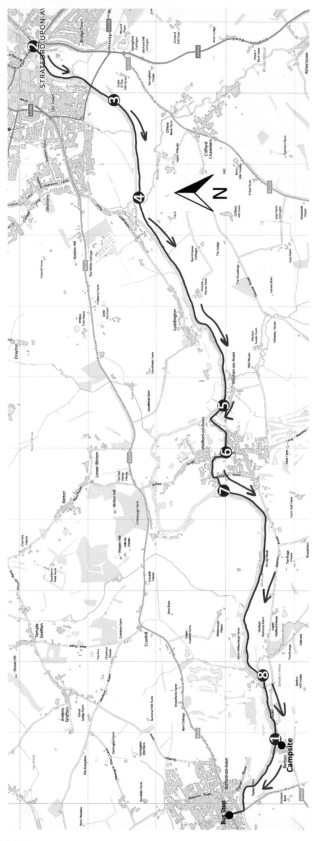

In Shakespeare's
Footsteps Route

Duration: 4hr (Easy)
Terrain: Riverside path, footpaths,
quiet roads, meadows, fields
mostly kissing gates, some stiles:
flat easy walking; one busy road to
reach campsite

To get to the start of this walk
catch the bus to Stratford (check
times). The walk time does not
include the bus journey or a trip
around Stratford on a red tour bus

Section 1: 0.75mi (1.2km)
- Exit campsite via right corner
  of camping field
- Turn right along top of
  embankment and round to left
  and down steps onto footpath
- Continue straight ahead along
  footpath, through four kissing
  gates and crossing three
  fields out to road by bridge
- Turn right and cross bridge
  (take care as very narrow but
  with special pedestrian
  waiting places)
- Turn left at junction with traffic
  lights
- Continue along road out to
  main B439
- Turn left and cross road to bus
  stop outside Budgens for 18X
  to Stratford

Section 2: 1mi (1.6km)
- At Stratford continue to town
  centre and Tourist Office on
  Bridge Foot by the river
  (here you can book an open
  red top tour bus to explore the
  town and surrounding area and

Shakepeare Way riverside path, passing Holy Trinity Church on the opposite bank where Shakespeare is buried.

a boat trip with Stratford Waterways Information Centre across the road)
- Cross A3400 (Bridge Foot) towards river and Gower Memorial
- Bear left past theatre on left and follow footpath over footbridge
- Turn right, then bear right across green to riverside path
- Follow path with river on right
- Turn right, cross footbridge and continue along riverside path
- Straight ahead under bridge and through gate onto narrow footpath, still with river on right

Section 3: 1mi (1.6km)
- Turn left at lock, then up steps and into wood
- Follow path, signposted, through wood and out to field
- Bear right, following path along edge of two fields with river on right into third field
- Turn right in 30yd (27m), signposted, and under tunnel
- Turn left along edge of field
- Continue straight ahead at corner onto narrow path
- Turn left up slope onto disused railway line

Section 4: 1.75mi (2.8km)
- Continue along rail line for short way, then bear right off rail track and through kissing gate
- Straight ahead along edge of field towards river
- Turn left and cross footbridge into field, and cross second footbridge into next field, then through kissing gate into third field
- Bear right at corner onto narrow path close to river and into next field
- Continue along edge of field as path meanders, keeping close to river on right, then over footbridge into fifth field

Section 5: 0.75mi (1.2km)
- Turn right through gap in hedge, signposted, and follow path across field onto track
- Straight ahead, passing church on right

- Turn right at T-junction along road
- At next T-junction turn left onto stony track, follow round to right and along edge of field: right again in 50yd (46m)
- Continue along edge of field and through kissing gate onto narrow footpath beside tarmac driveway, then another kissing gate onto road

Section 6: 0.75mi (1.2km)
- Bear left to road opposite (Millers Close)
- Continue along Millers Close to main road (High Street)
- Bearing slightly left, cross road and through kissing gate into lane
- Follow path between houses, turning right then left several times, passing graveyard and out to road
- Straight ahead along Mill Lane, ignoring driveway on left
- Turn left into caravan park, signposted

Section 7: 1.5mi (2.4km)
- Continue straight ahead onto grassy path, keeping close to river on right
- Follow footpath through wood and through kissing gate into field
- Bear right towards river and through another kissing gate into next field
- Follow path beside river, then through kissing gate into copse and out to riverside path
- Continue along riverside path through several kissing gates

Section 8: 1mi (1.6km)
- Follow path round edge of field at lock and cross footbridge into small car park
- Cross car park onto stony track and follow to road
- Turn right along Welford Road to pub and campsite (take care as although minor road there is quite a lot of traffic)

In the vicinity

Stratford-upon-Avon

There are so many interesting places to see, not only in the town but also just outside – Anne Hathaway's cottage, for example – and the best way to get an overview is via the red open-top bus tours. The commentary is especially enlightening, and tickets are valid for 24 hours so you can get off and on again at various stops en route. Dogs are allowed on the buses and in many of the gardens, but frequently not in the buildings. Tickets and advice are available at the Tourist Information office on the Bridge Foot.

Stratford and Avon Canal

This canal feeds into the River Avon right in the heart of Stratford at the Bancroft Basin, close to a lovely park and recreation field, with paths criss-crossing the attractive surroundings. The backdrop to all of this is the imposing Royal Shakespeare Theatre.

The canal is, in fact, relatively short at just 25 miles (40km), heading north to Kings Norton on the outskirts of Birmingham where it joins the Grand Union Canal. Building started in 1793, but it was not until 1816 that the final stretch was completed at Stratford.

Among the many places along the canal route is the small village of Wilmcote, where Shakespeare's mother, Mary Arden, lived before she married.

Several companies run boat trips along the river or the canal, leaving from Bancroft Basin. Information can be found here or at the Tourist Information office, as well as online. Check which companies allow dogs onboard.

WARWICK CASTLE

Warwick Castle's location on the banks of the River Avon was considered ideal for defence fortifications, and the Anglo-Saxons were first to build a settlement on the small hill, surrounded by a wall and ditch, because it commanded a clear view of the river. This was upgraded by William the Conqueror in 1068 to a motte-and-bailey castle (a fortification with a wooden or stone keep situated on a raised area of ground called a motte, accompanied by a walled courtyard, or bailey, surrounded by a protective ditch and palisade), and enhanced again in the 12th century when it was rebuilt in stone. Since then the castle's fortunes have fluctuated considerably, and it has been repaired on several occasions; increasing in size and magnificence each time.

In the 17th century it was converted to a country house by the Greville family, who lived there for the next 200 years or so until selling it in 1978 to the Tussards Group. It is now a theme park run by the Merlin Group, with a whole host of activities and attractions in both the building and the grounds. It is still one of the most imposing and intact medieval castles in the country.

BIDFORD-ON-AVON

This settlement grew up on an ancient route that crossed the River Avon at a ford known as Byda's Ford; hence the name of the village. It was such a convenient place to cross the river that even the Romans found it useful.

By the 15th century a stone bridge had been built just a few hundred yards to the west at the current location. It is a most unusual bridge: on one side, every few yards there is a triangular outcrop where pedestrians wait as traffic passes. Over the centuries this bridge has been repaired many times, most recently in 2015. Because it is Grade I listed it's classed as a scheduled

Bidford-on-Avon: one of the many villages on the River Avon.

monument (a nationally important archaeological site or historic building, given protection against unauthorised change).

There are many interesting buildings in the village, including the Church of St Laurence, which stands proudly overlooking the river. The original building was medieval but was substantially altered in the 19th century.

WELFORD-ON-AVON

This village, too, just a few miles east of Bidford, lies on the south bank of the River Avon, but nestled within a loop in the river. It has many interesting features; probably the most unusual being its maypole, which is the largest in the country at 65ft (20m) high. It is now aluminium as the wooden one was recently struck by lightning and damaged. The oldest part of the village, which has been occupied for thousands of years and is mentioned in the Domesday Book, is near the church, and it is here that there are several fascinating houses from many different eras. The many picturesque buildings and historical associations make this charming village a delight to wander.

Worcestershire – hills, rivers and market towns
OS MAPS EXPLORER 190 MALVERN HILLS & BREDON HILLS

Worcestershire is a very ancient county: one of the original Anglo-Saxon kingdoms that became part of the influential Kingdom of Mercia that, in 927, formed the unified Kingdom of England. Since then, the borders of Worcestershire have waxed and waned a great deal: in recent times this has been due to the growth of Birmingham. In an effort to rationalize the situation, the 1972 Local Government Act virtually abolished Worcestershire, dividing it between the new West Midlands area and the reconstituted Hereford and Worcester region.

Needless to say, many people were unhappy about this, and further local government changes in 1986 resulted in various Acts during the 1990s that ultimately restored the county of Worcestershire, albeit as a smaller, more rural region.

Being in such a central position Worcestershire has a rich cultural and political history, and several significant battles have taken place within its boundaries, one of which was the Battle of Evesham on August 4, 1265, the result of yet another attempt to limit the power of the king, led by the Earl of Leicester, Simon de Montfort. Unfortunately, his support drifted away and, at the battle, not only was Simon de Montfort's army defeated but he was killed. This battle is regularly re-enacted in August on Evesham's Crown Meadow.

Despite his defeat, Simon de Montfort is considered the 'Father of Democracy.' He called two parliaments in June 1264 and January 1265 which, for the first time, included representatives of several towns and shires as well as the church, with the aim of monitoring how the king used his authority. It was the failure of these parliaments that culminated in the fateful battle.

Then, in the 17th century, another constitutional tussle occurred: the English Civil War. Control of Worcestershire was essential because of its iron production in the north of the county. The Royalists demanded extortionate taxes from the people, and press-ganged local men, whilst the Parliamentarians' frequent raids and various battle skirmishes harassed the population. Then, at the Battle of Worcester in 1651, Oliver Cromwell resoundly trounced the Royalist army, bringing to an end the English Civil War. Unfortunately, the city of Worcester was then ransacked, with extensive looting and damage to property.

In 1857 in the small village of Broadheath, the composer Edward Elgar was born. He grew up in and around Worcester, and throughout his life often returned to visit familiar places. Also with links to Worcestershire is the author JRR Tolkien, and it is thought that inspiration for The Shire in *Lord of the Rings* and Bag End in *The Hobbit* came from a visit to his Aunt Jane's farm, Dormston Manor, known colloquially as 'Bagend.' The green tranquil countryside and the richly historical farmhouse had a profound effect on Tolkien, as he had just come from the smog-filled city of Leeds.

Also of note is the local paper, the *Berrow's Worcester Journal*, claimed to be the oldest paper in the world, in continuous and current production since 1690, though nowadays it is a freebie.

Then, of course, synonymous with the county since 1876 is Worcestershire Sauce, first concocted in 1837 by two chemists – John Wheeley Lea and William Henry Perrins – hence its subsidiary title of Lea and Perrins Sauce. This unusual and very versatile sauce can be added to a range of foods and recipes as well as drinks, and, as with many unique curiosities, mystery and folklore surround its origins and process.

Though the M5 scythes north to south through the middle of the county, rivers also dissect it into interesting pockets of land. The River Severn snakes down the western part of the county, creating a huge river valley. Rising up from the western edge are the renowned Malvern Hills, an AONB; a natural border with Herefordshire. Along the south of the county the River Avon meanders, creating the famous Vale of Evesham, where market gardens and orchards proliferate. The Cotswolds spill over into the south east corner of the county, and in the north east pocket lie the intriguingly-named Lickey Hills.

Apart from the sprawl of Birmingham to the north, and the county's capital of Worcester, there are many intriguing market towns and villages. Agriculture is important in such an extensive area of gently rolling hills: nowadays, mostly arable and dairy farming.

Often overshadowed by more well-known adjacent counties, there is a lot to see and do in Worcestershire, and with more than 3000 miles of footpaths and bridleways, there are some wonderful walking routes with amazing scenery.

The Malvern Hills; an AONB.

CAMPSITE – THE TURBLES CARAVAN SITE

The camping field is a large,

The campsite is a large grass field.

flat, grass field situated behind a row of white holiday lets; the electric hook-up sites, each with a tap alongside, are around the edge. There is a summerhouse stocked with games, etc, on the far side next to a toilet and shower. (I cannot give any details of the amenities as they were locked during my visit, but, from the outside, they appear rather basic.) The chemical toilet is located in a hut nearer the entrance at the far end of the white holiday lets. There is no reception; all bookings and payments are done online.

This is an ideal base for walking as there are many footpaths nearby, one of which goes through the campsite to Castlemorton Common, and there is a dedicated dog exercise area.

Pubs

There are two pubs close by, at one time accessible via footpaths across the fields. Unfortunately, one footpath has become very overgrown, and the private campsite path to the local has been closed because irresponsible dog owners have been leaving poo bags on the pub fence. However, both pubs are just a short distance along the main road, which has a grass verge on one side.

The Plume of Feathers

This is the closest to the campsite, and is considered to be the 'local.' It's a typical old-fashioned pub with a dedicated games room containing a pool table, and the menu reflects this. There are regular music nights, and the pub is popular with bikers.

Robin Hood

Adjacent to a static caravan park, this is a well organized and efficient pub. There is a large, welcoming outside area, including a children's play area, and the menu is typical gastro-pub food (delicious) with tempting specials.

Pearls of wisdom

A-ma-zing! A special place for me to run around, and what a place! A very large field with lots of interesting smells, especially doggie ones, and plenty of space to chase my frisbee! And all just a bounding leap and tail wag away through a small gate.

As an extra bonus this field leads along a lane to another big, open space, with oodles and oodles of places to explore and doggie companions to meet and greet. All

The Plume of Feathers is popular with bikers.

The Robin Hood has a static caravan park behind it.

the outings were fantastic, even though there was lots of tarmac. This place definitely has a paws-up from me!

SHORT WALK – A HINT OF 'THE SHIRE'

Distance: 5.5mi (8.8km)
Duration: 2.5hr (Easy)
Terrain: Fields, footpaths, stony tracks, gates, stiles (some sheep-proof), minor roads, some gentle climbs

Section 1: 1.25mi (2km)

- Exit campsite via holiday let cottages at entrance, and through gate onto Drugger's End Lane
- Turn left along road past houses
- Turn right just past second metal gate and field with horses and stables to cross stile
- Continue straight ahead along edge of field with hedge on right, passing kissing gate
- Follow edge of field to right, then left and cross stile in right corner into field
- Turn left along edge of field
- Turn left through gap in hedge, then immediately right, continuing along edge of field with hedge now on right
- Follow edge of field round to left to cross footbridge in hedge on right into next field
- Straight ahead along edge of field and over stile in corner
- Bear left towards church and through kissing gate in corner onto road
- Turn left along road to church

Section 2: 1mi (1.6km)

- Turn right down School Road, passing church on left corner and school on right
- Turn left onto track immediately after sewage works
- Follow track through gate round left-hand bend beside stream on right, then round another left-hand bend, signposted; ignore all paths off to right and left

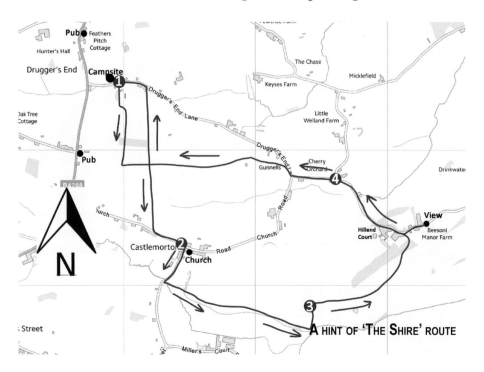

A HINT OF 'THE SHIRE' ROUTE

- Turn right at next right-hand bend and through kissing gate in hedge into field

Section 3: 1.5mi (2.4km)
- Follow path ahead along edge of field with fence on right, and through gate in corner onto wide, grassy track
- Continue along track through copse
- Turn left at T-junction along stony track out to road (turn right along road to just past Besons Farm for a wonderful view)
- Turn left and continue along road, passing Hillend Court on right

Section 4: 1.75mi (2.8km)
- Turn left along road at T-junction
- Straight on at next junction and through gate into field
- Bear right across field and over stile (sheep-proof) in fence
- Bear right across field and over stile beside gate into next field
- Straight across field, keeping close to hedge on right, and over stile (broken, so very difficult for dogs)
- Continue ahead along edge of field; through gap into next field and over another stile in right corner
- Cross next three fields and over stiles, keeping close to hedge on right
- Straight ahead along edge of fourth field with hedge now on left
- Turn right BEFORE stile and continue along edge of field with hedge on left as it

The scenery is simply idyllic ...

winds down, then over stile onto road
- Turn left along road to campsite entrance

LONG WALK – UP HILL AND DOWN DALE
Distance: 8mi (12.8km)
Duration: 4hr (Moderate)
Terrain: Fields, footpaths, tracks, gates, stiles, minor roads steps, steep climbs; amazing views

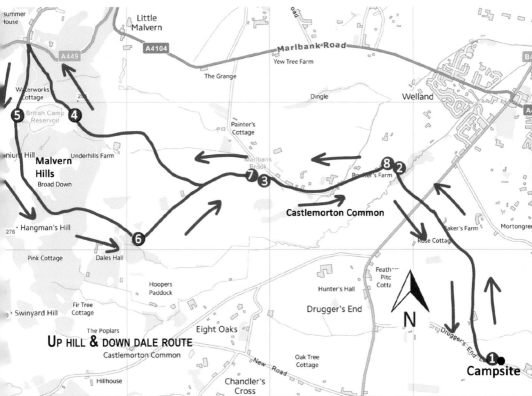

Section 1: 0.75mi (1.2km)
- Exit campsite via dog exercise area
- Bear left and through kissing gate into small field

- Through kissing gate in corner and right onto narrow footpath
- Follow path to junction
- Turn left and continue along path as it widens to track, then through gate, past house and out to busy road (B4208)
- Bearing right, cross road to minor road opposite (surprisingly busy)
- Continue on minor road and cross bridge

Section 2: 1mi (1.6km)
- Bear left immediately along wide, earth track which quickly becomes grassy
- Follow wide, grassy track, passing close to white house ahead and road on right
- Turn right onto narrower grass path, then on to right-hand bend of road to cross bridge ahead
- Continue along tarmac driveway round to left and past cottages on right
- Turn left onto wide earth track via single-plank bridge before gate across driveway
- Follow track out to field and cross, bearing right onto earth track at corner of field

Section 3: 1mi (1.6km)
- Continue along track and through gate into field
- Follow path ahead, bearing right, keeping close to fence on right, then through gate onto wide, stony path
- Continue along path past farmyard and out to tarmac driveway
- Turn left and through gate into field at brow of hill
- Bear left across field towards trees and through gate into wood
- Follow path through wood, climbing steadily with stream on left
- Take right path at junction with stream still on left, then green metal fence, climbing very steeply to reservoir and British Camp
- Bear left onto path just after house on right

Section 4: 1.25mi (2km)
- Follow tarmac path through car park to road (a good place for refreshments before climb to viewpoint)
- Retrace steps along tarmac path to house by reservoir
- Follow path around base of hill then up very steep hill with some steps to T-junction (a convenient seat here to rest before the next climb)
- Turn right and continue along stony track
- Turn left up slope, then steps (VERY steep)
- Turn left at junction and follow stony track and steps up to view point (views are magnificent but it can be very windy and cool)

Section 5: 1mi (1.6km)
- Straight ahead and down large, cobbled steps to wide path clearly visible ahead
- Follow path down and then up the next hill

- Continue straight ahead to top of hill and along wide, stony track, which zig-zags down via large cobbled steps to a large, round, stone signpost
- Turn right along earth track and follow down hill
- Straight ahead at junction, still descending
- Turn sharp left along wide track towards house

Section 6: 1.25mi (2km)
- Continue along track past house and onto narrow footpath up bank
- Follow footpath through trees
- Turn right at T-junction, descending then immediate left
- Continue along footpath through trees and out to field
- Bear right across field to wide track beside hedge on right
- Turn left along track and follow to corner
- Turn right at corner along grass path with hedge still on right
- Straight ahead along track across field and through gate in left-hand corner

Section 7: 1mi (1.6km)
- Turn right along edge of field, keeping close to hedge on right, then through gate in right corner
- Continue along wide, muddy track out to field
- Follow path round to left with hedge on left onto track and over bridge onto tarmac driveway
- Turn right and follow driveway past cottages, then over bridge to left-hand bend.
- Continue straight ahead onto grass track, bearing round to left

Section 8: 0.75mi (1.2km)
- Follow grass path, keeping right, and cross bridge on right
- Continue along road and cross busy road (B4208), bearing right to driveway opposite
- Follow driveway onto track and through gate into copse
- Continue along track to left-hand bend
- Turn right onto narrow path and through kissing gate into small field
- Straight ahead and through kissing gate in corner to campsite dog exercise area

IN THE VICINITY
CYCLING
With over 35 miles (56km) of bridleways and woodland track, there are many cycle trails in the area for all levels of cyclist, including mountain bikers high in the Malvern Hills.

BIRDWATCHING/WILDLIFE
The hills and surrounding area are carefully managed to encourage as diverse an environment as possible, and a huge variety of birds and wildlife are often spotted.

More wonderful walks from **dog-friendly campsites**

The British Camp

At the top of the Malvern Hills is the British Camp, an ancient hill fort dating from 200BC. Despite the many investigations that have taken place over the years – the latest by English Heritage in 2000 – it still remains a mystery, however, and legends abound about it. What *is* known can be found online, and on an information board in the car park at the foot of the hills. This can be reached by extending Section 4 of the long walk along the lane to the car park before starting the climb to the top.

Castlemorton Common

At one time a large area around Malvern formed part of the royal hunting grounds. Castlemorton Common is the only unenclosed common land remaining, with more than 600 acres to explore and enjoy.

Lovells Vineyard

This vineyard was created in 2008, and in 2013 the Lovells took over management of nearby Tiltridge Vinery. The vineyard has been so successful that, in 2016, Marks and Spencer decided to stock some of its wines. Various events are hosted here and the vineyard is open to visitors.

Malvern

Just 6ml (9.6km) to the north is this historic spa town, where there is so much to see and do that a visit to the Tourist Information office on Church Street is essential.

Upton-upon-Severn

This may be only a small town but its location on the west bank of the River Severn has been historically significant, as it was the only place at which to cross the River Severn between Worcester and Tewkesbury, and it was not until after WWII that this situation changed. As a result, the town was important and its location ideal, especially for many small, independent businesses.

The town has retained this bustling, thriving atmosphere, and there are many interesting buildings, of which the White Lion Hotel, a 16th century coaching inn, is probably the most impressive.

There is an array of independent shops – several connected with outdoor pursuits – and one such is the unique Map Shop. As the name suggests, this sells every conceivable type of map or book related to geography: a real treasure trove. Do visit.

If boats are your thing there is a marina, and if music festivals thrill you, the town hosts three: folk in May; jazz in June; blues in July. Something for everyone; a delightful place to spend time.

Walks in
South East England
(Kent, East Sussex, Suffolk)

East Sussex – ancient woodlands of the Weald
OS Maps Explorer OL25 Eastbourne & Beachy Head

Up until 1974 East Sussex was part of the historic County of Sussex; so called because it was the kingdom of the South Saxons. Sussex stretches along the coast of the English Channel south of London from Kent in the east to Hampshire in the west. With France only a few miles away across the water, Sussex was considered the gateway to Britain by invaders, from the Romans right through to World War II.

East Sussex was created from the larger county of Sussex as a result of the Local Government Act of 1972. It is one of the few counties without motorways but, even so, because it is so close to London, there is huge demand for houses and many of the roads are busy; even some of the minor ones. Despite this there are a lot of places to walk, particularly in the Weald, which is an AONB (Area of Outstanding Natural Beauty).

'Weald' is an old English term for forest, and, in ancient times, a huge forest covered much of the counties of Surrey, Sussex and Kent. Being somewhat forbidding, the forest was not inhabited, but was an abundant resource for those who lived on its fringes. Over the centuries the forest has shrunk a great deal, although the Weald is still one of the most densely wooded and unspoilt places in England.

Recently, the likelihood of seeing a wild boar here has increased: though hunted for sport and food to the point of extinction in the 1800s, some have successfully re-established themselves in the area, having escaped from boar farms.

There are three distinctive parts of the Weald –

* To the north and west can be found the highest areas – the 'Greensand Ridge'
* Around the edge is the 'Low Weald'
* The central part is the 'High Weald'

The High Weald covers nearly a third of East Sussex as well as straddling the border into Kent, though many of its ancient woodlands have disappeared.

Pearl exploring the remaining forest of the Weald.

Many of those that remain are privately owned, with some not open to the public. However, this is not so with Ashdown Forest: an area of heathland and woodland in the centre of the High Weald on the highest sandy ridge, created by the Normans for hunting deer. Though now much smaller and managed by Ashdown Forest Trust, it is still an amazing place to visit, renowned as the inspiration for A A Milne's *Winnie the Pooh* and his Hundred Acre Wood. It is possible to relive the stories by playing pooh sticks from the exact same bridge.

In ancient times the woods of Sussex Weald were considered mysterious and magical; the haunts of fairies and spirits, and this seems to apply even today in Sapperton Woods: ghostly spiders and their webs adorning the trees and tiny coloured fairy doors at the base by the roots. Pearl and I even found a tiny wheelie bin for collecting fairy dust ...

Now, only remnants of woodland remain because, over the centuries, this fantastic resource has been exploited by various industries, including shipbuilding. Henry VIII used wood from here to expand the recently-formed navy, and his flag ship, the *Mary Rose*, at present docked in Portsmouth, is an incredible example of this. Nowadays, in the coastal region tourism is the main industry and inland it's agriculture – arable and livestock – the latter with its own special breed of cow, known as Sussex Cattle. Recently, vineyards have been established for wine production, with several in the area.

The inhospitableness of the Weald has resulted in only a few small villages and hamlets scattered about, often just a short walk apart. Larger settlements are mostly on the outskirts, and used to be connected by the railway. This was closed in 1968, and the line has subsequently been converted to a cycleway, the Cuckoo Trail. This is a marvellous trail: a wonderful way to explore the area either by bike or on foot.

CAMPSITE – HORAM MANOR COUNTRY PARK

Located on the outskirts of Horam village, the entrance is not immediately evident as it is tucked away opposite the village hall, behind a small commercial estate. The approach – a drive – eventually opens out to a parking area beside the reception and shop.

Though actually a large site with approximately one hundred pitches for both tents and caravans, it feels small and intimate because it is spread over two fields, each with a facilities block, and is encircled by numerous shrubs and trees. In the first field are 20 hardstanding pitches as well as grass pitches, all with electric hook-up. Space to manoeuvre here was tight in places, so it is just as well that the second field is spacious; ideal for larger units and as an overflow area.

The advantage of the site is that not only is it adjacent to the well resourced recreation field but it is also part of Horam Manor Country Park. Among the various amenities the Country Park offers, just a short walk away is the Lakeside Bistro. With an extensive patio garden area overlooking the fishing lake, this bistro is aptly named; moreover, it is conveniently located just a short distance from the campsite along a track, and offers a range of food from breakfast to late afternoon (not evening). It is popular locally so booking is advisable.

PUB – THE MAY GARLAND INN

In the other direction across the playing field on the main A267 is the pub. Although there

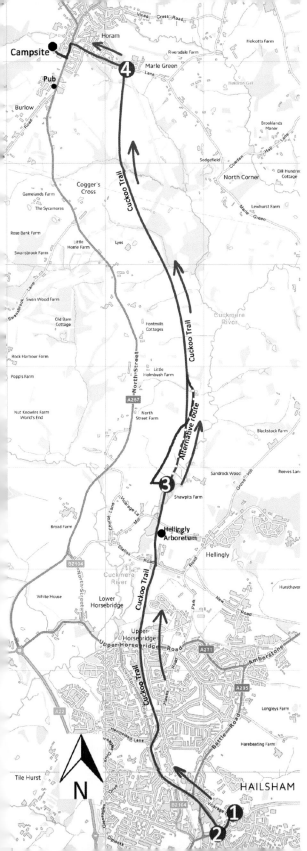

were people inside when I visited, it did not look very welcoming.

PEARLS OF WISDOM 🐕

What a wicked place! Two tail wags past the gate and there it was – the biggest field I had EVER seen. Yes, it was plain, and the grass was neat and tidy but just right for a frisbee – yay! Along the edges there were many trees and intriguing places; lots to explore.

Whenever I visited this amazing place there were so many buddies to meet and greet, and even run with! Fun! Fun! Fun! It was just a shame I could not have a dip in the water nearby – something about fish – I don't eat fish. And the walks! So many trees even close to the tarmac, though shame about the irritating bikes. So much to nose out and even chase; it was brill!

SHORT WALK – FOLLOWING THE CUCKOO

Distance: 5.25mi (8.4km)
Duration: 2hr (Easy)
Terrain: (A bus to Hailsham to start) Fields, footpaths, tracks, cyclepath some roads and pavements; a couple of gates and stiles

Section 1: 0.5mi (0.8km)

- Exit campsite via entrance and bear left across playing fields towards football pavilion
- Keep bearing left through car park to A267
- Turn right along road crossing

Chidingly Road, then right and cross A267 to bus stop for 51 and 51X buses
- Alight at Hailsham High Street (by Waitrose and Asda)
- Turn right and continue along High Street to traffic lights passing church on left
- Turn left into George Street and, passing police station on left, straight on at next traffic lights, crossing the road into car park.
- Continue ahead along edge of car park towards tunnel

Section 2: 2.5mi (4km)
- Turn right through tunnel and out onto rural track – Cuckoo Trail, signposted
- Follow well-signposted trail
- Keep left at arches and continue along lane/trail as it passes along the back of houses; then in front of houses along pavement
- Cross minor road to lane opposite between houses
- Continue along lane through long tunnel onto more rural track but still crossing some roads. (Watch for a really large oak tree on right: this is part of Hellingly Arboretum. An information board is on the trail)
- Also notice wooden plaques depicting local wildlife on bridge walls

Section 3: 2.5mi (4km)
- Turn left off trail just past bridge, and over footbridge and through gate onto footpath, then through kissing gate into field
- Straight across field and through gate into next field
- Bear right across field and over stile onto Cuckoo Trail
- Cross trail and up steps opposite out to field
- Bear left across field and left round shrub, then along edge of field and through gap ahead and over footbridge
- Turn left along edge of field with hedge on left, passing gap to stile
- **Either:** turn left before stile back onto Cuckoo Trail
- **Or:** Over stile and continue along edge of fields parallel to Cuckoo Trail on left and where Cuckmere River passes join trail
- **Then:** Follow Cuckoo Trail to Horebeech Lane Bridge

Section 4: 0.5mi (0.8km)
- Turn right after bridge and up exit ram out to road
- Turn right along road to roundabout junction
- Cross A267 at zebra crossing
- Turn left then right along Merrydown Way to Horam Manor Farm entrance
- Continue along driveway towards farm buildings
- Turn left at signpost towards bistro/café and follow path round to right with lake on right ;then round to the left
- Straight ahead, passing car park on right, and through gate to campsite entrance on right

The Cuckoo Trail.

LONG WALK – TO THE WOOD
Distance: 7.5mi (12km)
Duration: 4hr (Easy)
Terrain: Fields, woods,
footpaths, cyclepath, tracks
and roads, kissing gates,
gates and stiles (some
sheep-proof), and a short
but steep gully

Section 1: 1mi (1.6km)
- Exit campsite via reception out to A267, passing Village Hall and playing fields on right
- Turn left along road to roundabout, then right onto Horebeech Lane
- Continue along Horebeech Lane, passing new houses and crossing bridge over Cuckoo Trail to Laundry Lane
- Turn left and over stile in corner onto footpath
- Follow path over stile into field
- Cross field and over stile opposite beside beautiful carved horse's head into next field

Section 2: 0.75mi (1.2km)
- Bear left downhill and over stile into next field and cross, bearing left over bridge opposite with 'dog gate' on right side into field
- Bear right across field and over stile under large tree in corner onto narrow fenced footpath between houses and out to road
- Cross road to stony driveway
- Continue along driveway towards gate with hedge and vineyard entrance on right, passing garage on left
- Follow footpath with gate on right over stile into vineyard car park and reception (an ideal place to learn about wine)
- Passing vineyard entrance continue straight ahead onto stony track with field of vines on left, ignoring path on right, and over stile into copse
- Follow path between trees with fields on each side, and over stile onto short track with pond on right

Section 3: 0.75mi (1.2km)
- Cross track and over stile into field on right
- Continue ahead, keeping close to hedge on right
- Turn right to go over stile in hedge beside gate
- Turn left along edge of field with hedge now on left, and over stile in corner
- Continue ahead, keeping close to fence on right and over stile in 100yd (91.4m)

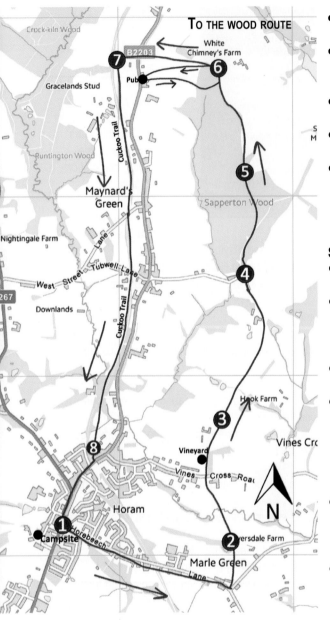

TO THE WOOD ROUTE

- Bearing left, cross track and over stile (sheep-proof)
- Straight on, passing barns on left and over half-stile beside rusty gate
- Bear left and through gate on left
- Turn left, crossing field down to wide track
- Turn right along track and through gate, passing houses and stile in fence on right to left-hand bend

Section 4: 1mi (1.6km)

- Turn right onto footpath into Sapperton Wood
- Follow path through wood, taking right fork in 50yd (46m) onto narrow path and again at signposted junction
- Take right fork a third time with a fence visible on right
- Turn left along narrow winding path between large fallen trees and roots. (If you pass a log with flat bench-like shape cut near kissing gate, you've gone too far)
- Follow narrow path over several fallen trees round an up-ended root ball to wider path
- Continue along woodland path (occasionally, fields are glimpsed through trees on right) to 'The Ravine' (so-called by locals)

Section 5: 1mi (1.6km)

- Cross ravine at easiest point and, keeping right where possible, continue out to field along path parallel to fields visible through trees on right
- Turn left towards fence corner, keeping close to wood on left
- Bear left through gap in hedge, signposted

- Turn right across field towards telegraph pole and though gap in hedge
- Straight on along edge of field and through gate in left corner
- Turn right immediately along narrow path to road
- Turn left to pub (a good place for refreshments)
- Exit pub through gate in left corner in garden, and another gate into field
- Turn left along edge of field through gap in hedge and into field

Section 6: 1mi (1.6km)
- Straight across and into wood through gap in trees by broken fence
- Follow path round to right (look for decorations on trees)
- Bear left down dip and continue along path over gully; round to left then left again between holly bushes
- Left between more holly bushes at junction and follow path parallel to fields visible through trees on right (this is now the same path as previously)
- Follow path out to field
- Straight across field, bearing slightly right towards pair of large trees, and through gap under one on right onto narrow footpath
- Continue along path to B2203
- Cross road to driveway opposite and under height barrier onto Cuckoo Trail

Section 7: 1.5mi (2.4km)
- Turn left along Cuckoo Trail
- Follow the Trail under and over bridges and past exit ramps to Horam Station

Section 8: 0.5mi (0.8km)
- Turn left by bike stand and along access road to B2203
- Turn left, cross bridge and continue along road to junction with A267
- Straight ahead and cross road at zebra crossing
- Turn left and continue along A267
- Bear right onto footpath at corner of Old Vicarage Close beside street sign
- Continue along path to village hall and turn right to campsite entrance

IN THE VICINITY

FISHING

Just a short walk away on part of the Horam Manor Estate can be found a wide variety of waters for coarse fishing at Horam Manor Fisheries. This fishery is family-run, and a daily fee provides access to the 11 ponds on site, many surrounded by woodland, which are well stocked with a variety of fish, including tench, carp and perch.

CYCLING

With many miles of quiet country roads and cycle trails across the Weald, there are routes for all types of cyclist. Nearby is the Cuckoo Trail created from a disused rail line for walkers, horseriders and cyclists. The 12-mile (19km) track from Heathfield to Polegate is

Hidden Springs: a Sussex vineyard.

a delightful tree-lined route linking villages, pubs and cafés as it traverses the High Weald.

HORAM

What an evocative name; perhaps a location in a dystopian sci-fi parallel universe? No, just a delightfully typical Sussex village on the Weald. Beside a number of shops, cafés and pubs, on the outskirts of the village lies a large recreation field with multiple sports facilities, an outdoor gym, and a vibrant village hall. Access to walks is easy as nearby are several rights of way across fields, as well as the Cuckoo Trail.

HORAM MANOR COUNTRY PARK ESTATE

Horam Manor Farm used to be a dairy farm but, over the past fifty years, the Goulden family diversified by leasing land and outbuildings to various concerns. Though the family still lives in the farmhouse the rest of the estate is a hub of different activities. Besides the campsite there is a riding stable, a family-run fishery, nature trails, a bistro, and a small museum – Sussex Farm Museum – which houses local artefacts, as well as several workshops where a range of arts and crafts are taught and exhibited. A varied and lively community.

HIDDEN SPRINGS VINEYARD

This vineyard is situated just a little way along the road to the adjoining hamlet of Vines Cross. When the two enthusiastic owners took over in 2015 they closed the campsite that had only recently been established, and resurrected the vineyard, replanting over 24,000 vines. In a few short years not only have they established their own award-winning wine, but also set up tours and tasting sessions; information about which is available online.

HEATHFIELD

A charming, pleasant market town situated on one of the many ridges of the High Weald, surrounded by lovely East Sussex countryside. A vibrant and pleasant place with a variety of shops, pubs and cafés on the busy high street, there is also a regular monthly farmers' market as well as several annual events. Tucked away in a corner of the Co-op car park is the entrance to the fabulous Markley Wood, which is well worth a visit.

HAILSHAM

Located on the edge of the High Weald, this market town has a long history, and is mentioned in the Domesday Book. In 1252 it was granted a Market Charter by Henry III, and a street market is still held every Saturday, with a farmers' market every second Saturday. Hailsham is an attractive town with an imposing church, delightful market square, and lively high street. There is a clear link to the Cuckoo Trail, which snakes through some interesting tree-lined sections.

WINDMILL HILL

This village is so named because of the tallest Post Mill that dominates the area. Built over 200 years ago, it had ceased to be viable by the advent of WWI, and quickly fell into disrepair. In 2003 restoration began and was completed by 2006, and the mill is now open to the public.

HERSTMONCEUX CASTLE

The Fiennes family built this imposing moated castle, set in 550 acres of woodland and magnificent garden, during the 1440s and 1450s. In the intervening centuries various families have owned the castle, although, during the 1700s, it degraded into a mysterious and eerie ruin until 1932, when Sir Paul Latham bought it and restoration began.

Now, Dr Alfred Bader owns the castle and grounds, and they are used by Queen's University of Canada as an international study campus. Visitors are welcome, including dogs on a lead, although castle tours are for people only. In addition, throughout the year there are various events, with the Medieval Festival being the most renowned.

Kent – the link with the European Continent
OS MAPS EXPLORER 148 MAIDSTONE & THE MEDWAY TOWNS
The characteristics of Kent are quite unique –

• It is the oldest recorded county name in Great Britain, having been identified by Greek and Roman writers in 55BC as 'Kention,' with the tribes who lived in the region known as 'Canti.' It is not clear what the derivative of this is, although the Celtic root 'canto' means edge or rim, and probably alludes to the fact that Kent forms the southeast edge of the country.

The river Medway slices through the county from the Thames Estuary to the High Weald on the southwest border with Sussex. Those born to the west of the river are known as 'Kentish Men' or 'Kentish Maid' (ordinary people), whilst those born to the east are 'Men of Kent' or 'Maid of Kent': people of high honour. The origin of this discrepancy is uncertain, but one suggestion is that the Anglo-Saxons settled to the west of the river, pushing the Jutes tribe to the east of it. Then again, it could be that the ordinary folk (Kentish Men) succumbed to William the Conqueror whilst those of honour (Men of Kent) resisted. Whatever the reason, establishment of the Association of the Men of Kent and Kentish Men in 1913 preserves this distinction.

• Kent has a long, varied and spectacular coast, and at Dartford it runs along the south bank of the Thames before jutting out into the North Sea. The coastline along the English

More wonderful walks from dog-friendly campsites

Between all of the roads lies the Garden of Kent.

Channel is comprised of chalk and, over the centuries, sea erosion has created the renowned white cliffs immortalized during WWII by Vera Lynn's hit song *There'll be Bluebirds over the White Cliffs of Dover*. Continuing west along the coast are the distinctive Romney Marshes.

• Kent has the distinction of being the closest county to mainland Europe, with only 21 miles (34km) of water separating Great Britain from France. In fact, on a clear day it is possible to see the French coastline. Because of this the county is a buffer between the capital, London, and potential hostile incursions. Consequently, there are defence fortifications all over the county: Roman forts; castles built by the Normans and throughout the medieval period, such as Dover and Rochester castles; Martello towers built during the 1800s, and airfields and anti-aircraft batteries during WWII.

• The cathedral in the city of Canterbury was the seat of the head of the Catholic Church in England for many centuries, until the reformation in the 16th century, when it became the religious capital of the Church of England. Though the Supreme Governor of the Church of England is the Queen, the Archbishop of Canterbury is the religious head of the worldwide Anglican Communion.

• More miles of motorway and major roads traverse Kent than any other county; undoubtedly due to the ferry traffic – all types of vehicles, including large freight lorries – that uses the Port of Dover, and the High Speed Channel Tunnel terminal. Nevertheless, squeezed between these ribbons of asphalt are picturesque towns and villages, farms and country lanes. Because of the proliferation of orchards, hazel nut production and hop gardens, especially in the south of the county, Kent is often referred to as the 'Garden of England.' Dotted throughout the county are Kent's unique oast houses, with their pointed triangular roofs. Originally used for drying hops, with the decline in agriculture many of these have been converted to holiday and residential accommodation.

The location of the campsite exemplifies this apparent contradiction, and the pub appears suddenly on a quiet country lane near a small hamlet that is closely bordered by two major roads. Despite this, it is surprisingly quiet.

Campsite – Hook and Hatchet

This small campsite of just eight pitches with electric hook-up has only recently been created (in 2017). The field, situated behind the pub car park, slopes, with the flattest part

The campsite is a simple field. In the next field is the start of a wooden sculpture trail.

at the top by the hedge (levelling blocks are necessary, even so). It is here that the electric hook-ups are located, with all other facilities at the bottom of the slope close to the pub – including the chemical toilet. Several water taps are dotted around.

The two toilets and showers are unisex, and are very modern and swish. Adjacent is a large field, part of the Hucking Estate, which is managed by the Woodland Trust, and is an ideal place to exercise your dog.

Pub – Hook and Hatchet

Travelling carefully along very narrow country roads, the white clapperboard building, its name emblazoned on the side, looms suddenly out of the hedge at an intersection. Large and sprawling with various outside spaces, this is a freehouse selling a range of beers, wines and spirits, and offering traditional pub food.

Though the Hook and Hatch has a long history, like many pubs nowadays it has faced difficult times, unoccupied for two years until the current owners reopened it in 2016. They have done a magnificent job in revitalizing the pub, and it is now a thriving business, despite its remote location. An assortment of events are on offer, from music nights to sports fixtures, including dog shows, so a stay here is never dull.

Pearls of Wisdom 🐾

I love places like this! It may be small but, by meaty bones, it's great. Just the other side of the fence is this huge field; shame there isn't a gate directly into it. We have to walk around the building to the gate: it's not far but it is an annoyance. Here, I can chase my frisbee if I like or explore all the enticing smells: oodles of these as a lot of other dogs use the field.

Then there are the gates leading out; three of them, in fact. We mostly used the one into the woods because it kept my owner drier in the rain, and because often in the open spaces were more of those pesky sheep.

The pub also welcomes local horseriders, providing hay and a place to tie up the horses whilst the riders socialize.

The jaunts went on and on. Only a couple of sections were tarmac, but I could still roam freely on my extended lead because there were few cars.

Also, I could go with my owner into the pub, where they did spoil me with lovely treats.

Short walk – Hucking Estate
Distance: 5.5mi (8.8km)
Duration: 5hr (Easy)
Terrain: Fields, woods, footpaths, tracks and roads, some kissing gates, gates, stiles and some gentle slopes, and amazing wooden sculptures dotted about the estate, celebrating the ongoing woodland restoration

Section 1: 0.75mi (1.2km)
- Exit campsite via car park
- Turn left along road, passing pub
- Turn right and through gate into field: Hucking Estate
- Continue straight ahead keeping close to fence on left, with campsite on left and first sculpture 'Tranchet Axe' on right
- Turn left and through kissing gate immediately after campsite
- Straight on along edge of field, keeping close to fence on left
- Continue ahead between trees and through kissing gate onto road

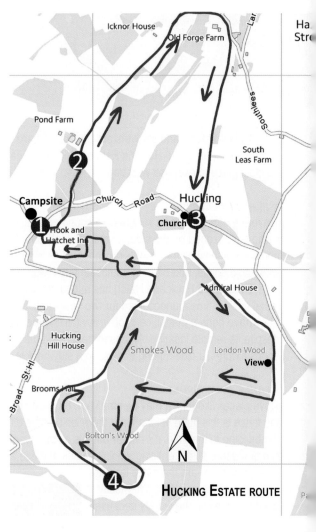

Hucking Estate route

- Bear right across road and climb over large wooden gate (dog through bars of metal gate)
- Continue straight ahead along path parallel to road on right and through gate ahead, passing signpost on right
- Turn left along edge of field with fence on right
- Cross field, bearing slightly left, and cross stile in fence into wood

Section 2: 1.25mi (2km)

- Follow path through wood with fence on right, passing two yellow way-markers
- Turn right just before metal gates and follow path into field, signposted
- Continue along edge of field with hedge on left
- Bear right to corner of fence ahead
- Turn right in five paces along footpath across field, signposted, and follow path along valley, over stile, across second field and over another stile
- Bear right towards trees and way-marker post
- Continue along edge of field with trees on right
- Bear left at corner (way-marker), through trees and over stile and through kissing gate into field
- Straight ahead, keeping close to fence on right, and through kissing gate on right into wood
- Follow path through wood with fence now on left, and through gate to lane
- Turn left towards road and church, (Hucking)

Section 3: 2mi (3.2km)

- Turn left, then right immediately after church, signposted, and through gate
- Follow track towards wood
- Turn left and zig-zag through wooden posts immediately before wood
- Follow grass track between fence on left and trees on right
- Turn left at corner along track, then right onto grass track immediately before bushes by dog bin
- Follow grass track out to stony track, keeping close to hedges/trees on left
- Turn right and continue along track to bend
- Turn right towards gate and noticeboard
- Continue straight ahead through gate and along grass track
- Turn left at 'Living Log' sculpture
- Continue along grass track to T-junction passing two way-markers.
- Turn left and follow track through gate into meadow
- Turn immediate right and follow wide grass track towards hills past 'Shepherd' sculpture

Section 4: 1.5mi (2.4km)

- Continue along wide grass track parallel to hills and through gate into another meadow
- Turn right and follow fence on right to 'Boar' sculpture at corner

The shepherd watching his flock ...

- With sculpture on right straight ahead along grassy track towards fence and trees, and through kissing gate in fence on right
- Turn left along track with fence now on left, ignoring all paths on right, and through kissing gate
- Turn left, cross track and through kissing gate opposite
- Follow path as it winds through trees
- Turn left up wooden steps and continue along path and through kissing gate into field
- Bear right across field towards pub and campsite, passing 'Tranchet Axe' sculpture

LONG WALK – ALONG THE RIDGE
Distance: 7.75mi (12.5km)
Duration: 4hr (Moderate)
Terrain: Fields, woods, footpaths, tracks and roads, some kissing gates, gates, stiles and some gentle slopes

Section 1: 1.25mi (2km)
- Exit campsite via pub car park, turning left along road, passing pub on left
- Continue straight ahead along road at T-junction
- Turn right at next junction along cul-de-sac
- Continue along road, passing Stanhope Farm on left, and through Scragged Oak Farm farmyard out to field
- Bearing slightly left, cross field and over flat stile in fence opposite

Section 2: 0.75mi (1.2km)
- Turn left along path (North Downs Way) with fence on left
- Turn left immediately after going through gap in hedge, then through kissing gate onto path
- Follow path down steps, cross road and up steps opposite (did not follow signposted detour to views as this was part of short walk)
- Turn left along wide stone track, signposted

- Turn right and through kissing gate onto wide grass track, signposted but confusing

Section 3: 1mi (1.6km)
- Follow North Downs Way as it snakes along, going through kissing gates (views are spectacular)
- Turn right down field/meadow,

View from North Down Way.

signposted, way-marker on wooden post, towards arch in trees, and through kissing gate at other side into field

- Continue straight ahead along edge of field with hedge on right
- Follow hedge round to left and down to road (busy)
- Bear right and cross road towards pub, Dirty Habit (refreshments available)

Section 4: 1mi (1.6km)

- Exit pub, turn right and right again down lane beside pub, signposted, past large sign for cricket club
- Turn right along footpath with fence and driveway on right, and through gate into lane
- Continue straight on toward road
- Turn left before road between wooden fence and small metal fence
- Turn right along path parallel to road and down steps to Greenway Court Road
- Turn left along road

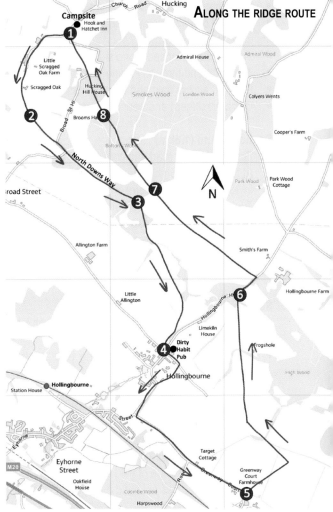

ALONG THE RIDGE ROUTE

Section 5: 1.25mi (2km)

- At junction turn left along wide track signposted 'Byway'
- Turn right at footpath junction onto wide stony track (North Downs Way), then left at next track junction
- Continue up wide stony track through wood
- Turn left through small gap in hedge and across small ditch at end of wood
- Straight ahead along edge of field with wood on left
- Turn left in middle of field and through gap in hedge onto wide path
- Turn right and follow path through wood
- Turn left at T-junction and left again in 50yd (45m) along a wide track through wood, going slightly down, through kissing gate and second kissing gate into field
- Along edge of field to corner

- Turn right through small gap in hedge 20 paces after telegraph pole
- Bear left down steps and continue down narrow path to stone track visible below (take care, rather overgrown)
- Turn left and proceed along stony track for just a few paces
- Turn right and through kissing gate into field
- Bear left across field and through kissing gate at foot of hill ahead
- Climb hill (steep) and bear left to go through kissing gate onto road (busy)

Section 6: 1mi (1.6km)
- Turn right along road and continue for 500yd (457m)
- At top of hill by Smiths Farm turn left onto overgrown track signposted 'Bridleway'
- In 100yd (91m) cross broken stile into field
- Turn right then left along stony track
- Follow wide track across field
- Turn right at corner, then left over two large fallen logs and along narrow footpath back out to wide track
- Bear right and through kissing gate opposite

Section 7: 0.75mi (1.2km)
- Continue along wide grass track and through kissing gate ahead into wood, then second kissing gate out to meadow
- Bear right across meadow, passing 'Boar' sculpture on left, and through kissing gate into young wood
- Continue along path and through kissing gate into established wood

Section 8: 0.75mi (1.2km)
- Follow path through wood out to road
- Bear right, cross stile opposite
- Continue along edge of field and over stile in corner
- Follow path across field and over stile onto road
- Cross road and over stile opposite into field
- Bear left to pub and campsite

IN THE VICINITY

HUCKING ESTATE

Next door to the pub is the car park for the Hucking Estate, so access to this is simple. This amazing 574-acre site is typical of Kent countryside: an AONB (Area of Outstanding Natural Beauty), it encompasses not only fields, hedges and woodland but also narrow country lanes, pubs, and the village of Hucking after which it is named. (Hucking is a very old English name.) Now, it is managed by the Woodland Trust (since 1997) but was known as the Howe Court Estate prior to this.

It's a wonderful place to explore as there are so many paths of various kinds criss-crossing the area, the changing seasons painting a different picture every month and the wooden sculptures dotted about enhancing the experience.

WILDLIFE/BIRDWATCHING

The flora and fauna of the Hucking Estates is extensive and increasing all the time. There is something to attract everyone from tree-huggers to flower buffs, and insect spotters to birdwatchers. There aren't any designated structures such as bird hides, though there is seating dotted about.

CYCLING

There are many designated cycle routes in the county, one of which passes close to Hucking and another through Hollingbourne. In addition, though narrow, surrounding roads are quiet.

LEEDS CASTLE

Unusually, this castle is not in Yorkshire but near Maidstone in Kent and only 5 miles (8km) from the campsite. It is considered the 'loveliest castle in the world' because of its position occupying two islands in a lake of the River Len. With a building recorded on the site since 857AD, and a stone castle since Norman times that has been extended often, it has a long and illustrious history.

Through the years the castle has had many royal visitors, especially Queens, and also Henry VIII. In 1976 it was bequeathed to the nation. It is a very interesting place to visit, although dogs are not allowed in the building – or even the magnificent grounds!

NORTH DOWNS

This ridge of chalk hills runs from the white cliffs of Dover northwest across Kent and round the south of London into Surrey. All along the Downs, which pass through two AONB are villages, farms, ancient drove roads and quiet county lanes, all accessed by the North Downs Way, opened in 1978, that runs from Dover to Farnham.

HOLLINGBOURNE

Situated on the south side of the North Downs is this attractive, fascinating village. The North Downs Way passes through it, as does the Pilgrim Way: an ancient route used by pilgrims on their way to Canterbury. Many of the buildings, therefore, have a long history, and are listed, including one of the pubs, The Dirty Habit.

DODDINGTON PLACE GARDENS

Just 8 milesl (13km) to the east lies Doddington, on the edge of the village that the 850-acre Edwardian Estate is situated in. Here, the Oldfied family still lives as it has done for over a hundred years. The magnificent gardens – featured in various articles and magazines – are open to the public, and dogs on leads are welcome.

BREDGAR & WORMSHILL LIGHT RAILWAY

This narrow gauge track has been built from scratch by a group of enthusiasts. On the days it is open assorted exhibits are on show, and there are various activities, including train rides.

Suffolk – a secluded place

OS MAPS EXPLORER 196 SUDBURY, HADLEIGH & DEDHAM VALE

The Romans' arrival was a major event for the region. Moving northward from the south coast into Suffolk, they built many roads and settlements on the flat terrain. Needless to say, the Celtic tribes in the area were not especially welcoming, and there were misunderstandings and disputes. Confrontation escalated to such an extent that the various Celtic tribes put aside their differences to unite against the Romans.

One of the Celtic leaders was Boudicca; wife of the King of the Iceni tribe. He died and left his family and kingdom, which was in Norfolk, under the protection of Rome, or so he thought, but, in fact, his family was dispossessed and assaulted. Boudicca led a revolt against the Romans, marching south through Suffolk, and initially had considerable success. However, even though the Celts had the bigger army, they were no match for the efficient, disciplined Romans, and were eventually defeated. Nowadays, it is as a folk heroine that Boudicca is revered; perhaps because she was an underdog.

When the Romans departed there was no army to fight off various other invaders, and, over time, the Anglo-Saxons swept over East Anglia, eventually settling in the area. This was an extensive region, and inhabitants of the north were known, somewhat unimaginatively, as the 'north folk,' whilst those from the south were, yes, you've guessed it, the 'south folk.' Over time this became the Norfolk and Suffolk counties we know today, and Roman influence waned, allowing the Anglo-Saxons to retain their religion, traditions and culture. So it is that we speak English in Great Britain.

The community the Anglo- Saxons established in Suffolk must have been important. The mound at Sutton Hoo puzzled archaeologists for years, and it was only in 1939 that, with the support of landowner Edith Pretty, Basil Brown set about finding some answers. The pair discovered that Sutton Hoo was a burial site for Anglo-Saxon kings with some unique artefacts. Their story has recently been made into a film, appropriately called *The Dig*, and starring Carey Mulligan and Ralph Fiennes. Further information about the site and the finds is obtainable from the nearby visitor centre.

So, north of Suffolk is Norfolk, whilst to the west is Cambridgeshire, with Essex to the south, and to the east is a long coastline; another AONB. This bulges out into the North Sea to be continuously battered by waves and storms. The rocks in the area are soft, and erosion is constantly changing the shoreline: 547yd (500m) of Suffolk coast has fallen into the sea during the last 500 years alone.

Along the southern border of the county is the River Stour and its large estuary, and leading off from this is the smaller River Orwell estuary, with the town of Felixstowe, the largest container port in Britain, on the coast nearby. The River Orwell flows north through Ipswich. It was whilst living in the area that George Orwell took his pen name from the river.

Most of the rest of the county is very flat although there are some small hills in the west close to Cambridgeshire. Throughout Suffolk agriculture – mostly arable – is important. Farm size varies enormously, from small holdings to large farmsteads, and most of the businesses in the area support agriculture in some way: Branston Pickle and the large Birds Eye factory in Lowestoft, for example. Because agriculture is so crucial, every May Ipswich hosts the Suffolk Show organized by the Suffolk Agricultural Association. Here, the best of Suffolk's food, farming and agricultural achievements are celebrated and promoted. In existence for 189 years, this is one of the oldest county shows in the country.

Suffolk may be rather secluded and sparsely populated, but its gentle, soothing landscape is restful, and exploring the county reveals many hidden gems.

CAMPSITE – WHITE HORSE

The campsite is a simple, sheltered flat field behind the pub, with a wind turbine in the corner. There are 27 pitches, four of which have electric hook-up. The modern amenities block is small with just one separate toilet and shower for men and another for the ladies, and is solar-powered, with outside dishwashing facilities. A large hedge separates the campsite from the holiday lets.

Across the road from the campsite is The Millenium Green, which has a children's play area and wood at the rear. This is an ideal place to exercise dogs.

PUB – WHITE HORSE

Located in the heart of the Suffolk countryside, environmental sustainability is of immense importance to the owners, so the pub uses renewable energy as far as possible. For those excited by craft beers, there's a micro-brewery next door, so a range of special beers are always on tap. The vegetable garden at the rear supplies the kitchen.

The pub is very large with four rooms: the public bar, the lounge, the nook, and green room, in addition to an outside garden and patio space. During my visit the kitchen was closed but was expected to open shortly.

PEARLS OF WISDOM 🐕

Wow – what a surprise! This little gem is a tasty morsel. No exercise area for me, BUT just a bound across the road there's a thrilling humongous doggie playground with new friends to meet, frisbee to chase; sooo many exciting smells!

And then there's the wood, a fab place to visit – and the walks: fields, fields, and more fields with exciting hedgerows to investigate. And NO sheep, so I could freely mosey about most of the time. Loved it loved it loved it!

SHORT WALK – AMBLING ROUND THE FIELDS

Distance: 4mi (6.4km)
Duration: 2hr (Easy)
Terrain: Fields, woods, footpaths, tracks, footbridges, lanes, many gaps in hedges, minor roads, the odd gate and stile

Section 1: 1mi (1.6km)
- Exit campsite onto road via pub

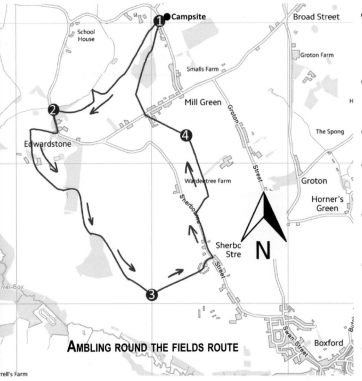

AMBLING ROUND THE FIELDS ROUTE

- Turn left; in 25yd (23m) turn left again onto footpath between two houses, signposted
- Follow path to right between garages and out to field
- Turn left through gap in hedge, then sharp right
- Continue along path through trees, glimpsing field on right
- Turn right through gap in hedge just after left-hand bend
- Turn right, following path along edge of field with hedge on right, ignoring steps down on right
- Follow path out of field and across wide grass track, then back onto path along edge of another field and through gap in hedge by large tree
- Continue along path round to right, keeping close to hedge on right
- Bear right down steps and along path out to road

Section 2: 1.25mi (2km)
- Turn left along road, turning right along drive under the magnificent arch of Edwardstone Manor
- Continue along driveway flanked by huge horse chestnut trees to church (churchyard is a lovely place to explore with pleasant views)
- Turn left along path with church on right
- Straight ahead at bend into wood, way-marker
- Bear left across field and through gap into field by an amazing tree
- Continue along edge of field to corner with hedge on left
- Bear left round pond on left, then bear sharp right onto path into wood (not clear)
- Continue through wood, crossing wide track to way-marker beside footpath along edge of field ahead with hedge on left
- Turn left through gap in hedge and over footbridge into another field
- Follow path along edge of this field with hedge now on right
- Straight on at corner and over footbridge into next field, passing way-marker on right, and into fourth field

The magnificent arch: all that remains of Edwardstone Manor.

Section 3: 1mi (1.6km)
- Turn left at way-marker and across field and through gap in hedge, then over bridge into next field
- Cross field and onto lane between houses ahead out to road
- Turn left along road, then right at signpost onto wide track
- Bear left at bend onto wide earth track, crossing field towards trees and through gap, then over bridge

Section 4: 0.75mi (1.2km)
- Turn left along edge of field out to road
- Turn left along road for 25yd (23m)
- Turn right along footpath just after two small while thatched buildings, signposted
- Continue ahead round right and left bends, then onto path between tall hedges and into wood
- Keep right at junction to follow path as it winds through wood
- Turn left at junction out to field
- Turn right along edge of field
- Straight ahead out to road, passing garden on left
- Turn right to pub and campsite

LONG WALK – RETURN TO BOXFORD, PLEASE
Distance: 10mi (16km)
Duration: 5.5hr (Easy)
Terrain: Fields, woods footpaths, grass tracks, stony tracks, footbridges, lanes, many gaps in hedges, minor roads, the odd gate and stile

Section 1: 1.25mi (2km)
- Exit campsite onto road via pub
- Turn left; in 25yd (23m) turn right through gate onto footpath, signposted
- Follow path over footbridge along edge of field, with wood on right, then down steps into field
- Turn right, following footpath along edge of field with wood still on right
- Continue along path across field, keeping to left of buildings ahead, and passing large wooden shed and pond on right

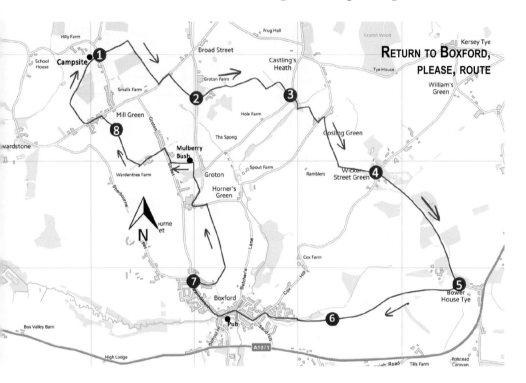

- Bear right along path over footbridge out to road
- Turn left along road
- Turn right just after slight bend at wide gap in hedge, keeping right onto narrow footpath with fence on left
- Continue straight ahead along edge of field out to road, passing group of trees on right
- Turn left along road, taking second footpath on right, signposted (there are two paths very close together)

Section 2: 1mi (1.6km)
- Follow path as it bears slightly left past gate and up steps
- Continue along path and over stile opposite, then through copse and over another stile
- Straight on, crossing two wide tracks and down slope by way-marker
- Bear left, away from horse jumps on left, keeping close to shrubs on right, then bear right up slope
- Bear left at top of slope, passing close to large, wooden jump on left
- Turn sharp right at hedge on right
- Straight ahead, passing more jumps, to white temporary fencing and white flag
- Turn right onto footpath, then left out to field
- Continue along edge of field with hedge on left and over footbridge into field
- Turn right along path, keeping close to hedge now on right, round corner and down to next corner

- Turn right over footbridge, following path ahead out to road
- Cross road to grass path opposite

Section 3: 1.5mi (2.4km)

- Continue along path and over footbridge on left, then turn sharp right along narrow path winding out to field

Most of the footpaths run along the edges of fields.

- Turn left up slope along edge of field with hedge on left, passing house on left, and over footbridge out to road
- Turn left along road, passing house on left
- Turn right opposite barn, signposted, and along very wide track, keeping right, onto path along edge of field with hedge on left
- Continue along path across field and through large gap into next field
- Turn left along edge of field, passing several large oak trees on left, then round to driveway
- Turn right along driveway out to road

Section 4: 1.25mi (2km)

- Bear right across road to tarmac track between wooden fence (Bleesem Hall)
- Continue along driveway onto track (which becomes grass path with house on left
- Follow footpath as it widens and narrows to wide junction at fence corner, signposted

Section 5: 1.25mi (2km)

- At junction turn right onto grass track with fence on right
- Continue straight on, ignoring all paths and tracks leading off, passing farm on left to join wide track curving in on left
- Follow track across field, round big left-hand bend with wood on right
- Turn right at bend into wood

Section 6: 1.25mi (2km)

- Continue along path and through wood out to road, passing houses on right
- Turn left along road, passing garage, then right at junction to pub (White Hart) on left (an ideal place for refreshments)
- Exit pub and cross road, bearing left to path between houses, signposted 'Bowls Club'
- Continue along stony track and out to playing fields, passing Bowls Club on left
- Cross playing fields to left corner and through gap in hedge by wooden fence

Pearl received special treatment in the White Hart at Boxford!

Section 7: 1.75mi (2.8km)

- Turn right along edge of field with hedge on right
- Turn left at corner, following path across field, along edge of next field and out to road by open barn
- Turn left along road, right at junction, then left again along access path to gate
- Through churchyard then gate opposite onto footpath
- Turn right then left at fence corner
- Follow path round to left into wood through gate into field
- Continue along path ahead to junction by fence corner
- Take second grass path on right heading towards sprawling, fenced 'tree' (this is the famous 'Mulberry Bush')
- Retrace steps to fence corner and continue straight ahead along stony track and through gate to road
- Turn right along road, then left along wide path
- Follow path along edge of field over footbridge and past farmyard on right
- Turn right down steps and cross footbridge; then up steps and along path to wide track ahead, keeping close to hedge on left
- Turn left then immediately right onto wide path across field towards trees, and through gap over bridge

Section 8: 0.75mi (1.2km)

- Turn left along edge of field out to road
- Turn left along road and proceed for 25yd (23m)
- Turn right along footpath just after two small white thatched buildings, signposted
- Continue ahead round right and left bends onto path between tall hedges and into wood
- Keep right at junction to follow path as it winds through wood
- Turn left at junction out to field
- Turn right along edge of field
- Straight ahead out to road, passing garden on left
- Turn right to pub and campsite

IN THE VICINITY

CYCLING

Suffolk is an ideal county for cycling because it is so flat, although there are *some* hills, and there are quiet lanes and light traffic only on most roads. There are plenty of delightful places to stop for a break. Several suggested routes are to be found on the internet.

BIRDWATCHIMG

With so many RSBP and Wildlife Trust reserves – many of which provide hides – dotted around there is plenty of opportunity to spot birds. The range of birds that can be seen is extensive due to the diverse landscape. Located in the county is Suffolk Birding, which offers various bird courses, including identification and photography.

EDWARDSTONE

Like many small settlements in Suffolk, Edwardstone – in the heart of the county – is strung along the road, and has a long history, being documented in the Domesday Book. It did have a big manor, but this was demolished in 1952 with only the grand entrance arch remaining.

During the 15th century Edwardstone was a prosperous place but is much more peaceful nowadays, with a delightful park established to mark the millennium, situated next to the wood.

ST MARY THE VIRGIN CHURCH EDWARDSTONE

It seems as if this church is in the middle of a field, and access is via a rough track apparently leading to nowhere in particular. There is evidence of a church on the site for many centuries, though the current building shows no indication of this. The interior is fascinating, having been extensively refurbished by architect G F Bodley in the late 1800s. The views are arresting.

BOXFORD

This large village, just 2 miles (3.2km) south of the campsite, straddles the River Box; hence its name. With a school and several shops (including a welcoming pub, the White Hart), the village is a bustling community. In honour of Tornado Smith, a daredevil motorcycle rider whose parents ran the pub, a 'Wall of Death' event is occasionally held. This is a carnival sideshow featuring a silo- or barrel-shaped wooden cylinder, typically ranging from 20 to 36 feet (6-11m) in diameter, and made of wooden planks, inside which motorcyclists travel along the vertical wall and perform stunts, held in place by friction and centrifugal force.

GROTON WINTHROP MULBERRY TREE

This tree was planted in around 1550 by Adam Winthrop, grandfather of John Winthrop who was born in 1588, a Puritan who, in 1630 led a group of colonists to America. They arrived at Massachusetts Bay where they set up a colony, of which John Winthrop was governor for a number of years, establishing a government in Boston that became a blueprint for other early American colonies.

Winthrop died in Boston in March 1649. He was so influential in the United States that his writing is often quoted, and a number of places are named after him.

THE GROTON WINTHROP MULBERRY TRUST

This Trust was set up for four reasons –

- To look after the 'Croft,' an open space in the hamlet of Groton
- To maintain and protect the Winthrop Mulberry Tree – one of the oldest Mulberry trees in Britain – in the middle of the Croft
- To preserve links between Groton and New England. To mark the 350th anniversary of John Winthrop's death, in 1999, an oak tree was planted in the Croft by Philip Lader, then US Ambassador to Britain. In 2015, another oak tree was planted in the Croft, on which occasion the US Ambassador, Matthew Winthrop Barzun attended A descendant of John Winthrop, Barzun also visited his ancestral home
- To support the Groton parish and church

LAVENHAM

Six miles (9.6km) north of the campsite is the village of Lavenham, which has a long and rich history. It is considered one of the most representative Medieval villages in Great Britain, with a huge number of listed buildings.

Over 750 years ago Henry III granted the village 'market status,' which allowed it to grow and prosper. Nowadays, it is a bustling community with shops, art galleries, restaurants, cafés and pubs.

Walks in South West England
(Devon, Dorset, Gloucestershire, Hampshire)

Devon – wild places
OS MAPS EXPLORER OL28 DARTMOOR

Devon is a very distinctive county. Because it straddles the South West Peninsular, most unusually, it has two coastlines: to the north of the county is the Bristol Channel, whilst in the south is the busy English Channel. Separating these two coastlines is a mostly rural Devon, remarkably containing two moors: Exmoor to the north, which extends across the border into Somerset, and Dartmoor which lies wholly in the south west corner of the county.

Dartmoor has long been considered an exceptional place; so much so that, in 1951, it was one of the first areas in Great Britain to be given National Park status. Dartmoor is probably so popular because in southern England it is a rare area of wilderness. Unexpectedly large at 368sq ml (954sq km), it is a desolate and austere place. The soil is thin and impoverished; the shallow valleys are marshy; the vegetation is just coarse grasses, bracken or heather, and towering over all are huge, weathered rocks. Yet this inhospitable place is home to a huge variety of unique and endangered flora and fauna. In recent years otters have made a comeback on Dartmoor, and seem to be thriving. Just as exciting, beavers have been re-introduced to one of the Dartmoor rivers, and they, too, seem to be doing well.

The moor gets its name from the River Dart which rises at two points high on the moor, and then merges at the appropriately named Dartmeet. This single river, now the Dart, meanders across Dartmoor to Buckfastleigh, and out into the English Channel at Dartmouth. In fact, most of Devon's rivers start on Dartmoor, flowing both north and south out to the sea. They are generally fast-flowing, and levels quickly rise when it rains.

Because there are so many streams and rivers criss-crossing the moor, and because of high rainfall, there is a profusion of water, most of which is quickly and easily absorbed by the layer of peat (decaying vegetation) that covers much of the moor. Peat is like a sponge so the water does not drain away. In some places a great deal of water is stored

The Devon countryside viewed from Dartmoor.

in the soil, which results in bogs of various types and sizes that can occasionally be hazardous. So even if walking on bright, sunny days, be cautious as the ground can be very wet and soggy.

Another distinctive feature of Dartmoor are the 'tors': piles of weathered granite boulders shaped around 280 million years ago that crown many of the hills, some of which are impressively lofty. Dotted all over the moor, some are quite spectacular, and some are topped with stone crosses that were medieval signposts indicating routes across the moor. As so many of the tors are remote they are ideal habitat for wildlife, and they also fire the imagination and inspire adventure, hence the annual Ten Tors Challenge which takes place every May. As the name suggests, the idea is that teams of six young people aged 14-20 visit ten specific tors using designated routes. There are three levels: bronze (35ml (56km) distance); silver (45ml (72km) distance), and gold at a distance of 55ml (88km).

Fortunately for this event and outdoor enthusiasts, access to the moor has been free and open since the Dartmoor Commons Act of 1985, even including those areas the military has been using for over 200 years. So, besides the bridleways, permitted footpaths and 450ml (724km) of public rights of way, walkers can wander wherever they wish.

These days the moor is managed by the Dartmoor National Park Authority, comprising representatives from several local councils as well as the government, even though since 1348 the centre of Dartmoor has been owned by the Duchy of Cornwall. In Saxon times it was a royal forest, and the 'burghs' (strongholds) that were built, as well as the later Norman fortifications, became the foundation for some of the settlements, mostly on the edge of the New Forest. One of the remotest and largest villages on Dartmoor, Princetown, was, in fact, only established in 1806, as a result of the creation of Dartmoor Prison to hold captives in the Napoleonic Wars. Today, the prison contains serious offenders, as it has done since 1850.

Apart from tourism the moor is really only suitable for rough grazing, ideal for the indigenous ponies as well as sheep and hardy cattle. The abundance of water ensures an easy supply for local towns and villages, in addition to providing local tin mining and quarry mining with a source of power. Also, the water is so special it is used in the distillation process of Plymouth Gin, which no doubt contributes to this spirit's distinctive flavour.

This amazing, wild place has something for everyone, as the 33,000 people who live there will attest: an ideal location for the outdoor junkie or the gentle rambler; the wildlife enthusiast or the birdwatcher; the historians or the literary buffs, and families or individuals looking for space. The stunning views of the moorland, wooded valleys and soaring tors invoke a spirit of freedom and exploration.

CAMPSITE – FOX AND HOUNDS

Situated behind the pub is a large, gently sloping field divided into three areas. The first, next to the rear of the building, is occupied by several static vans. A truncated, small wooden fence divides the remainder of the field into more or less two equal sections. The top of the site is mostly favoured by tents, whilst tourers opt for the middle section, primarily because this is where several hardstanding pitches are situated. Trees and shrubs that border the site on the right offer welcome shade for both campers and the

There's welcome shade at the campsite for everyone!

horses in the adjoining field, who seem to especially enjoy watching the antics of the crazy bipeds.

Several water taps and electric hook-up points are scattered around the field, with the Elsan point and bins located near the static vans. There are toilets and showers that have recently been refurbished, though these are small in both size and number (ladies have two toilets and one shower cubicle; men the same). These are located off-site on the opposite side of the entrance track in the upper storey of a building. When the site is busy, queues quickly form.

PUB – FOX AND HOUNDS

The pub building is rather large and imposing, stretching out along the A386. This is, perhaps, not surprising considering that it is also an hotel with several rooms available in addition to a camping barn and the campsite. Besides two small, cosy, intimate bars, the pub also has a restaurant and a games room that includes a pool table and dartboard. At the side of the pub is a patio and large, pleasant garden. A variety of drinks are available and, although the menu is conventional, it is locally sourced and enjoyable.

PEARLS OF WISDOM

Just a short trot across the site and we were out to a wide trail, but, oh my poor pads, it was full of stones; some were very sharp. This was not too bad as the grass on the sides was softer and full of enticing smells. In a few tail wags we were through a gate and into wide, open grassy spaces, BUT oh, lots of those pesky sheep, so occasionally I was tethered to my owner. What silly animals: they run away then suddenly stop and stare at me. At least they are small, not like the beasts at the campsite (my owner called them horses). When I jumped up onto the top of the wall I was right next to them. I did not like the air rushing out of their noses: first time I have been this close to one.

I would rather chase my frisbee, and there were plenty of

The Fox and Hounds stretches along the road.

nearby fields for this. My least favourite was the one down a road; I don't like roads!

Campsite – Lydford Caravan and Camping Park
This campsite is located on the outskirts of Lydford village, and is a spacious, well organized and efficient site with shrubs and trees dividing it into various sections. Tents are assigned to the top meadow, with hardstanding pitches mostly in the lower section close to the entrance, and grass pitches in-between. As many of the pitches are laid out in a pleasing curve there is plenty of space, and this has helped create an atmosphere of calm and tranquillity.

The facilities block is modern and generous. Reception houses a shop that sells basic grocery items in addition to camping accessories, and it has a small off-licence.

Pearls of wisdom
Wow! The best part of this campsite was the large field just across a road, with oodles of space and a lovely smooth, green surface; perfect to chase my frisbee. Much, much more fun than the narrow strip around part of the campsite: the 'dog walk' my owner said. Not so good was the tarmac I had to pad along before we got to more interesting places, especially when it was hot, and oh! there were so many bicycles.

I was able to swim in several places, though at times I was jabbed by some of the plants. Not pleasant.

Short walk from Fox and Hounds campsite – To the top
Distance: 3.5mi (5.6km)
Duration: 2.5hr (Very challenging in places)
Terrain: Very steep climb to top of tor, boulders to scramble over to Widgery Cross, easy descent but muddy, even in dry weather. Wide and narrow grassy tracks, footpaths, stony tracks, stile. Sheep and horses roam freely on the moor, so be vigilant if accompanied by a dog

Section 1: 0.75mi (1.2km)
- Exit campsite via entrance
- Turn right along wide, stony track, going uphill and through gate on right
- Turn immediately right along grassy path between wall on right and mound on left
- Bear left over mound and up slope away from wall, signposted
- Continue, keeping mound now on right, bearing left to log
- Cross mound again, bear right and through gate or over ladder stile ahead

Section 2: 0.75mi (1.2km)
- Turn left and cross River Lyn via stepping stones
- Straight ahead along middle stony track climbing up
- Follow path uphill (very, very steep) as it becomes a wide, rocky grassy track to Widgery Cross on top of Brat Tor: halfway up is a tree that offers shade on bright days and a place to pause and take in the scenery

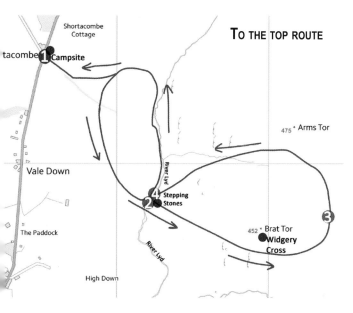

To the top route

Section 3: 1mi (1.6km)
- Exit opposite side of Widgery Cross, following grassy path down over moor towards outcrop at Arms Tor ahead
- Turn left along wide, stony, ditch-like track going downhill and over a stream
- Bear right along a narrow grassier footpath at large boulder on right, next to buried boulder just before really marshy section of main track
- Continue downhill along path to stepping stones and footbridge
- Bearing slightly right cross footbridge

Section 4: 1mi (1.6km)
- Turn immediately right along grassy path, keeping river on right and fence on left (need to scramble over rocks and trees roots where river is close to fence)
- Turn left at corner of field along wide, grassy path, going uphill with wall now on left
- Continue straight ahead along path and through gate onto stony track
- Follow track downhill to campsite entrance on left

Short walk from Lydford campsite – Lower moors
Distance: 6mi (9.6km)
Duration: 3hr (Moderate)
Terrain: Footpaths, quiet roads, lanes, tracks, gates, stiles and cyclepath (beware bikes)

Section 1: 1.25mi (2km)
- Exit campsite via entrance
- Turn immediately left along road
- Turn right onto stony path just past white house (Bolts House), signposted

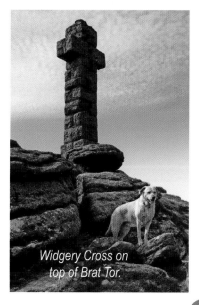

Widgery Cross on top of Brat Tor.

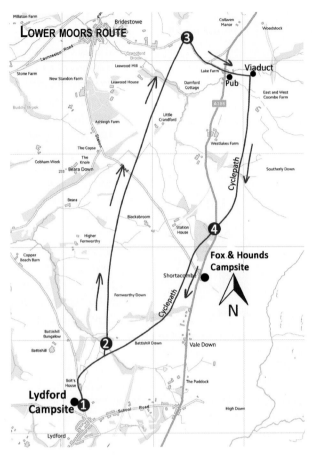

- Follow path to junction
- Turn right along stony track and through gate
- Bear left over stone footbridge
- Keep bearing left onto stony track going uphill
- Continue straight ahead along track, ignoring fork off to right, then over moor and through gate onto tarmac driveway

Section 2: 1.5mi (2.4km)
- Follow path and cross road to track opposite
- Continue along track past fields (lovely views; watch for viaduct to right) and over stone footbridge
- Turn left in 25yd (22.8m) over wooden footbridge
- Turn immediately right along wide track to road, passing stream on right

Section 3: 1.75mi (2.8km)
- Turn right along road
- In 50yd (46m) cross A386 onto track opposite beside Bearslake Pub (ideal for refreshments)
- Continue along path, keeping close to river, and under huge viaduct
- Turn right through gate before entrance to moor
- Follow path up onto cyclepath (Granite Way)
- Straight on along cyclepath to road

Section 4: 1.5mi (2.4km)
- Cross road back onto cyclepath
- Follow cyclepath past two gated animal crossings
- Turn immediately right at the second one through gate onto moor
- Continue straight ahead along wide, grassy track, down and then uphill
- Straight on along brow of hill and down to stony track

- Turn left and then right at ford over footbridge
- Follow stony track through gate
- Turn left at junction along another stony track and uphill to road
- Turn left along road to campsite entrance

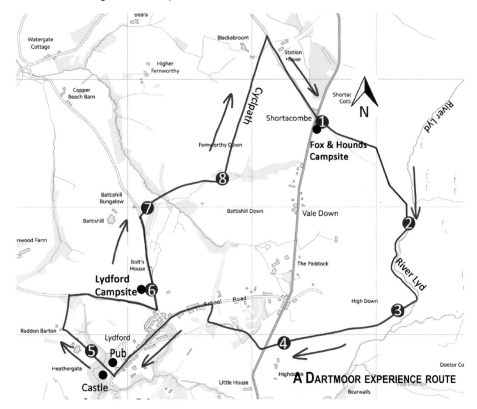

A DARTMOOR EXPERIENCE ROUTE

LONG WALK – A DARTMOOR EXPERIENCE

Distance: 7.5mi (12km)
Duration: 4.5hr (Challenging in places)
Terrain: Several steep hills, rocks to scramble over beside river, wide, grassy tracks, footpaths, stony tracks, quiet roads, stiles and cyclepath (beware bikes). Sheep and horses roaming freely on the moor: be vigilant if accompanied by a dog

Section 1: 0.75mi (1.2km)

- Exit campsite via entrance
- Turn right along wide, stony track, going uphill and through gate on right
- Turn immediately right along grassy path between wall on right and mound on left
- Bear left over mound and up slope away from wall, signposted
- Continue, keeping mound now on right, bearing left to log
- Cross mound again, bear right and through gate or over ladder stile ahead

Swimming in the River Lyd.

Section 2: 1mi (1.6km)
- Turn left towards stepping stones over River Lyn
- Turn right before river along wide, grassy path
- Follow path (rocky in places, requiring a bit of a scramble), keeping close to river on left as it narrows, twists and turns, passing several pools; some deep enough for your dog to swim
- Turn right uphill along stony track, at junction with large stones and boulders making a river crossing

Section 3: 1mi (1.6km)
- Turn left at brow of hill along wide, grassy track
- Follow path along crest of hill high above and parallel to river
- Take right fork at junction along less defined, narrower track that becomes wide grass track
- Continue straight ahead across wide junction
- Straight on across wide open,grassy space towards two clumps of trees and telegraph pole onto stony path between tree and pole

Section 4: 1mi (1.6km)
- Follow path through gate and down to A386
- Cross road (take care, busy) to very minor road opposite
- Follow road which soon becomes a track, then footpath, round left-hand bend and right- hand bend onto stony track to junction
- Continue straight ahead along grassy track to minor road
- Straight on along road to main Lydford village thoroughfare
- Turn left along road to Castle Inn (good place for refreshments)

Section 5: 0.75mi (1.2km)
- Exit pub via garden and car park at rear
- Left corner of car park has a footbridge leading to castle and church (interesting to visit)
- Take wide, gravelly path in right corner of car park, passing two stone buildings
- Follow path as it winds along to road, passing Lydford Ancient Spring on right and ignoring all paths leading off

- Turn right along road to bus turning area
- Turn left through bus area

Section 6: 1mi (1.6km)
- Continue along road past Lydford campsite on left
- Turn right onto stony path just past white house (Bolts House), signposted
- Follow path to junction
- Turn right along stony track and through gate
- Bear left over stone footbridge
- Keep bearing left onto stony track, going uphill

Section 7: 1mi (1.6km)
- Take right fork and continue uphill (steep) along wide, grassy track
- Take left fork at brow of hill
- Continue straight on at wide grass junction, heading for white building under hill (Fox & Hounds)
- Follow wide grass track downhill and up again and through gate onto cyclepath

Section 8: 1mi (1.6km)
- Turn left along tarmac path (beware of bikes) to road
- Turn right along road to A386 junction
- Cross A386 to pub

IN THE VICINITY
WIDGERY CROSS
Behind the pub, high on Brat Tor, Widgery Cross soars skyward, dominating its surroundings; a monument that is unusual on three counts –

- It is very recent, having been erected by local artist William Widgery in 1887 to commemorate Queen Victoria's Jubilee
- It is the largest and tallest of all the crosses on Dartmoor as it is constructed of several granite blocks instead of being carved out of a single block
- It is the most conspicuous of all the Dartmoor crosses as it can be seen far and wide

CYCLING
Though cycling over common land and open moorland is prohibited, Dartmoor is still an ideal place for cyclists, as not only are there a variety of quiet country lanes, but also over 220ml (350km) of bridleways, as well as several designated cyclepaths, the most popular of which in NW Dartmoor is 'Granite Way,' an 11ml (8km) trail from Lydford to Okehampton, mostly along a disused rail line that crosses the spectacular Meldon Viaduct. The viaduct was built in 1874, over the remains of mineral mines, and has a span of 341ft (165 metres). Close to the viaduct a path leads off to Meldon Dam, built in 1972, and reservoir.

LYDFORD

A tranquil, charming village, Lydford was, during Saxon and Norman times, a very important place: a Saxon 'burgh.' Though a substantial settlement, it was built primarily for defence and commerce. Interestingly, during this time it had a mint that manufactured silver pennies, as the road name Silver Street indicates, and the pub has four 'Lydford Pennies' hanging on the wall. Replicas are available to buy, but at the considerably higher price of £2.00.

The Normans used Saxon foundations to build their defences, and the remains of a castle stands proudly on a mound overlooking the gorge, between the aptly-named Castle Inn pub and St Petroc Church; both also interesting places.

LYDFORD GORGE

Over many, many thousands of years the River Lyd has sliced its way through the edge of Dartmoor, creating the deepest, most spectacular gorge in the area that incorporates the longest waterfall in the South of England: 'White Lady Waterfall' and a series of whirlpools, 'The Devil's Cauldron.' The National Trust owns and manages the gorge and surrounding area, and has done since 1947. There are designated walks of various lengths and for various abilities, and information about these is available online or at the visitor centre. Dogs on leads welcome

The gorge has two entrances: one is just under 1 mile (1.6km) from Lydford campsite, and for much of the way there is a pavement, and the other is about 2 miles (3.2km) from the campsite, though it does not make for pleasant walking, with or without a dog. There is, however, a bus from the pub or campsite to this gorge entrance.

Unfortunately, I was unable to visit the gorge and surrounding area as it was closed

MARY TAVY

Just 5 miles (8km) south of Lydford is the village of Mary Tavy, that, during the 1800s, was a thriving mining community, though now is a much smaller, peaceful, rural village. Its unusual name derives from a combination of the local 13th century church (St Mary) and the nearby river (Tavy).

On the other side of the river, about 1.5 miles (2.4km) away is 'sister' village Peter Tavy. The bridleway between them makes access easy.

TAVISTOCK

About 7 miles (11km) south of Lydford on the south west edge of Dartmoor National Park lies the ancient tin mining town of Tavistock, that, nowadays, is a thriving market town. It is home to several small independent shops, as well as a farmers' market and the renowned pannier (indoor) market (dogs welcome). Tavistock's claim to fame is that it is the birthplace of Sir Francis Drake.

OKEHAMPTON

Approximately 8 miles (13km) to the north of Lydford, on the northern edge of Dartmoor, is another charming market town, Okehampton, considered the walking centre of Dartmoor.

This, too, gets its name from a local water source: convergence of the east and west Okement Rivers.

Okehampton has a long history, having been established in the Bronze Age, so there are plenty of interesting things to see, including the Norman Okehampton Castle, the attractive Simmons Park, the Dartmoor Railway, and the Museum of Dartmoor Life.

Dorset – sensational Jurassic Coast
OS MAPS EXPLORER OL15 PURBECK & SOUTH DORSET

It's no surprise that Dorset is so popular as the county has many attractive rural places as well as a stunning coastline, which is so unique it was declared a UNESCO World Heritage Site in 2001.

Dorset's 88ml (142km) coastline borders the English Channel from Lyme Regis in the west to Bournemouth in the east. As it meanders along, so the sea, through erosion, has carved out cliffs, arches, stacks and beaches, exposing rocks and fossils that document 185 million years of the Earth's history. It is called the Jurassic Coast because most of the exposed rocks are from the Jurassic period; the geology of the area is so exceptional as to be of global importance.

The unique Dorset coastline was declared a UNESCO World Heritage Site in 2001.

Among the many exceptional coastal landforms is Chesil Bank, usually referred to as Chesil Beach. This barrier beach is an astonishing 18 miles (29km) long, stretching from the Isle of Portland to West Bay, and, with the South West Coast Path running parallel to it, the stunning views it offers during all weathers can be fully appreciated by everyone.

The name Chesil evolved from 'ceosel' or 'cisel': Old English words meaning gravel and shingle. As the name suggests, this is a shingle beach comprising flint and chert pebbles from Jurassic and Cretaceous rocks. Unusually, they can be found in a range of sizes: at the eastern end near Portland they are large, mostly potato-size, gradually getting smaller until about the size of a pea at West Bay, the westernmost point. In days gone by, this was useful for smugglers as it allowed them to estimate their position when they landed on the beach at night.

Despite having been in existence for more than 5000 years, the origin and formation of Chesil Beach is still a mystery that ongoing research hopes to explain. It's a surprisingly substantial structure – as high as 50ft (15m) in places and 660ft (201m) wide. The seaward side of the beach shelves rapidly into the sea, eventually levelling off at a depth of roughly 60ft (18m) around 980ft (299m) offshore. The beach is constantly moving because of the incessant action of the water battering the shore, and there are very few plants as a consequence. Where it exists, the opposite shore is much more sheltered and quiet, and here can be found some plants, lichen and mosses.

A barrier beach – a large body of water known as Fleet Lagoon – separates Chesil Beach from the mainland. Because it is such a long stretch of water the upper reaches are known as West Fleet, which is where the campsite is located, and the lower reaches as East Fleet. The lagoon, too, varies in width, at over half-a-mile (804m) in the middle of East Fleet and just over 200ft (61m) at its narrowest point. Similarly, it is as deep as 16.5ft (5m) in some places, but mostly – especially in the upper reaches – it is less than 6.5ft (2m), which is why Pearl found so few places to swim.

Sea water enters the lagoon in several ways: seepage through the barrier, tidal ebb and flow via the opening at the Isle of Portland, and during terrific storms when waves crash over the beach and beyond. The upshot is that Fleet waters are rather salty, but somewhat offset by streams and brooks that feed into the lagoon. Being neither fresh nor salty, the Fleet is therefore classified as 'brackish.'

The area is a Site of Special Scientific Interest (SSSI) because of the abundance of wildlife. It is also a birdwatcher's joy, especially as there is a nesting colony of mute swans at Abbotsbury.

The military has found the area useful, too, and there are rifle ranges, some of which are still used today, as well as the remains of concrete pillboxes and anti-tank blocks. In fact, the lagoon was one of the locations used during WWII to test the Bouncing Bomb, as told in the film *The Dam Busters*.

This unique area offers so much to the visitor: dramatic landscapes; striking seascapes; fascinating wildlife and countless varieties of bird, as well as interesting places to visit, several easily accessible by public transport.

Campsite – Bagwell Farm Touring Park

This is a big campsite (320 pitches) with a range of on-site facilities, including a shop, restaurant and bar. To make best use of the sloping area the site has been terraced. At the top of the slope is a large field that has been put aside to exercise dogs in. At the bottom are the entrance and communal facilities such as toilet block, shop, etc, and the field for tents. In-between are two or three terraces that have many level pitches for touring units.

When these are occupied the units look like massed ranks of soldiers on parade.

Shrubs section off parts of the site but it is large and imposing even so. The undoubted gem of this campsite is its easy access out into a field and down to the coastal path at West Fleet by Chesil Beach.

Bagwell campsite from the field at the rear of the site near Chesil Beach.

Pubs

There are, in fact, three pubs close to this campsite –

• THE RED BARN AND GRILL

This is the on-site restaurant and bar, that, during my visit, was open for takeaway meals only. Normally, the inviting interior and attractive outside seating area overlooking the pets corner and donkey field are open for a range of meals and drinks. During high season it is open daily, though less often in spring and autumn.

• VICTORIA INN

Though this pub is situated on the main road it is easily accessed, in just a few minutes, via a footpath across a field. When I dropped by it had not opened, and, sadly, I was unable to ascertain whether or not it would ever resume trading.

• ELM TREE INN

This pub is just over 1 mile (1.6km) away in the nearby village of Langton Herring. The quickest route is through the woods adjacent to the dog walking field; a delightful walk. As the short walk passes this pub, Pearl and I took the opportunity to stop off. The food is slightly more upmarket than usual pub grub and was delicious.

The pub had been refurbished, and is a lovely place to spend some time.

PEARLS OF WISDOM 🐆

What a surprise! When we arrived here I received a welcome pack: delicious treats (yum), and a coloured bag (poo bag, so my owner said), in a pretty paper bag (looked okay, but not edible). With a huge field for me to stretch my legs and meet some pals, it promised to be fabulous, although I had to stay on a lead in the field, so no playing with my frisbee

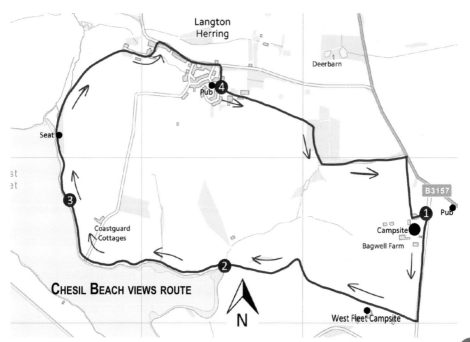

(site 'rules' I heard my owner mutter). Never mind, we found a field on the other side of the track on the way to the pub where I *could* chase my frisbee all day.

There were so many different places to explore: woods, fields, beach, sea (not deep enough to swim but still fun), and all just a tail wag away. A really cracking place!

SHORT WALK – CHESIL BEACH VIEWS
Distance: 5.25mi (8.4km)
Duration: 2.5hr (Moderate)
Terrain: Footpaths, a few quiet roads, lanes, tracks, gates, stiles and coastal path, fields, some steep climbs

Section 1: 1.25mi (2km)
- Exit campsite via shop and reception
- Continue along driveway, passing play area on right, and through gap in fence onto stony track
- Turn right and up slope, passing campsite on right
- Turn right at junction towards West Fleet Campsite reception
- Follow driveway, passing reception building on left and turning right at the corner
- Turn left in 25yd (22.8m), over stile into field
- Turn left along edge of field, passing houses on left and keeping close to fence on left
- Continue around three sides of field and over stone stile into next field
- Turn immediately left and follow path down along edge of field to coastal path

Section 2: 1.5mi (2.4km)
- Through gap in wall ahead and turn right, signposted
- Turn left in 25yd (22.8m), signposted
- Continue along path, keeping close to water on left, through kissing gate, cross slipway and back onto path
- Follow path (with water still on left) to bench by noticeboard with information about birds (a good place to take time out)
- Path now climbs uphill away from the water

Section 3: 1.25mi (2km)
- Turn left through kissing gate, signposted
- Continue along edge of field and under some amazing trees
- Straight ahead along path and under more trees, ignoring signposted path and stile on left, and path into field on right
- Follow path out to a field and across to corner of fence, then over stile ahead into road
- Continue along road and round bends to T-junction
- Turn right along road and take second turning right onto 'The Knoll' in Roses Lane
- Straight ahead at junction, passing church on left
- Follow road round to left to pub Elm Tree Inn (a delightful place to stop for refreshments)

Boats on the waters of West Fleet.

Section 4: 1.25mi (2km)
- Exit pub and turn left
- Turn right at junction onto Shop Lane, then turn left towards Driftwood Studio
- Continue straight ahead through gate between barns into Higher Farm Yard
- Bear right, then turn left along stony track with fence on left
- Straight ahead at junction onto wide track with hedge now on right
- Follow round to right into wood and then left at bottom of slope, signposted
- Continue along woodland path with stream on right, then round to right now parallel to road
- Follow path back into wood along edge of field and out to verge of road and campsite entrance on right

Long walk – Tracking the Sand Bar
Distance: 8mi (12.8km)
Duration: 5hr (Easy)
Terrain: Coastal path, wide, grassy tracks, footpaths, stony tracks, fields, a few quiet roads, stiles and gates (note practice times at army rifle range)

The footpath from the campsite to the coastal path.

Section 1: 1mi (1.6km)
- Exit campsite via access route at bottom of slope, going towards sea and away from reception and shop
- Follow path straight ahead out of campsite along edge of two fields to coastal path
- Turn left along wide track with wall and hedge on right
- In 25yd (23m) turn right at junction and through gap in wall, then immediately left onto grassy trail, signposted, with wall now on left
- Follow path to noticeboard, bearing left going through wall again

Section 2: 1mi (1.6km)
- With bay on right continue along path and through gate, then over footbridge, passing hotel on left, and over wooden walkway and through gate into field
- Turn right along edge of field into next field (on left are horseracing gallops, so keep to

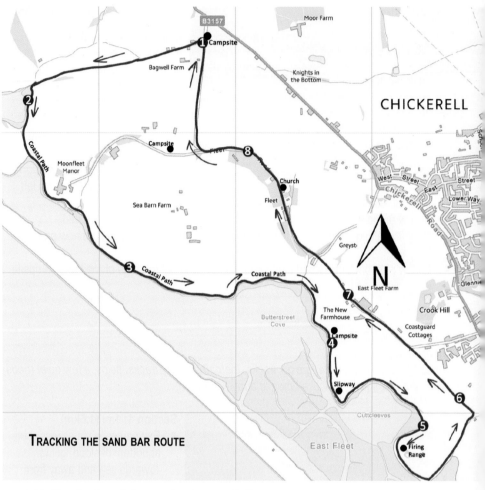

TRACKING THE SAND BAR ROUTE

right side of path and dogs under close control)
- Follow path over footbridge into next field

Section 3: 1mi (1.6km)
- Continue along edge of field as it winds around the bay, and through gate
- Straight on down slope, through gate, over footbridge and through another gate into next field
- Follow narrow, stony path parallel to coastline through another two kissing gates and out to a lovely, grassy area (possible picnic site though it is near campsite's recreation area)

Section 4: 1mi (1.6km)
- Cross green, keeping close to fence on left, and through gate onto stony path
- Continue along path between fence and hedge, passing campsite on left, up a slope

and through gate onto slipway
- Cross slipway, passing bench left (good rest stop)
- Follow path round edge of large field, over footbridge, and along edge of further three fields, then through gate into army firing range (if red flags flying follow diversion instructions in section 5 to section 6, and turn left at army pillbox)

Section 5: 1mi (1.6km)
- Straight across path and through gate
- Follow path round headland and through gate, signposted
- Turn left through another gate and along wooden walkway, signposted 'Diversion Coastal Path'
- Continue along path as it winds about and through gate
- Straight ahead onto concrete track
- Turn left, signposted 'East Fleet Farm'
- Continue along track and cross tarmac to footpath opposite
- Follow footpath round to left

Section 6: 1mi (1.6km)
- Turn immediately right at white army pillbox (guardhouse) onto narrow path between hedges and round static kissing gate and over footbridge into field
- Straight on along edge of field, keeping close to hedge on right, and cross stile into next field
- Continue ahead, keeping barn on left, and over stile beside it onto road
- Turn left along road through East Fleet Farm Campsite, passing shop, etc, on right.

Section 7: 1mi (1.6km)
- Continue straight on through campsite, passing houses on right then barn at top of slope; round right-hand bend to Fleet Road T-junction
- Turn left along Fleet Road, passing church on right

Section 8: 1mi (1.6km)
- Continue uphill to left-hand bend
- Straight ahead along Private Road to West Fleet Holiday Farm
- Follow driveway round right-hand bend
- Continue straight on to wide, stony track at left-hand bend
- Follow track to campsite entrance

IN THE VICINITY
PUBLIC TRANSPORT
The X53 Weymouth to Axminster bus runs along the B3157 past the campsite entrance about every two hours: check timetable at Traveline. The nearest bus stop is just across the field, outside the Victoria Inn. There are many interesting places to visit along the route, and walking back to the campsite is easy as the coastal path is not far away.

More wonderful walks from **dog-friendly campsites**

BIRDWATCHING

There's a big variety of birds to be seen in the area, thanks in large part to the continued efforts of the Fleet and Chesil Nature Reserve. Though there are no bird hides on the coastal path, there are several benches dotted about, thus providing the opportunity to scan the skies, so binoculars would be handy.

At Abbotsbury is the celebrated swannery that, for over 600 years, has been home to around 600 swans, among which it is possible to walk whilst they are feeding, nesting, etc. Free-flying birds who could choose to nest anywhere, the swans are obviously attracted by the Fleet Lagoon. The only such place in the world but, of course, definitely not for dogs.

FISHING

At one time the seaward side of Chesil Beach supported commercial fishing, but nowadays, apart from a small eel fishery in mid-Fleet, fishing is recreational only. In the lagoon angling is only permitted in the waters around Ferrybridge at the start of the causeway to Portland. The unique Chesil land formation is hugely popular with anglers; Portland, Weymouth Pier and Abbotsbury being well-liked fishing sites. Several websites detail types of fish and top fishing sites in the area.

LANGTON HERRING

This small village, just a stone's throw from the coastal path, has an unexpectedly old church, as well as some interesting houses. Unique with a long and intriguing history, remarkably, it is one of only a few villages in Britain known as a 'Thankful' village: so called because all of the local men who fought in WWI returned home safely. Astonishingly, the same thing happened in WWII, so it is a doubly thankful village! Consequently, it does not have a war memorial.

The village's name derives from Old English 'Lang+Tun,' meaning farmstead, and it is mentioned in the Domesday Book. There are many smuggler tales about the place, and, in more recent times, Barnes Wallis stayed at the local inn whilst testing his bouncing bomb on the Fleet. And even Churchill is said to have dropped by for a drink!

In the 1960s the pub was supposedly the rendezvous for Russian spies. All very exciting, indeed, though nowadays it's a quiet, peaceful village with a delightful pub, an interesting church, and an intriguing art studio and gallery.

FLEET EXPLORER

The glass-bottomed *Fleet Explorer* makes regular 1.5 hour trips along and around the Fleet, and into Portland Harbour from Weymouth. Its crew is very knowledgeable, discussing the importance of the area, pointing out local wildlife above and below the water, and recounting thrilling tales of smugglers and shipwrecks. This service has recently been taken over by Dorset Wildlife Trust, so contact this organization for details. Well-behaved dogs are allowed at the skipper's discretion: enquire before booking.

HARDY MONUMENT

On Black Down Hill above the village of Portesham is a 72ft (22m) monument in the shape of a spyglass (telescope), erected in 1844 to commemorate Admiral Thomas Hardy, a naval officer from 1790 to 1839 who took part in many naval battles, but is primarily remembered for the immortal phrase "Kiss me, Hardy," uttered by a dying Nelson at the Battle of Trafalgar in 1805. Hardy's family, who come from Portesham, wanted the monument to be a landmark for shipping, and, since 1846, it has featured on shipping charts. The monument is open during peak season and visitors can climb the 120 steps to the top for a magnificent view. Dogs are welcome in the surrounding area but may not be allowed in the tower.

ABBOTSBURY

Just a short bus ride away is the charming village of Abbotsbury with its many thatched cottages and buildings, some of them dating from the 16th century. A delightful place to explore, besides the useful village store and post office there are a couple of pubs and cafés, and a variety of intriguing shops. Plus, of course, the aforementioned swannery.

ABBOTSBURY SUB-TROPICAL GARDENS

Just 1ml (1.6km) outside of the village, en route to the coastal path, are these 20-acre subtropical gardens, café and giftshop, established in 1765 and full of exotic plants. Well-behaved dogs are welcome.

BENNETTS WATER GARDENS

When the Putton Brickworks in Chickerell closed in the 1950s, Norman Bennett saw in the flooded pit works a possibility to use them to grow the pond plants and water lilies he loved. He modified the 8-acre site and, in 1958/9, created Bennetts Water Gardens, showcasing an assortment of water plants. Most impressive is the display of water lilies, many of which are the same variety as those painted by Claude Monet. An interesting and informative place to visit, especially as dogs, too, are welcome.

CHESIL BEACH VISITOR CENTRE

Located on the outskirts of Weymouth in Ferrybridge car park, this, too, is now managed by Dorset Wildlife Trust. Here there is a wealth of information about Chesil Beach, Fleet Lagoon and local wildlife, as well as details of walks along Chesil Beach and boat trips on the Fleet. A range of family activities are organized throughout the year. Dogs are generally welcome but under strict control so as not to disturb the area's ecosystem.

MOONFLEET

In 1898 J Meade Falkner's novel *Moonfleet* was published: a story of smuggling, shipwreck and treasure set around Chesil Beach and the Fleet, with Moonfleet village an amalgam of several local villages. The book was hugely popular and has been adapted for theatre, TV and film many times; most recently in 2013. There are, therefore, several local 'Moonfleet' places: near the campsite on the coastal path is Moonfleet Hotel, and in Weymouth Moonfleet Adventure Sail Training offers courses and experiences in tall ship sailing.

WEYMOUTH

Ever since George III's visits in the late 1700s, Weymouth has been a popular family seaside resort with its golden, sandy beach and shallow waters. However, there is much to see and do in Weymouth as it has a long, interesting history and busy harbour. It was here that the sailing events for the 2012 Olympics were held.

Gloucestershire – sliced by the Severn

OS MAP EXPLORER 179 GLOUCESTER, CHELTENHAM AND STROUD

The River Severn slices diagonally through this county from north east to the Severn estuary in the southwest, neatly dividing Gloucestershire into three distinct sections.

To the east are the iconic Cotswolds, with many small and charming stone villages and gently rolling hills. To the west is the Forest of Dean, less populated and with many walks that meander through the trees, extending towards the Welsh border and the undulating area foreshadowing the mountains of Wales. Separating these two distinctive features is the third area, the wide valley carved out by the River Severn.

Unusually, over the years, the river has had several different names. Its Celtic name was 'Sabrinna,' the origin of which is unclear, though a possible explanation is that in Celtic mythology Sabrina (the Latin derivation) was the goddess of the River Severn, so thought because of an elaborate fable about a nymph known as Sabrina who drowned in the river. This, perhaps, explains why the Romans referred to the river as 'Sabrina.' In Wales the river was known as 'Hafren', the Welsh translation of the Roman name, and the English translation was 'Severnin.'

Nowadays it is known as the River Severn along its entire length and, at 220ml (354km), the river is the longest in Britain, rising in the Cambrian Mountains in mid-Wales, and eventually flowing out to the Bristol Channel and Atlantic Ocean. Meandering through the countryside in a semi-circular pattern, it passes through Wales into England via the county of Shropshire, and on through Worcestershire and Gloucestershire. It then sculpts an ever-widening estuary that splits Wales from England.

Discharging into the mighty Atlantic Ocean has a considerable impact on the river. Sea tides stretch over 40ml (64.4km) upstream to Maisemore village just a few miles northwest of Gloucester, and the tidal range is huge at 48ft (15m); claimed to be the second largest in the world. This prevented ships from sailing inland and so, in the 18th century, work began on the Sharpness and Gloucester Canal , but it was over 25 years later, in 1827, before the 16 mile (26km) direct waterway was finally completed.

Then there is the infamous 'Severn Bore.' During especially high tides, the water is squeezed up the tapering estuary into the ever-narrowing river, so creating a

The Severn is the longest river in Britain.

large wave, or bore, that moves rapidly upstream from Sharpness towards Gloucester. The size of the bore varies considerably depending on tide and weather conditions. The largest usually occur in spring when the wave can be as high as 49ft (15m), at times reaching speeds of 20mph. When a particularly large bore is expected, the river banks heave with surfers eager to 'ride the bore,' as well as numerous spectators enjoying the show.

Being such a long river there are many bridges giving access to both banks. It has been estimated that there are as many as 107 bridges, 31 of which are listed because of their importance for either historical or engineering reasons. One of the most well-known is the Iron Bridge, the first constructed of iron in 1779, and erected to span the gorge the river chiselled out of the countryside. Then there are the two Severn Bridges that span the wide estuary to connect Wales with England. These have only recently been built. The first was completed in 1966 and was considered revolutionary; the second, completed 30 years later in 1996, was opened by Prince Charles.

For many centuries the Cotswolds area of Gloucestershire was celebrated throughout England and Europe for its sheep and wool production, and during the 15th century this was England's main source of finance. Since then, the wool trade has gradually declined, although Gloucestershire is still mainly an agriculture county. The sheep have been superseded by cattle and arable farming; chiefly wheat and barley, with several fruit orchards in the north east part of the county.

In the western part of the county are the woodlands of the Forest of Dean. This Royal Forest was the first to be designated a National Forest in 1939. Though for many centuries the forest was a source of timber, these days the emphasis is on re-forestation.

The flat valley of the River Severn at the Vale of Gloucester has always been an ideal road and rail route between the Midlands and the south west, but just off these busy thoroughfares the county's true character can be found.

Campsite – Red Lion

This campsite is very conveniently situated beside the pub and, although they bear the same name, they are two separate concerns.

The spacious flat field is subdivided into smaller areas, and although there are only a few hardstandings there are 72 hook-up pitches in total, mostly situated around the edge of the field with the middle free for tents and campervans. There are several static vans that, being grouped in a field behind the pub, do not impinge on the touring areas.

The amenities block is well appointed with laundry and

The campsite is in the river valley and so is prone to flooding.

More wonderful walks from dog-friendly campsites

The pub garden overlooks the river, though is across the road from the campsite.

dishwashing facilities. There is an information area and a shop, which is useful as the campsite is in a very secluded spot, even though just a few miles from the motorway.

Because this campsite is so close to the river it is prone to flooding. It's advisable to check the status of the site before departing.

Pub – Red Lion

The large garden of this pub overlooks a long section of the River Severn, which is relatively clear of shrubs and undergrowth, and watching the life of the river is an enchanting past-time. Unfortunately, the road that separates the pub and garden is a drawback, even though it is only a very minor one.

Inside, the pub has two dining areas as well as a large, L-shaped room with a bar, and another eating area, all of which are decorated with various historical and pertinent memorabilia.

The owners of the pub endeavour to offer a range of wines, beers, etc, many locally brewed. The food is mostly the usual pub grub but of high quality, as locally-sourced seasonal food is used and meals are freshly made to order.

The pub has been a favourite meeting place since the mid-1800s, and is as popular today, with many customers bringing along their dog, especially on bright, sunny days. It is best to book for meals, particularly at the weekend.

Pearls of wisdom 🐾

There was a smell of water as soon as we arrived at the place. Yipee! I thought, swim time. But what a disappointment as it was difficult – practically impossible – to climb down to the water. However, just a short distance from the garden was a small area where the water splashed up over the shore: an ideal place for a swim. It was fabulous swimming in the river – what a delight!

Even though the campsite did not have a special area for me to stretch my legs, there were lots of places to chase my frisbee, and one of the nicest was the long, green area next to the garden, although it was a shame we had to cross a road to get there. Over the stile in the campsite we found a big field to explore, with lots of interesting smells.

Later, in the pub, everyone made a big fuss of me, which I really enjoyed!

Short walk – Beside the Severn
Distance 5mi (8 km)
Duration: 2hr (Easy)
Terrain: River path, wide, grassy tracks, footpaths, stony tracks, fields, stiles and gates

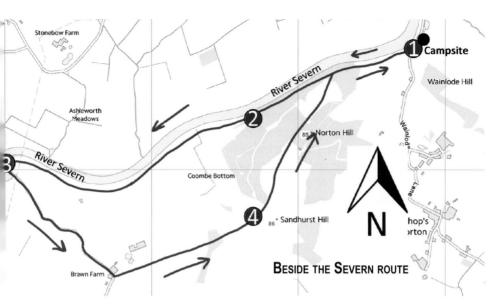

BESIDE THE SEVERN ROUTE

Section 1: 1.25mi (2km)
- Exit campsite onto road via entrance and cross to riverside garden
- Turn left along grass verge, keeping close to the road
- Bear right towards hedge and pass close to kissing gate on right, then over wooden planks into field
- Up narrow footpath, keeping close to hedge on right, and through kissing gate set in hedge
- Continue along path between fence on left and hedge on right and through kissing gate
- Turn right in 20 paces and through another kissing gate into wood
- Turn left and follow path through trees, over footbridge and out into field
- Bearing right cross field back into wood
- Follow footpath and over stile, signposted, then down steps
- Continue along path and down more steps towards river, along path with – finally – some river views, then over stile into field

Section 2: 1mi (1.6km)
- Bear right and continue along edge of field, keeping close to hedge on right
- Cross footbridge (under trees) or through gate gap on left
- Cross next two fields, keeping close to hedge/river on right, and through small gate beside large one into next field
- Continue straight on then bear right towards church spire; at pylons, bear left and through gate onto track (Rodway Lane)

Section 3: 1.5mi (2.4km)
- Turn left and continue along Rodway Lane to Brawn Farm

- Turn left at T-junction and continue on past large pillars, then through gate onto stony track
- Follow track, keeping right at farmyard as it winds up hill to trig point and bench

Section 4: 1.25mi (2km)
- Bear left along wide, grassy track towards wood signposted 'Bridleway'
- Continue straight ahead past barns on left and gated entrances
- Follow track downhill, keeping close to hedge on left, and round to right out into field
- Turn left along edge of field and through kissing gate in corner into next field
- Continue straight on along narrow footpath at edge of field, still going down and passing on left kissing gate used at start of route
- Follow path through kissing gate and down between fence and hedge to pub riverside garden and campsite

LONG WALK – THE SEVERN VALLEY
Distance: 9mi (14.5km)
Duration: 5hr (Easy)
Terrain: River path, wide grassy tracks, footpaths, tracks, stony tracks, fields, embankments, stiles and gates

Section 1: 0.75mi (1.2km)
- Facing toilet block turn left along tarmac track with static vans on right
- Bear left at bend to right and cross grass to stile in hedge
- Exit campsite by crossing stile into field
- Continue straight ahead along edge of field, keeping close to hedge on left
- Follow path round to left, then right, still close to hedge on left
- Turn left immediately after passing stile in hedge on left and through gate
- Bear right across field towards pylons visible between gap in trees, and cross stone bridge in gap
- Continue straight ahead to river embankment
- Turn left along embankment and cross bridge on left

Section 2: 1.25mi (2km)
- Follow path along the edge of field, keeping close to hedge on right, and cross another stone bridge
- Continue ahead, bearing slightly left of hedge and still along edge of field, keeping hedge on right. Cross two stiles and a stream in corner into next field (there may be nettles here)
- Straight on, still keeping close to hedge on right
- Turn right at corner and thorough gate into field
- Bear slightly right and cross field, then through gate by house onto wide track
- Continue on track through farmyard and past church onto road
- Follow the road to houses

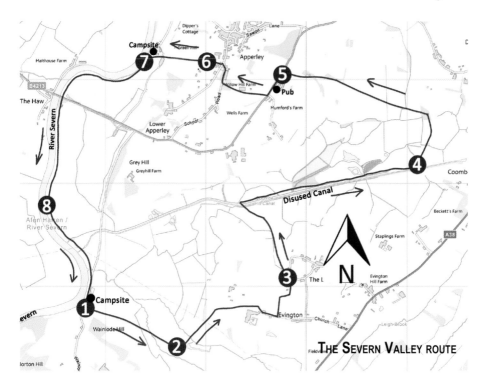

THE SEVERN VALLEY ROUTE

- Turn left and cross stile, signposted, into field
- Straight across and through gap in hedge to corner, keeping close to hedge on left
- Bear left round tree/hedge and then immediately right to cross stile in wooden fence onto grassy path
- Follow path past house and through gate onto road

Section 3: 1.75mi (2.8km)
- Turn left along road past several houses to pond on left
- Turn left at pond signposted 'Public Bridleway' and follow track through gate into field
- Follow path round to left, keeping close to fence on right, then through gate and over a small brick bridge
- Round to the left along footpath and cross metal footbridge over disused canal
- Take right fork and follow grassy footpath with disused canal on right and 'long water' on left (partway along this path is a seat, a good place to stop for lunch and to watch the wetland birds)
- Continue on path past bridge to bird hide

Section 4: 1.25mi (2km)
- Turn left into meadow signposted 'Grundon Hide via meadows'
- Follow path straight ahead, past kissing gate on left and over stone bridge
- Bear left, passing gate on left and yellow way-marker beside brook, then over stone

A gentle walk in the sunny Gloucestershire countryside.

bridge, passing yellow way-marker, with gate to reserve on left (dogs not allowed)
- Bear right along footpath and over stone bridge, then through kissing gate on right
- Turn left and follow path to gate, keeping close to hedge on left
- Turn right before gate and cross half-stile into field
- Continue straight ahead along edge of field
- Turn left at corner and right at next corner onto wide track
- Continue straight across field, bearing slightly left into copse, and cross stile
- Follow path through trees and cross stile into field
- Bear right across field, heading toward white building, and through gap in hedge
- Bear left across field between caravan park and house, signposted, and cross stile into a lovely garden (take care: possibly dogs here)
- Exit garden onto B4213 via garage and gate

Section 5: 0.75mi (1.2km)
- Turn left along road and then 50yd (46m) to pub
- From pub, turn left along road and in 20 paces (end of car park) turn right (opposite Wick Road) and cross stile into field and orchard
- Bearing slightly right, straight ahead up hill
- Keeping house on right, follow path close to fence to tarmac driveway.
- Follow driveway and cross stile to road
- Turn right along road and turn right past house opposite; then cross stile into field
- Bear right across field towards white house and through kissing gate onto road
- Turn right along road, passing church on right
- Turn left just before junction, signposted, along tarmac driveway and through gate into field

Section 6: 0.75mi (1.2km)
- Continue straight ahead, keeping close to fence on left, and cross stile in corner
- Turn sharp right and cross stile in adjacent corner.
- Straight ahead to corner, turn left, keep close to hedge on right and through gate
- Turn left along edge of field and cross stile ahead into next field
- Bear left down field and through gap in hedge, then straight on out onto road by pub through gate opposite
- Turn left and follow road between pub and caravan park
- Turn left towards caravan park and enter 'Severn Way,' keeping close to fence on left, then cross stile ahead into field

Section 7: 1.5mi (2.4km)
- Continue straight ahead along edge of field and cross stile into next field
- Follow path across field and through two gates to road
- Cross road and through gate opposite signposted 'Severn Way'
- Bear right along top of mound and cross stile into field
- Bear left and cross stile opposite
- Turn left along edge of field with river still on right and cross stile into next field
- Follow path along the edge of next four fields, through gates and over stiles

Section 8: 1mi (1.6km)
- Continue on path across top of disused lock into field under pylon
- Follow path round to the left, then over stile on right into next field
- Continue along path round to right then left and over stile onto road by bridge
- Cross bridge and turn immediate right onto wide grass path
- Continue along path to riverside garden and campsite entrance on left

IN THE VICINITY
FISHING
With the river so close, coarse fishing is on offer. Ask at the shop or the pub for further information about day and half-day tickets.

BIRD WATCHING
With several nature reserves dotted about the floodplains of the Severn Vale, binoculars are essential. Some reserves have designated bird hides; some have walking trails, and some will allow dogs as long as they are under control. The range of birds to be seen increases significantly during the winter because this area floods easily, and thus makes an ideal wetland for over-wintering birds. Such diversity contributes to the region's Site of Special Scientific Interest designation.

APPERLEY
Just over 2ml (3.2km) away is the charming village of Apperley, so called because in old English the name translates as 'apple-tree wood.' Nowadays there are few orchards but at one time the region was renowned for the number and variety of its trees.

It is a peaceful, tranquil place possibly because there is now no shop (so just as well there is one at the campsite), although it is a lively community with lots of activities locally.

Apperley has a long history, information about which can be found on the Community Website. With several footpaths passing through the village, there are lots of places to explore.

WALLSWORTH HALL
This magnificent building was built by Samuel Hayward in the 1740s, and his family lived in the hall until 1903, when it was sold so that the estate could be divided among his surviving relatives.

Purchased by James Dorrington, when his wife died in 1943 the hall and its contents were sold to Gloucester City Council, and it became a residential nursery during WWII, and later a training centre for nursery nurses. In 1953, it was sold again and remained largely unused until 1987 when it was bought by the Nature in Art Trust.

Wallsworth Hall is now the only museum and art gallery inspired by nature, and exhibitions and courses are held there throughout the year.

ASHLEWORTH

On the other side of the River Severn is the historic village of Ashleworth. A ferry used to connect the village to Sandhurst, 3ml (4.8km) south of the campsite, but now access is via a bridge several miles north of both the campsite and Ashleworth.

TEWKESBURY AND GLOUCESTER

These interesting and historic cities are only a short drive from the campsite, although there is no bus to either destination.

Hampshire – kings' playground
OS MAP EXPLORER OL22 NEW FOREST

Situated mostly in Hampshire between Southampton and Bournemouth is the New Forest. Confusingly, three regions have this name. The largest is the New Forest local government district, a subdivision of Hampshire County Council; then there is the actual geographical area, and lastly is the National Park. Although the New Forest has been a unique feature of this area for many years, it was not until March 2005 that it was finally awarded National Park status, which should ensure its continued existence as a valuable recreational and ecological area.

Its *New* Forest moniker is a misnomer, in fact, as it has a long, long history, with hunting being a common practice in these deciduous woodlands. Some parts, though, were cleared for cultivation, but, because the soil was so poor, it quickly became heathland. There is evidence of both Bronze Age and Iron Age settlements in the area, though, as in many other parts of the country, it was the Romans' arrival that had the greatest impact. Their settlements were larger; their cultivation more intense. They even established a pottery industry as indicated by the many remnants of Roman pottery found in the vicinity. Then, on the western edge of the forest at Rockbourne, the remains of a large Roman villa were discovered

The forest was first called 'Nova Foresta,' Latin for 'new forest,' by the Normans in 1079. William the Conqueror (King William I) realised that the area was ideal for hunting – a favourite royal pastime – so he earmarked a huge section for his personal use, which included heathland and open moorland as well as woods and forest. To ensure there was always plenty of game he introduced special restrictive Forest Laws that outlawed many activities but specifically the erecting of fences. To pacify disgruntled local inhabitants he allowed them 'commoning,' the right to gather fuel, both wood and peat, and to graze their animals in the forest; they thus became known as commoners. The penalties for infringing these Forest Laws were very severe, and they have had a considerable impact upon the character of the New Forest, and continue to do so even now in the 21st century.

Responsibility for policing these laws fell to 'Verderers,' a position specially created by William I, and part of his newly-formed judicial and administrative system. The term loosely translates as 'Custodians of the Greenery,' and is derived from the Norman word 'vert,' meaning green. Verderers dealt with the day-to-day business of the forest, including investigating minor transgressions, but it was the peripatetic Chief Justice who dealt with more serious offences.

Over the last 150 years Verderers' roles and responsibilities have been updated to reflect the changing times, and the various New Forest Acts of 1877, 1949 and 1964. Nowadays they work closely with the Forestry Commission and local authorities, and comment on issues pertaining to the forest. Their role is to protect and administer commoning practices: conserve the landscape, wildlife and character; ensure a viable future. The Verderers' Hall in Lyndhurst still holds sessions once a month where any matter relevant to the forest can be raised by the public. Verderers are not paid but are, by statute, allowed annually from the forest a doe, a buck, a bundle of wood and a bag of coal. A truly distinctive remuneration!

William I and his family enjoyed hunting in his newly-acquired domain, but misfortune appeared to stalk them. In 1081 his firstborn son, Robert, was killed in a hunting accident. When William died in 1087, his middle son, known as William Rufus because of his ruddy complexion, became king. Not a very popular ruler, in 1100, whilst out hunting in the forest, Rufus was accidentally struck by an arrow and died, though the circumstances are unclear. It was indeed suspicious that all the King's hunting companions immediately absconded, supposedly because they were afraid. Was it truly an accident, or was it intentional? And, if the latter, on whose orders?

It is known that the arrow belonged to Walter Tyrell, but what exactly happened was never ascertained and remains a mystery to this day. A memorial stone, known as the Rufus Stone, now stands at the spot where this incident is supposed to have occurred.

Surprisingly, large tracts of the New Forest

New Forest ponies freely roam and graze.

– around 90 per cent – are still owned by the crown. Rather than hunting, the major occupation nowadays is preservation and conservation under the auspices of the Forestry Commission. Local farmers still have 'common rights,' so not only do the indigenous New Forest Ponies horses freely roam and graze but so, too, do cattle, donkeys and occasionally pigs, an activity that is vital to maintain the eco-system of this ancient woodland area.

More wonderful walks from **dog-friendly campsites**

With three rivers burbling their way to the sea, and several charming villages dotted about, the New Forest provides a perfect opportunity to enjoy and appreciate the countryside.

CAMPSITE – RED SHOOT CAMPING PARK

This family-run site is situated behind the pub of the same name, actually in the New Forest on one of its minor roads. The large, mostly flat field is surrounded by trees, heathland, and fields of sheep and donkeys, which enhances the relaxed and tranquil atmosphere. There is little incentive to venture far with the adjacent pub and well-stocked shop that supplies morning bread and croissants to order.

This is a well organized, spacious site with comprehensive facilities that include a modern toilet block, laundry and play area. The 100+ pitches, 47 of which have electric hook-up, are generally informally arranged in the assorted sections demarcated by numerous trees and shrubs. At the entrance is the obligatory cattle grid to prevent forest horses, donkeys and cows from entering the site and assisting the lawn mower with grass trimming.

The location of the campsite is idyllic, the staff are friendly and helpful, and the walking is marvellous as there are so many footpaths close by.

PUB – RED SHOOT

Conveniently situated next to the campsite but a separate concern is this country pub, providing, as it states on the website, 'pub classics from Wadsworth range from beer-battered fish & chips to a delicious Hunter's board with cheddar, honey roast ham, chutney, piccalilli & rustic bread.' I was delighted to discover it also offers a gluten-free menu. This is a popular venue so to be sure of a table booking is advisable.

The Red Shoot is unusual in that there is also a micro brewery on-site. Thus, there is the opportunity to experience unusually-named beers such as Tom's Tipple or New Forest Gold. To showcase the produce several beer and cider festivals are held during the year. Another plus is that dogs are welcome throughout the pub – there are even treats for them on the bar.

The Red Shoot pub also has a micro brewery.

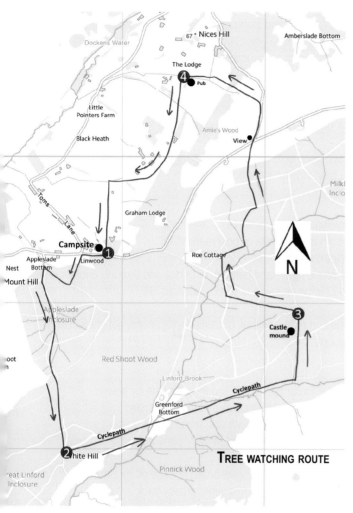

TREE WATCHING ROUTE

Wow whee! What a fabulous place, even though there wasn't an actual special area for me to run. Within a frisbee fling there was so much for me to inspect, and the grassy area just across the road was perfect for a frisbee-chasing game.

This grassy area led straight into the forest, where I could run and run and run. I stumbled upon squirrels to chase until they leapt up a tree, and rabbits until they went down a hole. The other creatures I came across – horses, cows and funny, long-eared ones that made an odd noise, donkeys, I think, were all rather big and scary but slow and impassive. I kept well clear of them and they took no notice of me.

Only a short trek down a very quiet road was a vast, open heathland to rummage around. All just sooo exciting. The same cannot be said of the pub, even though I was allowed inside. Sitting and waiting was rather boring, even though there were treats on offer and people to fuss me.

SHORT WALK – TREE WATCHING
Distance: 5.5mi (8.8km)
Duration: 2.5hr (Easy)
Terrain: Woodland tracks, wide and narrow, muddy in many places, footpaths, cyclepaths, gates and kissing gates, stiles; short gentle climbs

Section 1: 1.25mi (2km)
• Exit campsite across cattle grid via entrance

- Straight ahead through pub car park and along pub driveway, then cross road and through barrier onto green
- Straight ahead through gap between two wooden posts and into forest
- Follow footpath ahead
- Turn right at T-junction and continue along path
- Turn left at junction onto wide, stony track with small car park on right
- Continue along wide track past barrier and on to huge junction (probably muddy), passing smaller junctions
- Straight ahead between two trees onto smaller track, going slightly downhill.
- Follow track through gate past crossroads onto gravel track

Section 2: 1.25mi (2km)
- Continue along track to cyclepath
- Turn left and follow cyclepath through gate at post marked '66'
- Turn left along path into clearing
- Continue along cyclepath round right-hand bend, over bridge and through another gate
- Continue along cyclepath to large crossroads by post marked '64'
- Turn left onto wide track
- Straight ahead past mounds on right (remains of castle fortifications; not immediately obvious) back onto gravel cyclepath

Section 3: 1.5mi (2.4km)
- Turn left along cyclepath over footbridge, uphill and through gate by house
- Turn right with house on right onto footpath parallel to trees and road
- Turn right through gate and continue along path with fence on left
- Turn left at fence corner, still following fence on left
- Turn left through gate onto wide, grassy track
- Continue straight ahead to road by forestry noticeboard at edge of car park on left
- Cross road, turn left then immediately right onto wide, grassy track
- Follow grassy track over moorland, past small car park on right and out to access road
- Turn left downhill to pub (good place to stop for refreshments)
- From pub cross car park out to access road
- Turn left along road to right-hand bend
- Turn left at bend onto track, signposted 'Middle Earth'
- Follow path round left-hand bend past shed and through gate
- Continue along path, round right-hand bend passing house 'Bag End' on right and through gate on left at top of drive by shed onto footpath

Section 4: 1.5mi (2.4km)
- Follow path across footbridge, round edge of field and over stile
- Continue along fenced path and over stile onto track
- Bear slightly left, cross track and over stile opposite
- Turn right along edge of field with fence on right

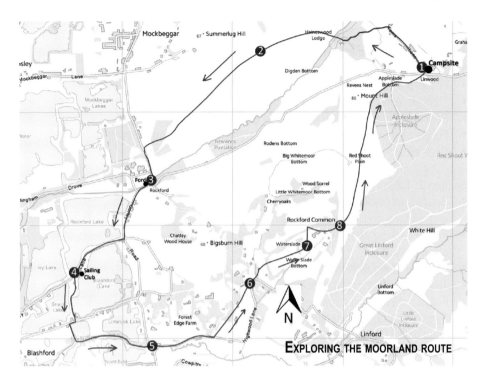

EXPLORING THE MOORLAND ROUTE

- Continue along edge of field and over three stiles close together onto fenced path
- Follow path onto stony track through gate by house
- Follow track as it winds along edge of moorland, passing several houses on left and out to tarmac road
- Continue along road round left-hand bend to campsite

LONG WALK – EXPLORING THE MOORLAND
Distance: 8mi (12.8km)
Duration: 4hr (Easy)
Terrain: Moorland tracks, wide and narrow, muddy in places, footpaths, short stretches of quiet road, gates and kissing gates, stiles, short gentle climbs

Section 1: 1.75mi (2.8km)
- Exit campsite via reception, crossing cattle grid and car park
- Turn right along road to right-hand bend
- Turn left off road and over stile onto fenced footpath
- Continue along footpath and over bridge onto moorland
- Straight ahead up slope and cross wooden plank bridge just before tree
- Bear left at tree, keeping stream on right
- Continue ahead onto clearly defined path going up and bearing left
- Follow wide track to large junction

- Turn right along path, going uphill towards small tree on skyline
- Straight ahead along narrow footpath
- Turn left onto wide track, going uphill towards tree on skyline
- Follow path to top of hill
- Turn left along narrow path, passing tree on left, heading towards copse
- Bear left at junction along wide, stony track, passing copse on right
- Follow path right round trees and then left onto narrow, stony path
- Bear left at junction onto wide, stony track

Section 2: 1.25mi (2km)
- Bear left off track onto grass trail by large gorse bushes (there is a pond on right deep enough for a dog swim. If you pass this you have gone too far)
- Follow track between two bushes and over stony track towards large clump of trees along brow of hill
- Continue along wide track, passing trees on right going downhill
- Take second turning on right into wood partway down hill
- Follow path through rhododendron bushes to open green space by gates
- Turn left through kissing gate at Newlands Farm onto fenced footpath signposted Avon Valley Path, passing stables on right
- Take second turning on right, signposted, then through gate onto path and another gate out to road

Section 3: 1mi (1.6km)
- Turn left along road using grass verge and cross ford via bridge on left
- Turn right, still along road, keeping close to stream on right
- Cross road at junction and through gate opposite onto narrow footpath
- Straight ahead along footpath with fence on right, hedge and road on left and through gate onto road with pub on right (good place for refreshments)
- From pub cross car park to green ahead, bearing right to road
- Turn right along road, crossing cattle grid
- Continue along road past Ivy Cottage on right and through gate on right just past house on right
- Turn right and follow narrow footpath past houses and round to right, then left to lakeside

Section 4: 1mi (1.6km)
- Turn right at sailing club onto wide, stony track
- Just past gate entrance turn left onto narrow footpath
- Follow footpath as it winds round lakes through wooded area, and through gate onto road
- Turn right and in 20yd (18m) turn left through kissing gate onto narrow footpath signposted 'Avon Valley Path'
- Take left fork along path, following green fence on left

The sailing club.

- Follow path beside stream and cross road to cul-de-sac

Section 5: 0.75mi (1.2km)
- Continue along road, passing bridge on right, farm and houses
- Turn left along footpath beside second thatched house, signposted
- Continue through trees and over wooden walkways round to left and through gate
- Take right fork, keeping close to fence on right
- Turn right down path to road at corner of house

Section 6: 0.75mi (1.2km)
- Continue straight ahead across grass triangle, bearing left, and follow road round to right
- Turn sharp left off road between trees onto track, signposted
- Follow path to road, turn right and right again onto wide track
- Follow track uphill and, as it narrows, through trees out onto moorland.
- Bear right to wide, grassy track with buildings on right

Section 7: 0.5mi (0.8km)
- Take left fork along narrower grassy track onto gravelly path
- Turn left then right between two small pillars just before barrier onto wide, grassy track
- Continue along track towards trees

Section 8: 1mi (1.6km)
- Turn left at crossroads and follow path, keeping close to trees on right
- Take right fork at next junction onto grassier track
- Follow path round right-hand bend, keeping close to trees on right
- Take stony path on right going downhill
- Cross track with small car park on right

- Straight ahead across green towards white house
- Follow path round house on right and parallel to road to pub/campsite entrance on left

IN THE VICINITY

CYCLING

Several cyclepaths criss-cross the New Forest, and many of the roads are 'cycle friendly.' Consequently, there are a number of mapped routes available. Bikes can be hired in both Fordingbridge and Ringwood.

BIRDWATCHING

Only 2 miles (3.2km) south west of the campsite is the Hampshire and Isle of Wight Wildlife Trust nature reserve. This 490-acre site of woods, grasslands and lakes teems with wildlife, especially birds of all kinds. At times as many as 5000 birds can congregate on Blashford Lakes, which is recognized as an internationally significant site. Six bird hides are dotted around the nature reserve. Access is particularly easy due to the numerous gravel paths.

RIDING

The proliferation of stables throughout the New Forest indicates the popularity of riding. Fir Tree Farm Equestrian Centre, which offers lessons and hacks for both adults and children, is only a couple of miles across the heathland or four miles by road.

OTHER ACTIVITIES

An introduction to other activities such as archery is available with Insight Activities at Midgam Farm, just four miles away on the outskirts of Fordingbridge.

BUS TOUR

During July and August an open-top bus travels around the New Forest on three separate but intersecting forest routes – red, green and blue – and, because it is a hop-on, hop-off bus it's very easy to change routes. A bonus is that bikes go free.

This is a unique way to experience the New Forest, riding through the tree tops listening to the commentary. The nearest pick-up point to the campsite is at Ibsley, about 4ml (6.4km) away, which is on the red route.

RUFUS STONE

A three-sided landmark supposedly marking the spot at which King William II was killed by an arrow shot belonging to Sir Walter Tyrell, after whom the nearby pub is named. A triangular stone just a metre high, what is known about the event is detailed on two sides of the stone. On the remaining side there is information about the monument itself.

CANADIAN MEMORIAL

Deep in the Forest between Bolderwood and Stoney Cross can be found a Canadian Memorial – a simple wooden cross beside a minor road overlooking sloping ground –

which marks the spot where Canadian forces regularly gathered for church services during WWII in the days leading up to D-Day in June 1944.

NEW FOREST CENTRE

The ideal place to find out more about the New Forest, in the heart of the New Forest at Lyndhurst; 9 miles (14.4km) from the campsite.

FORDINGBRIDGE AND RINGWOOD

Two interesting, charming places; not quite New Forest towns as they are situated on the edge of the forest, but well worth a visit, nevertheless. Fordingbridge is 6ml (10km) north of the campsite whilst Ringwood is 4ml (6.4km) to the south west.

Visit Hubble and Hattie on the web:
www.hubbleandhattie.com • www.hubbleandhattie.blogspot.co.uk • Details of all books
• Special offers • Newsletter • New book news

203

Walks in Scotland
(Aberdeenshire, Argyll and Bute, Dumfries and Galloway)

Rights of Access in Scotland are slightly different to the rest of Great Britain. The 2003 Scotland Land Reform Act established 'a statutory right of responsible access over most areas of land and inland water.' This means that, as long as you respect the countryside and behave responsibly, it is permitted to access practically all of the Scottish countryside (Appendix i). As a consequence, the only paths shown in the customary green dashes on OS Maps are the long distance trails such as the West Highland Way.

Most of these routes are linear. They are well signposted, and popular with walkers of all abilities, so are busy during the long summer days, even in inclement weather. Once having reached the correct path it is possible to walk many, many miles before the necessity to check location. (However, it is always prudent to refer to the map at regular intervals to ensure you are on the correct path.) It is interesting talking to walkers here, who come from all over the world. Some aim to complete the entire trail whilst others enjoy a short climb for the spectacular views.

I was surprised to discover on the Ordnance Survey Maps of Scotland that few tracks or paths appear to intersect these well known trails, and finding circular walks was problematic without local knowledge. Most such walks usually involve the busy popular routes as well as tracks generally only used by locals. It is possible, therefore, to experience the beauty of Scotland in the company of others, and also appreciate the remoteness and vastness of the country in solitude.

Whenever and wherever walking in Scotland, always check the weather conditions, as these can suddenly change and become inclement, making navigation even more difficult: because of the landscape and lack of human habitation, it is easy to get lost.

Aberdeenshire – mountains
OS MAPS EXPLORER OL58 BRAEMAR, TOMINTOUL & GLEN AVON

The character of the landscape gradually changes the further north one goes in Scotland. The colossal Cairngorm Mountains dominate the central area, so dictate walking routes: either circular, coastal roads or following rivers through the middle of the National Park. As Braemar is situated at the confluence of the Rivers Dee and Clunnie right in the heart of the National Park, the choice of roads is limited to the middle route. Almost imperceptibly the road narrows to one lane each way, and realisation slowly dawns that traffic and its accompanying roar has diminished. The deeper into the mountains the road meanders, the quieter it becomes ... until there's just you. I have experienced nothing like this before: no traffic; no noise; just me and my dog and the van. A passing vehicle is a rare event.

As the road snakes deeper into the mountain ranges, so the peaks and hills jostle one another like spectators at a football match, catching the sun's rays and tossing them this way and that in a lightning flash of colour. Other times, clouds float across the heavens, brushing the jagged mountain tops and leaving wisps of translucent vapour cloaking the range like a scarf, the peaks thrusting through resembling accusatory fingers jabbing at the sky. Even when the clouds descend the slopes, wrapping upper reaches of the mountains in a cross-patch quilt of grey, they constantly shift and shimmer. The secret life of these majestic mountains would reveal many a tale if only they could talk ...

The Cairngorms National Park is the largest national park in Great Britain, and, whilst the mountains here are the focal point as well as the largest, the area also encompasses other nearby mountains such as the Monadhliath range, and also hills, rivers and valleys. Over the centuries the tops of the Cairngorms have been weathered by wind, snow and rain, and in places there are uncharacteristic plateaux. At this height the environment is Arctic-like, with the possibility of snow at any time during the year: frequently, there are patches of snow on mountain peaks throughout the summer, and of course, in winter snowfall is significant enough to make the area very popular with skiers.

Braemar village is an ideal base from which to explore the park; a bustling community with various art and music events, including traditional ceilidhs. This compact settlement has a variety of buildings and narrow roads that straddle the Clunnie Water in the sweeping arch of the River Dee. With forest, hills and mountains surrounding it, the views are stunning. Then there is the intriguing Braemar Castle sited on a mound just over 0.5m miles (0.8km) away, that was occupied by a member of the Farquharson Clan until very recently when the village took charge of it. In 2008 it was opened to the public.

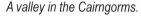

A valley in the Cairngorms.

More wonderful walks from dog-friendly campsites

In the first week of September the famous Highland Games take place on a recently purpose-built showground. It is thought that the idea for the games – a forerunner of the annual Braemar Gathering – was mooted in the 11th century by King Malcolm, who arranged competitions in order to identify the best soldiers. It has been traditional since Queen Victora attended in 1832 that members of the royal family are present at the games, and Balmoral Castle – the family Scottish holiday home – lies in the next village. A popular event generally, visitors from all around the world gather at the games. Whatever time of year you may visit Braemar, there is always something for everyone, and plenty to see and do.

CAMPSITE – BRAEMAR CARAVAN PARK

This campsite is conveniently situated on the outskirts of Braemar village, deep in the Cairngorm Mountains, and has spectacular views. Open all year round, it is ideally placed to explore the surrounding area, whether walking and climbing in summer or skiing or snowboarding in winter. A large campsite with 92 hard-standing pitches (extremely useful for winter visitors), and 11 grass ones, it is efficiently run with helpful staff. There are two heated amenities blocks, one of which is particularly comprehensive with laundry, drying room, and even a boot room. The reception houses a small shop but, being so close to the village, there is a more comprehensive choice at local shops.

PUBS

There is an extensive choice of pubs, cafés and restaurants in Braemar, some of which allow dogs and some of which have restricted opening hours. There are so many for such a small village because it is a popular tourist destination, especially during the Games. With the campsite so close to the village, all are easily accessible. Beside the castle ruins and across a car park is Farquharsons Bar & Kitchen which is most like a pub. This does accept dogs, and is a popular place to both eat and drink.

PEARLS OF WISDOM 🐕

This is a humongous place and one of the few campsites we have been to where there is a special area put aside for me to play. What an exciting place; far bigger than most. It has a stream: nowhere near deep enough for a swim, unfortunately, even though there is a bridge. At the other end are stepping stones, so just paws-wet depth. Crossing the bridge there is a wood; an actual wood with lots of trees

Braemar has a variety of eating establishments. At the end of the street is Farquharsons Bar and Kitchen.

The campsite dog walk in woods, complete with stream.

and several paths through it. A fun place with oodles of exciting things to sniff but nowhere to chase my frisbee. Walks were good: some tarmac but with very few fast machines: cars, I think. Quite a lot of uphill and down; also lots of water as we were near a river but I was disappointed that this was not deep enough for a swim either. The two walks from Braemar campsite are very similar in length, although the terrain is very different: the long walk is the more challenging of the two.

Overall a good place with lots of different things to explore.

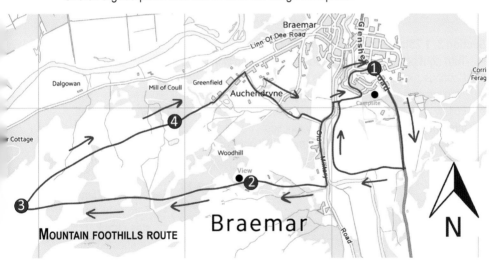

SHORT WALK – MOUNTAIN FOOTHILLS
Distance: 5.5mi (8.8km)
Duration: 3.5hr (Moderate)
Terrain: Footpaths, moors roads, lanes, stony tracks, gates, one steep climb

Section 1: 1.75mi (2.8km)
- Exit campsite via reception onto road
- Cross road to stony track, turning immediate right onto concrete path
- Follow path parallel to road to signpost
- Turn right, through gate, cross road, through gate onto path with golf course on left

- Continue along path round several bends, passing river on left, and through gate over footbridge
- Turn sharp left to cross another bigger footbridge (Society Bridge) onto road (Old Military Road)
- Turn left along road, passing houses and farms, and over cattle grid in road (ignore cattle grid at farm entrance on right)
- Bear right up track (which becomes grassy)
- Take right fork going up (steep) between static vans and through gate
- Continue along narrow path going uphill (very steep), and through gate out to wide track
- Turn left along track, passing house on right to signpost and viewpoint on right

Section 2: 1mi (1.6km)
- Exit viewpoint, turning right along path signposted 'Morrone Birkwood Circular'
- Straight on at left bend onto narrow footpath (way-marker hidden on left) and through gate
- Continue along footpath through heather and round hill on left, heading towards trees (amazing views)

Section 3: 1.25mi (2km)
- Turn right before gate into wood, following path with wood and fence on left
- Continue along path as it winds away from wood
- Turn left along stony path, initially going up
- Follow path as it steadily descends, crossing big boulders on down to trees and through gate, out to large, 4-way junction
- Straight across onto wide, stony track, still going down, then through gate
- Follow wide, stony track, passing pond on right (ideal for dog swim) onto tarmac road

Section 4: 1.25mi (2km)
- Turn right onto wide, stony track signposted 'Chapel Brae Gardens'
- Follow track, going slightly downhill and passing Morrone Outdoor Centre on right

The path down the Morrone Birkwood towards Braemar.

- Straight on at junction, still going down
- Follow track round left bend at next junction, passing Braemar Gathering Showground on left
- Turn right onto path, passing wooded shed on right, and through gap in fence into wood
- Straight ahead along path between trees, bearing round to left, then right up to way-marker on brown post
- Turn right at way-marker, following path to next one
- Bear left, following path across green and out to road
- Turn right along road with river on left
- Turn left at signpost to cross footbridge (Society Bridge)
- Bear left at steps onto path across field, heading towards gates between houses
- Through gate out to road, turning right then left along lane between white posts
- Follow lane out to cul-de-sac, turning right
- Continue along road between new houses out to A93
- Turn right along A93 to campsite entrance

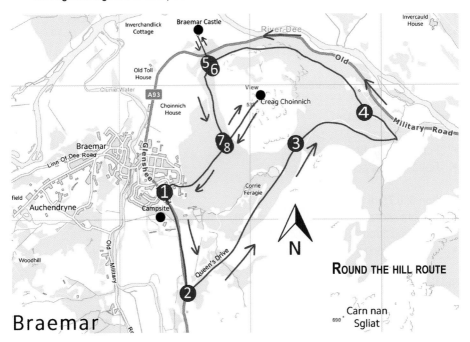

LONG WALK – ROUND THE HILL
Distance: 6.5mi (10.4km)
Duration: 5hr (Moderate/challenging in places)
Terrain: Footpaths, woods, roads, lanes, stony tracks, gates, narrow paths, rocky paths, several uphill and downhill, steep climb to the top

Section 1: 0.5mi (0.8km)
- Exit campsite via reception onto road
- Cross road to stony track, turning immediate right onto concrete path
- Follow path parallel to road, passing signpost and gate on right, onto a stony path zig-zagging up the hill away from road; through gate onto wide track
- Turn left (behind the track leads to gate out to road: Queen's Drive, the carriage route used by Queen Victoria)

Section 2: 1mi (1.6km)
- Continue along wide track, steadily climbing and passing footpath on left signposted 'To village' to bench (amazing views)

Section 3: 1mi (1.6km)
- Follow path, now going downhill through woods, over footbridge, round bend and over second footbridge, going down towards road and onto wide track

Section 4: 1mi (1.6km)
- Bear right off track and onto path beside gate to road just before watch tower
- Continue along path between trees, with road on right
- Keep right onto narrow footpath heading towards water and road over footbridge and uphill
- Follow path as it winds around the hill and eventually down to road through gate

Section 5: 0.5mi (0.8km)
- Turn right cross A93 to path opposite
- Follow path to Braemar Castle information tent
- Retrace steps across A93 to gate

Section 6: 0.75mi (1.2km)
- Straight ahead up steps, following path along hill between fences, then up more steps and through gate, passing viewpoint on right
- Continue along path round to right and over stepping stones to junction

Section 7: 0.75mi (1.2km)
- Turn left, signposted 'Creag Choinnich'
- Follow path uphill (very steep and rocky) as it zig-zags through trees with sharp right turn, then through heather to top (360 degree views)
- Retrace steps to junction

Section 8: 1mi (1.6km)
- Continue along path, going downhill and ignoring joining paths
- Bear right at large junction still going down towards signpost, noticeboard and house, and through gate ahead

- Bear left across grass to road
- Follow road round two right-hand bends; then left out to A93
- Turn left along road to campsite

IN THE VICINITY

FISHING

The River Dee is ideal for fishing, with over 80 miles of suitable waters. It is most famous for salmon fishing, although the river is home to other fish, too. If required, from February to October fishing guides (ghillies) are available. Details and information about permits, etc, can be found through 'Fish Pal' at www.fishpal.com/Scotland/Dee/fisheries.html?dom=Dee.

Braemar Castle is well worth a visit.

BIRDWATCHING/WILDLIFE

There's an abundance of diverse bird and wildlife in the National Park, including many rare and endangered species, although because the park is big and so much of it is remote, it can be difficult spotting any. Braemar Highland Experience and Wild Discovery arrange guided tours around the River Dee on private roads and isolated hills.

CYCLING

A good way to explore further afield is by bicycle. There are many bike trails in the National Park: family rides, challenging mountain routes, and everything in-between. Again, further detail and information is available online.

WILD SWIMMING

There are many places to wild swim in the Cairngorm Mountains, and there is plenty of information about this online. The area in the immediate vicinity of Braemar is not especially suitable as the waters are not really deep enough.

BRAEMAR CASTLE

Well worth a visit. Dogs are not allowed in the castle but can be supervised by a staff member during the castle tour.

GLENSHEE SKI CENTRE

This alpine snow-sports area is just 9 miles (14.5km) south of the campsite at the head of Cairnwell Pass. It is the largest alpine snow-sports area in Great Britain and, with 22 lifts, it is popular with both skiers and snowboarders. Because it is so remote there is plenty of parking, and also hook-ups for motorhomes. In addition, on site there are three cafés that open at different times of the year. The one which opens in the summer welcomes dogs. Further information and details are available online.

Argyll & Bute – two lochs
OS MAPS EXPLORER OL39 LOCH LOMOND NORTH

The Loch Lomond and Trossach National Park covers a huge area of SW Scotland just to the north of Glasgow, and is, in fact, the fourth largest national park in Great Britain, with a total area of 720sqml (1865sqkm). The landscape is spectacular and surprisingly varied, with undulating hills in the south, towering mountains in the north, plus extensive forests and woodlands, and numerous lochs and rivers. It is relevant to note that the countryside has been shaped by human interaction over many centuries, and is still evolving.

The suggestion that special areas of Scotland should be protected as designated National Parks was first mooted just after the Second World War, and among the four regions suggested was Loch Lomond and the Trossachs, although, astonishingly, no action was taken, even though another study in 1990 came to the same conclusion. Eventually, when the National Parks (Scotland) Act 2000 was passed by the newly devolved Scottish Parliament, two national parks were created: the Cairngorms National Park and the Loch Lomond and Trossachs National Park, which was officially recognized in July 2002.

The park is so called after a small forest in the central area and the largest loch. It also contains within its boundary several other forests, including the Argyll Forest Park on the SW peninsula, which is managed by Forestry Scotland, and, at the top of Loch Long, the popular peaks of the Arrochar Alps.

Then there are the 21 Munros, Scottish mountains over 3000ft (914m) in height, as well as numerous smaller hills and peaks; around 50 rivers and streams (or burns, as they are known in Scotland), and a multitude of small lochs (lakes, as they are generally known), as well as 22 bigger ones. The biggest of these is Loch Long which is very close in location to Loch Lomond.

The north end of Loch Long is just 2 miles (3.2km) from the shore of Loch Lomond, and this intervening narrow strip of land has profoundly shaped the area, though in the past it had been suggested that the two lochs be linked by a channel. Considering that the two lochs are so close the differences between them is stark. Firstly, Loch Long is relatively obscure, whereas Loch Lomond is one of the most

The landscape around Loch Lomond is varied: always striking and atmospheric ...

famous lochs, partly due to the song *The Bonnie Banks of Loch Lomond,* first published around 1841, and its catchy chorus –

> *O ye'll take the high road and I'll take the low*
> *And I'll be in Scotland afore ye*
> *For me and my true love will never meet again*
> *On the bonnie, bonnie banks o' Loch Lomon'*

Secondly, Loch Lomond is a fresh water lake, whereas Loch Long is a seawater inlet extending at the south western end into the Firth of Clyde. It is more of a fjord with the steep, wooded banks of the loch forming part of the coastline of the Rosneath Peninsula.

Then there is size. Both of similar length – 20mi (32km) – with Loch Lomond being slightly longer and Loch Long being much narrower; just 1-2mi (1.6-3.2km) wide. Loch Lomond is considerably wider, achieving nearly 5mi (8km) in places: as one of the largest inland lakes in Britain, several islands are dotted about it. Because it is so large there are not only boat cruises but also water buses connecting various settlements along its banks.

Because Loch Lomond crosses the faultline between the Highlands and Lowlands of central Scotland, it is often considered the gateway to the Highlands, and spectacular surrounding landscape – woods, hills, peaks, ponds and rivers – reinforces this view, as does the Gaelic name of the loch which translates as 'Lake of the Elms.'

The more utilitarian Loch Long decodes as 'Ship Lake'; no doubt as the result of intrepid Viking invaders who, in 1263, sailed up Loch Long and then dragged their boats overland the 2mi (3.2km) to Loch Lomond in order to attack the settlements there.

Two very distinctive lochs; both offering fantastic experiences.

Campsite – Glenloin House Caravan and Camping

This campsite is situated on the north tip of Loch Long on the outskirts of Arrochar. It is part of a bigger complex comprising a garage, a shop and a takeaway-cum-café, so although it is surrounded by spectacular scenery of woods, mountains and lochs, the bright lights of the garage are somewhat intrusive. The amenities block – functional, clean and tidy – is located at the rear of the shop/café. However, the chemical toilet is hidden away up the drive in the garden of the house, so is quite a trek.

The campsite is laid out around two circular access roads, with pitches and grass area for tents and

The campsite is situated at the tip of Loch Long.

games radiating off each side, creating an intimate, pleasant atmosphere. With the village of Arrochar stretching down the road, and parking place and picnic area across the road, it is a convenient base.

Pubs – Arrochar & Tarbet
Ben Arthur Bothy (Arrochar)
A short walk from the campsite, this pub has a fabulous outdoor seating area on the banks of the loch with spectacular views. Although a very popular venue, the atmosphere is more of a local pub than a tourist hotspot.

Loch Long Hotel (Arrochar)
A large, imposing hotel just a short walk from the campsite, seemingly set high into the mountain, with a long drive to the entrance. The outdoor garden is at the front, and has spectacular views over the loch.

Slanj Bar & Restaurant (Tarbet)
This restaurant is en route to the ferry on the outskirts of Tarbet, and I have included it because it is so exceptional. The building is unique as it is a decommissioned church, and, though conventional, the menu is delicious, offering a range of international flavours made with Scottish produce. More unusually, it also offers a choice of three meals and a dessert for dogs!

The owner has diversified, and a portacabin in the large car park is a village shop. Finally, there is a takeaway service for food *and* people: a free ride to the campsite so long as you eat in the restaurant.

Pearls of wisdom

From the minute we arrived there was a salty smell in the air, and, as we walked across the road to a car park, it got really strong. Water! My owner would not let me go in – something about mud – but what's mud? It washes off anyway! The path we walked along had lots of grass beside it with many smells to check out, and even a space for me to chase my frisbee. Great! The campsite itself was quite ordinary but I had a fabulous time.

Pearl waits patiently to enter and order her dinner at Slanj Bar and Restaurant.

In the next village we found a place for me to swim: sometimes with people, which was very strange! Then we went on what I think was a boat. It rocked a bit and the smell of water was very strong. Getting on was not very nice as the path was full

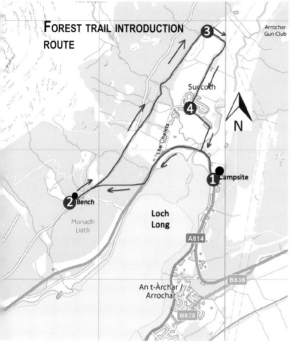

FOREST TRAIL INTRODUCTION ROUTE

of lots of tiny metal holes that really hurt my feet. Getting off was okay as there were just wood planks.

Best of all my owner took me out to dinner! Yes, I know we often do this but this time I had a meal, too! It was delicious. Gosh, my owner takes a long time to eat hers!

SHORT WALK – FOREST TRAIL INTRODUCTION
Distance: 3.5mi (5.6km)
Duration: 2hr (Moderate)
Terrain: Footpaths, roads, lanes, stony tracks, gates, some very steep climbs

Section 1: 1mi (1.6km)
- Exit campsite via facilities block, crossing road to car park
- Turn left through gate onto loch-side path
- Turn right along path, passing car park on right, and over bridge to far end of car park
- Bear right across car park to A83
- Cross road to forest track opposite, turning left onto track
- Follow track as it winds uphill through forest to bench at junction

Section 2: 1.25mi (2km)
- Turn right along wide, stony track
- Continue along path, taking right fork at junction signposted 'Arrochar Car Parks'

Section 3: 0.5mi (0.8km)
- Follow path downhill and round bend towards buildings
- Turn left along stony track just before row of new houses on right

Section 4: 0.75mi (1.2km)
- Continue along track, passing house on right, and through gate

The path winding up the hill to the bench in Section 1.

- Follow track towards trees, turning right to cross footbridge
- Continue along narrow footpath out to wide, stony track
- Turn right along track to road
- Turn left along road to campsite entrance

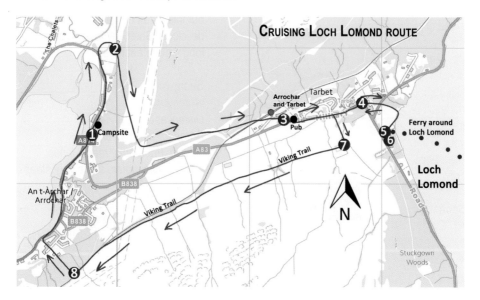

LONG WALK – CRUISING LOCH LOMOND
Distance: 6.5mi (10.4km)
Duration: 3.5hr (Moderate)
Distance (including West Highland Way): 14ml (22.5km)
Duration: 7.5hours (Challenging)
Terrain: Footpaths, roads, lanes, stony tracks, gates, several steep climbs (information about terrain of West Highland Way below)

This walk passes the jetty at Tarbet, from where it is possible to take several boat trips around Loch Lomond, including –
- Rob Roy Cruise
- Northern Highlight Cruise. Circular boat trips of about an hour around the Loch. Departs daily during the summer
- Ferry to Inversnaid. Sail to opposite side of Loch; explore area and return later same day. Runs several times every day during the summer
- Ferry to Rowardennan, offering two options –
- Climb Ben Lomond and return on afternoon sailing
- Walk West Highland Way to return on afternoon sailing from Inversnaid. Only operates at weekends during summer

I did the West Highland Way option and found my walking pole essential as this is a challenging walk. The first section to a small bay is easy, and then the path becomes very

Several boats offer cruises around Loch Lomond.

narrow, requiring some scrambling over various obstacles. The third section is easy underfoot but very steep in places. The final section after the bridge into the woodland is like the second section: narrow with many obstacles to clamber over. There is little opportunity to admire the view because not only is it obscured by trees, it is also necessary to watch your footing.

Dogs are allowed on all boats, and tickets can be purchased on the day from the crew.

Section 1: 0.5mi (0.8km)
- Exit campsite via entrance drive, turning left to road
- Turn right along road (necessary to cross road as pavement one side only)
- Turn right in 30yd (27m) onto wide, stony track
- Turn right onto narrow footpath, signposted, heading into trees ahead (steep climb)

Section 2: 1mi (1.6km)
- Turn right at junction still going up, signposted, to follow path through trees
- Take left fork at next junction going up (steep)
- Continue along path going up and down (steep in some places), passing bench on right to wide, stony track

Section 3: 1mi (1.6km)
- Cross track to path opposite
- Follow path going down, then up and round left-hand bend, signposted, and down under railway tunnel and out to car park
- Bear left across car park to A83
- Turn left along road (very busy), passing village shop and restaurant on left

Section 4: 0.5mi (0.8km)
- Straight ahead at bend onto lane
- Turn right through big black gates and across hotel car park to A82
- Cross road onto Lochside green
- Bear left across green to jetty

Section 5: West Highland Way
Boat trip (see above)

Section 6: 0.75mi (1.2km)
- Disembark from boat onto loch green, bearing right towards hotel
- Cross road into hotel car park and through black gates into lane
- Turn left along lane onto pavement of A83
- Continue along road to second gated turning on left (worth taking a detour along A83 to Slanj Restaurant for refreshments)
- Turn left onto wide track and through gate
- Follow tarmac track uphill, turning right at bend and through gate onto stony track

Section 7: 1.5mi (2.4km)
- Continue along track parallel to road as it crosses the hillside, passing footpath on right (amazing views)

Section 8: 1.25mi (2km)
- Turn right down track towards loch, signposted, and through gate under rail-line (watch your head)
- Follow path downhill into village, passing houses on left, and out to road by church
- Turn right, following road around church to A83
- Turn right along road to campsite entrance

IN THE VICINITY

FISHING

With so many lakes and rivers in the National Park there is plenty of opportunity to fish, especially in Lochs Lomond and Long. A fishing permit is required, and details of how to obtain one are available online.

CYCLING

With so many cycle routes suitable for all abilities, cycling is an ideal way to explore the National Park. Bike hire is available, and information on cycle routes can be found online.

TARBET

This fascinating village is at the Loch Lomond end of the narrow strip of land separating it from Loch Long. In Gaelic its name means, most appropriately, 'isthmus.' Besides the railway station (the Glasgow to Mallaig line) there is also a pier.

BOAT TRIPS

Regular Loch Lomond boat trips and ferries depart from the pier in Tarbet. A fleet of boats of varying sizes, mostly operated by Cruise Loch Lomond, allows visitors to explore the more inaccessible places, as well as linking settlements on both banks. It is a wonderful experience, cruising around the loch. Information and trip details can be found online.

ROWARDENNAN

This small settlement is on the eastern shore of Loch Lomond, and has a variety of accommodation to cater for the huge number of walkers passing through whilst trekking the West Highland Way. In prime position on the banks of the loch and with stunning views is Rowardennan Lodge Youth Hostel. The nearby car park is for those who wish to climb Ben Lomond. Access is via a narrow road or a more enjoyable boat trip.

Ben Lomond

The highest mountain in the National Park at 3193ft (974m), the loch is named after it. In 1995, the mountain and the land surrounding it were designated a war memorial to commemorate the fallen of WWI and WWII. The memorial is a short walk from Rowardennan car park: a circular stone and granite sculpture.

Arrochar

This rural village is strung out along Loch Long's banks at its head, and is surrounded by the Argyll Forest: gateway to the Arrochar Alps. The views are spectacular, especially the unusual rooky peak of the 'Cobbler' mountain – so called because it looks like a doubled-over cobbler at work, but its official name is Ben Arthur.

Being easy to reach, Arrochar is a lively place, well worth exploring for its off-the-beaten-track nooks and crannies.

Dumfries & Galloway – out west
OS Maps Explorer 311 Wigtown, Whithorn & the Machars

The shortest distance between two points is usually a straight line, and so it is that the majority of main routes in Scotland run in a north to south direction: particularly evident in the county of Dumfries and Galloway, a long county that stretches west to east along the coast of the Solway Firth out to the Irish Sea.

The county has three distinct sections: the coastal area; the eastern sector, through which the main north-south routes traverse, and the inland region of the western half of the county, where, in 1947, Galloway Forest Park was established.

Though Dumfries and Galloway is in the Scottish Lowlands, all this indicates is that the area is not part of the famous 'Highlands' of Scotland. Both districts are large so are subdivided again geographically. One section of the Lowlands is the Southern Uplands, which stretches west to east along the border with England. As the name indicates, these are ranges of hills and mountains – some quite high: in Galloway Forest Park, for example, the 'Merrick' rises 2764ft (844m), whilst the 'White Coomb' reaches 2696ft (822m). Both are classed as mountains as they each exceed 2000ft (609m).

The Scottish coastline is exceedingly long, in part due to the bays, estuaries, peninsulas and headlands that form so much of the shore, and typical of this is the 200 mile (322km) coast of Dumfries and Galloway. Such a tortuous coastline makes access complex and time-consuming, but the pay-back is amazing views and spectacular scenery. In these secluded places there are fewer towns and villages, and they are also smaller and more intimate, resulting in a calm and tranquil atmosphere; especially so in the western half of the county.

More wonderful walks from **dog-friendly campsites**

Wigtown is one such place, a small settlement in the south western part of the county that was, at one time, the main town of that region as the capital of the old county of Wigtownshire. Its position on a hill overlooking the large Wigtown Bay, which flows into the Irish Sea, contributed to its importance commercially and strategically. However, the advent of the railway and roads changed all that and the town found itself bypassed ... and so began a gradual decline.

In 1997 revival of the town's fortunes began with establishment of Wigtown as Scotland's national book town; buildings were refurbished, gardens planted, and a plethora of bookshops established. 1998 saw the first Wigtown Book Festival that is now an annual event attracting huge audiences. With over a thousand years of history and a nature reserve in the bay, Wigtown has much to offer besides books, and is a delightful place in which to spend time.

Garlieston is likewise another enchanting place in which to while away the time; just 7 miles (11.2km) south of Wigtown, and easily reached by bus. Originally where the Kilfilian Burn (stream) flowed out into the bay was a water mill and small settlement, which was developed into a port by Lord Garlies in 1780. Much of the village's current arrangement is the same as initially planned, with North Crescent running parallel to the coastline on one side of the burn and South Crescent on the other; the houses overlooking the bay.

During the 1800s Garlieston was a bustling port, with several trading vessels and various enterprises in the village connected with sailing. To increase harbour capacity a pier was constructed in 1816, and arrival of the railway in 1876 contributed to the town's prosperity, though changes during the early 20th century signalled its gradual decline as a commercial port. Nowadays, there may be the odd fishing boat but most vessels are recreational, and it is tourism that is important now.

A little known element of the village's history is its important contribution to the success of WWII. Because Garlieston Bay was similar to Normandy's beaches, it was the secret location for testing prototypes of various seaborne equipment, especially the 'Mulberry' floating harbours so essential to the D-Day landings. Dotted around the area are concrete remnants of these, and the village hall houses an informative display.

CAMPSITE – GARLIESTON CARAVAN AND MOTORHOME CLUB

A Caravan and Motorhome Club site, this is efficiently run, and the amenities are of the usual high standards. Situated at the southernmost end of Garlieston village, right on the seafront and adjacent to the pier and coastal path, the site is quiet and calm.

The 63 pitches are spread over two sections separated by a road. One section overlooks Garlieston Bay, whist the other is a more sheltered area known as the Walled Garden: an arrangement that makes the site disjointed and somewhat nondescript. However, the nearness of the beach and coastal path, as well as a regular bus service, means it is a convenient base

CAMPSITE – GARLIESTON LODGE CAMPSITE

This small campsite is situated in Garlieston village in the woodlands of Galloway House gate lodge on the south bank Pouton Burn, a charming stream. All of the five pitches have

Garlieston Caravan Club site is well-placed overlooking the beach.

hardstanding and electric hook-up, and overlook the pond and are surrounded by fields. It is essential that dogs are kept on a short lead as there are many other animals on the smallholding: besides fish in the pond (fishing is permitted) there are hens and ducks, whilst an adjoining field is home to a small drift of black pigs.

Pub – Harbour Inn

Just a few minutes' walk from the campsite is this traditional local pub, dating back to 1700, and situated on the main thoroughfare overlooking the bay. Besides a small, cosy bar there is a restaurant area and a garden, and the pub is popular as the meals, though traditional, are very enjoyable: booking is advisable.

Dogs are welcome in the bar but not the restaurant, although meals are also served in the bar. It's a friendly place with helpful staff.

Pearls of wisdom

Was this going to be a super-duper place? It smelt so – water, salt water. Would I be able to go swimming? Oh, I'm sooo excited! It won't be long before we set off on our 'finding out' walk ...

What a strange place: there are odd sections of the campsite all over the place. I could go here but not there; on the lead here but off there. I was right about the water, as there is lots of it, though not very

The Harbour Inn is on the main thoroughfare overlooking the bay.

good for swimming because it's not deep enough in some parts. I wasn't able to swim from the slipway because of the boats, but not much further on, just by a seat, we went across some stones and sand and found a fantastic place to swim that was plenty deep enough. Yipee! So close; just two tail wags away. My morning jaunt – a swim and a walk: fabulous.

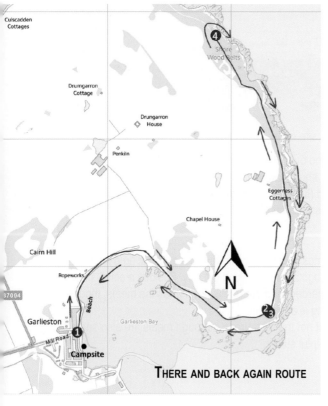

SHORT WALK – THERE AND BACK AGAIN

Distance: 5mi (8km)
Duration: 2hr (Moderate)
Terrain: Footpaths, fields, woods, beaches, tracks, roads, gates, stiles
To make this walk circular it is necessary to either walk several mile along roads – one of which is the main route to and from Garlieston village, or go through a field with lots of cows. I spoke to the farmer; he regularly uses this field for his cows, so it's not really a viable option

Section 1: 1.25mi (2km)
- Exit campsite via entrance, turning towards the sandy beach and passing the village hall on right
- Turn right onto beach just after the village hall, then left along the beach
- Bear left up to road at grassy area, turning right and keeping close to wall on right
- Turn right back onto beach at end of wall
- Turn left along beach, following curve of bay and heading towards third telegraph pole
- Watch for bench on road, turning left between grass hillocks along a clear path leading to the bench, then out to road

The path winds through the woods (Section 1).

- Turn right along road to left bend
- Turn right onto narrow footpath signposted 'Core Path 388/Innerwell'
- Continue along path, ignoring those on right going down to bay, passing way-marker on right, then through gate
- Follow path next to wall on left which then becomes a fence: through another gate
- Continue along path as it winds through the woods out to field

Section 2: 1.25mi (2km)
- Follow path along edge of field, keeping close to woods on right, then through gate into another large field
- Straight on along edge of field, keeping bay on right, and through gate into wood again, passing way-marker on right: over fallen tree
- Take right fork continuing along path
- Turn right along clear path going down slope, then bearing left to ivy-covered wall (Eggerness Castle Fort)
- Follow path around broken wall over three fallen trees
- Turn left through trees at junction onto path to begin return journey

Section 3: 1.25mi (2km)
- Straight on, passing footpath and ivy-covered wall on left
- Follow path over fallen tree and through gate into field
- Continue along edge of two large fields, going through gates as necessary, onto path leading into woods by way-marker on left (hidden)

Section 4: 1.25mi (2km)
- Follow path through woods under fallen tree that forms an arch
- At fork both paths lead to wide path alongside wall and then a fence: through two gates out to road
- Follow road into village and campsite entrance, keeping close to seawall on left

LONG WALK – STRANGE CASTLE RUINS
Distance: 7.25mi (11.6km)
Duration: 4hr (Moderate)
Terrain: Footpaths, fields, woods, beaches, coastal paths, stony tracks, roads, gates, ladder stile, a steep climb to castle ruin

Section 1: 1.25mi (2km)
- Exit campsite via entrance onto road
- Turn along road towards pier with main campsite on left
- Turn right through large, black gates onto wide, stony track
- Follow track past fields on both sides to 3-gate junction
- Turn right through gate along wide track, round left and right bend and through gate to driveway

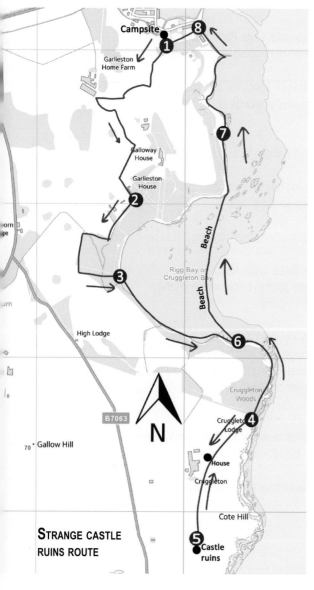

- Turn left along driveway, keeping close to fence on left
- Turn next right signposted 'Car Park,' passing first Galloway House on left (huge) and then car park on left and through gate
- Continue straight ahead through second gate, and round right bend beside tall wall (possibly Walled Garden)
- Through gate into wood

Section 2: 0.75mi (1.2km)
- Turn immediately right onto narrow footpath into wood
- Straight on at junction, then take right fork (not grassy)
- Follow path as it winds through woods, crossing six assorted footbridges
- Turn left at corner away from small, overgrown gate into field
- Continue along wide grass track, still in woods, and round left bend, ignoring path on right into field
- Turn right along slightly narrower path at junction
- Follow winding path past gate on right and out to bay by plank footbridge

Section 3: 1.25mi (2km)
- Turn right over footbridge with sea on left
- Follow path through woods over three more footbridges to large junction
- Take left fork, which soon follows stone wall on left
- Continue along path to small, mowed grass area with house (Cruggleton Cottage) on right and turrets on left (amazing views)

Section 4: 0.75mi (1.2km)
- Straight across lawn and through arch opposite onto path
- Follow path, first ducking under shrubs, then weaving through tall grasses, and

The ruins of Cruggleton Castle.

through gate in wall on right next to ladder stile into field
- Turn left along edge of field, and through kissing gate in corner into next field
- Straight on along edge of field with sea still on left, and through gate into third field
- Cross field to arch opposite; over ladder stile into castle ruin mound

Section 5: 1.25mi (2km)
- Retrace steps across field and through gate
- Carry on along edge of two fields and through gate in wall on right
- Fight long grasses and duck under shrubs to mowed grass area
- Cross grass onto coastal path opposite
- Continue along coastal path and over four footbridges

Section 6: 1mi (1.6km)
- Turn right along narrow path onto beach immediately after bridge
- Turn left along beach (ideal for dog swim)
- Exit beach at far end by large boulder near part of tree trunk and way-marker on small post
- Turn right along narrow stony path, keeping close to sea on right, passing gates on left and swing to junction by shelter

Section 7: 0.5mi (0.8km)
- Straight on along wider gravel path with sea still on right, then through two gates

Section 8: 0.5mi (0.8km)
- Follow coastal path to pier
- Turn left along road, passing pier harbour on right, and on to campsite entrance

IN THE VICINITY
CYCLING
The peninsular around the village of Garlieston is ideal for cyclists as there is little traffic on the roads. There are four signed cycle routes of varying difficulty and length: green (20mi/32km), yellow, red (17mi/27km) and orange (22mi/35km). Further information and a leaflet is available from Tourist Information Centres.

FISHING
At the village harbour there is mooring for several craft which are occasionally used by

commercial fishing boats. Just along the coast, Whithorn has several vessels available to hire for sea fishing as this is a popular local activity. There are also shops that sell bait and fishing tackle.

SORBIE TOWER

Just over 2 miles (3.2km) along the B7052 is this interesting structure: the ancient seat of Clan Hannay, thought to have been built by Patrick Hannay in the 16th century. The clan was outlawed during the 17th century as a result of disputes, and the tower was sold to the Earl of Galloway. From 1748 it gradually deteriorated into a formidable ruin when the last of the line died out.

Then, in 1965, it was gifted back to the Clan Hannay and the gigantic task of restoration began. Though a great deal of work has been undertaken with surrounding grounds landscaped, the castle tower cleared, information panels erected, toilets installed and picnic area created, there is still much to do. Even so, it is an imposing structure. The local shop at Garlieston has information about viewing the interior.

WHITHORN

On the southern part of this SW peninsular is the historic Whithorn region. It was to Isle of Whithorn that, in 397, Christianity was bought to Scotland by St Ninian. When he died in 431 he was buried in his church in the village of Whithorn. Because of this, for many centuries Whithorn was a place of pilgrimage, especially St Ninian's Cave on the west side of the peninsular where, traditionally, it is thought the saint went to pray and meditate.

The town still retains much of the original street pattern, with several listed buildings as well as the unique churches associated with St Ninian It is also home to the smallest theatre in Great Britain, at which is held a regular annual Arts and Crafts event.

THE WHITHORN TRUST VISITOR CENTRE

Not only does the centre provide useful information about the area, it also houses interesting artefacts and regular exhibitions.

Appendix i
Countryside codes

UK Government: Rights of Way and Open Access Land

PUBLIC RIGHTS OF WAY

You can walk on all public rights of way.

Some public rights of way are also open to horseriders, cyclists and motorists. You can use –

- Footpaths – for walking, running, mobility scooters and powered wheelchairs
- Bridleways – for walking, horseriding, bicycles, mobility scooters and powered wheelchairs
- Restricted byways – for any transport without a motor and mobility scooters and powered wheelchairs
- Byways open to all traffic – for any kind of transport, including cars (but mainly used by walkers, cyclists and horseriders)

Rights of way in England, Wales, and Northern Ireland

Public rights of way are marked with signs or coloured arrows: for example, yellow for footpaths; blue for bridleways

You can find the route of public rights of way –

- On Ordnance Survey and other maps
- On some council websites

RIGHT TO ROAM

You can access some land across England without having to use paths: this land is known as 'open access land' or just 'access land.'

Access land includes privately-owned mountains, moors, heaths and downs, common land registered with the local council, and some land around the England Coast Path. Your right to access this land is called the 'right to roam,' or 'freedom to roam.'

WHAT YOU CAN AND CAN'T DO

You can use access land for walking, running, watching wildlife and climbing. There are certain activities you can't usually do on open access land, including –

- Horseriding
- Cycling
- Camping
- Taking animals other than dogs on to the land

- Driving a vehicle (except mobility scooters and powered wheelchairs)
- Water sports

But you can use access land for horseriding and cycling if –
- The landowner allows it
- Public bridleways or byways cross the land – horseriders and cyclists can ride along these
- There are local traditions, or rights, of access

DOGS ON OPEN ACCESS LAND
You must keep your dog on a lead of no more than two metres long on open access land –
- Between 1 March and 31 July – to protect ground-nesting birds
- At all times around livestock

On land next to the England Coast Path you must keep your dog under close control. There may be other local or seasonal restrictions, but these don't apply to public rights of way or assistance dogs.

EXCEPTED LAND
On access land some areas remain private ('excepted land'), and you **don't** have the right to access these areas, even if they appear on a map of open access land.
Excepted land includes –
- Houses, buildings and the land they're on (such as courtyards)
- Land used to grow crops
- Building sites and land that's being developed
- Parks and gardens
- Golf courses and racecourses
- Railways and tramways
- Working quarries

Use public rights of way to cross excepted land.

PRIVATE LAND
You may be able to access private land if the landowner has agreed to let the public use it: for example, for walking, cycling or horseriding (sometimes known as giving 'permissive access'). Look for signs.

Scotland: Outdoors Access Code 2003
Everyone has a statutory right of access to all land and inland waters, unless specifically excluded. These access rights are for outdoor recreation, and for crossing land and water.
There are some obvious common-sense restrictions, including –
- Private houses and gardens
- Farm buildings and yards

- Farmland that has been planted or has crops growing
- School land and sports or playing fields when in use
- Golf courses (but you can cross a golf course provided you don't interfere with any rounds)
- Airfields, railways, telecommunication sites, military bases and installations, working quarries and construction sites, and visitor attractions or other places that charge for entry

ON OR IN WATER
- The access rights apply to non-motorised crafts only, and open water swimming
- Respect anglers and their desire for peace
- Take care when entering or exiting water so as not to damage the environment
- Avoid areas of commercial fishing unless you have spoken to the landowner
- Access rights extend to swimming (subject to any local bylaws)

IN WOODLAND
- Never light fires during dry periods in woodlands or on peaty ground
- Never cut down or damage trees
- Pay attention to signs, and follow any advice from the forester or land manager

ON FARMS
- Access rights do not usually apply to farmyards. However, if a right of way or core path goes through a farmyard, you can follow this at any time
- Use a gate or stile where one has been provided. Do not climb over walls or hedges unless there is no alternative
- Leave gates as you find them, even if they are open
- Keep away from fields of farm animals or growing crops
- Do not take your dog into fields containing growing crops, calves, lambs, or other young animals

HILLS AND MOUNTAINS
- Avoid areas where red stag stalking is taking place. This is usually between July and October. and notices will give full details of restricted areas
- The same applies to grouse shooting
- Do not let your dog roam near ground-nesting birds, or worry sheep or cattle
- Take responsible care when walking in hills and mountains so as not to damage the environment or disturb wildlife

WILD CAMPING
Scotland's generous outdoor access rights extend to wild camping, except where there are seasonal camping restrictions such as on the shores of the east side of Loch Lomond
- Wild camping should be lightweight, done in small numbers, and only for two or three nights in any one place

- Always responsibly consider where you are camping, and try to avoid causing problems for local people and land managers by not camping in enclosed fields of crops, or near farm animals
- Take extra care to avoid disturbing deer stalking or grouse shooting. If you wish to camp close to a house or building, seek the owner's permission

LEAVE NO TRACE
- Take away all your litter
- Remove all evidence of your tent pitch, and of any open fire
- Not cause pollution

Country Code
www.gov.uk/government/publications/the-countryside-code/the-countryside-code

RESPECT OTHER PEOPLE
Please respect the local community and other people using the outdoors. Remember your actions can affect both lives and livelihoods.

CONSIDER THE LOCAL COMMUNITY, AND OTHERS ENJOYING THE OUTDOORS
Respect the needs of local people and visitors alike: for example, don't block gateways, driveways or other paths with your vehicle.

When riding a bike or driving a vehicle, slow down or stop for horses, walkers and farm animals, and give them plenty of room. By law, cyclists must give way to walkers and horseriders on bridleways.

Co-operate with people at work in the countryside: for example, keep out of the way when farm animals are being herded or moved, and follow directions from the farmer.

Busy traffic on small country roads can be unpleasant and dangerous to local people, visitors and wildlife: slow down and, where possible, leave your vehicle at home; consider sharing lifts and use alternatives such as public transport or cycling. For public transport information, phone Traveline on 0871 200 22 33 or visit www.traveline.info.

LEAVE GATES AND PROPERTY AS YOU FIND THEM, AND FOLLOW PATHS, UNLESS WIDER ACCESS IS AVAILABLE
A farmer will normally close gates to keep in farm animals, but may sometimes leave them open so the animals can reach food and water. Leave gates as you find them, or follow instructions on signs. When in a group, make sure the last person knows how to leave the gates.

Follow paths unless wider access is available, such as on open country or registered common land (known as 'open access land').

If you think a sign is illegal or misleading, such as a 'Private – No Entry' sign on a public path, advise the local authority.

Leave machinery and farm animals alone – don't interfere with animals even if you think they're in distress. Try to alert the farmer instead.

Use gates, stiles or gaps in field boundaries if you can – climbing over walls, hedges and fences can damage them, and increase the risk of farm animals escaping. Our heritage matters to all of us: be careful not to disturb ruins and historic sites.

PROTECT THE NATURAL ENVIRONMENT

We all have a responsibility to protect the countryside, now and for future generations, so make sure you don't harm animals, birds, plants or trees, and try to leave no trace of your visit. When out with your dog, make sure he is not a danger or nuisance to farm animals, horses, wildlife or other people.

LEAVE NO TRACE OF YOUR VISIT, AND TAKE HOME YOUR LITTER

Protecting the natural environment means taking special care not to damage, destroy or remove features such as rocks, plants and trees. These provide homes and food for wildlife, and add to everybody's enjoyment of the countryside.

Litter and leftover food doesn't just spoil the beauty of the countryside; it can be dangerous to wildlife and farm animals – so take it home with you. Dropping litter and dumping rubbish are criminal offences.

Fires can be as devastating to wildlife and habitats as they are to people and property, so be careful with naked flames and cigarettes/pipes at any time of the year. Sometimes, controlled fires are used to manage vegetation, particularly on heaths and moors between 1 October and 15 April, but if a fire appears to be unattended report it by calling 999.

KEEP DOGS UNDER EFFECTIVE CONTROL

When you take your dog into the outdoors, always ensure he does not disturb wildlife, farm animals, horses or other people by –
- Keeping him on a lead, or
- Keeping him in view at all times, being aware of what he's doing, and confident that he will return to you promptly on cue
- Ensure he does not stray off the path or area where you have a right of access

Special dog rules may apply in particular situations, so always look out for local signs: for example –
- Dogs may be banned from certain areas that people use, or there may be restrictions, bylaws or control orders limiting where they can go
- The access rights that normally apply to open country and registered common land (known as 'open access' land) require dogs to be kept on a short lead between 1 March and 31 July, to help protect ground-nesting birds, and all year round near farm animals
- At the coast, there may also be local restrictions that require dogs to be kept on a short lead during bird breeding season, and to prevent disturbance to flocks of resting and feeding birds during other times of year

It's always good practice (and a legal requirement on 'open access' land) to keep your dog on a lead around farm animals and horses, for your own safety and the welfare of the animals. A farmer may shoot a dog who is attacking or chasing farm animals without being liable to compensate the dog's owner.

However, if cattle or horses chase you and your dog, it may be safer to let your dog off the lead. Your dog will likely be much safer if you let him run away from a farm animal without impedance from you – and so will you.

ENJOY THE OUTDOORS

Even when going out locally, it's best to get the latest information about where and when you can go. For example, your rights to go onto some areas of open access land and coastal land may be restricted in particular places at particular times. Find out as much as you can about where you are going, plan ahead, and follow advice and local signs.

PLAN AHEAD AND BE PREPARED

You'll get more from your visit if you refer to up-to-date maps or guidebooks and websites before you set off. Visit Natural England on GOV.UK, or contact local information centres or libraries for a list of outdoor recreation groups offering advice on specialist activities.

You're responsible for your own safety and for others in your care – especially children – so be prepared for natural hazards, changes in weather, and other events. Wild animals, farm animals and horses can behave unpredictably if you get too close, especially if they're with their young, so give them plenty of space.

Check weather forecasts before you leave. Conditions can change rapidly, especially on mountains and along the coast, so turn back if in doubt. When visiting the coast, check tide times on EasyTide: don't risk being cut off by rising tides, and take care on slippery rocks and seaweed.

Part of the appeal of the countryside is that you can get away from it all. You may not see anyone for hours, and there are many places without good mobile phone signals, so let someone know where you're going and when you expect to return.

FOLLOW ADVICE AND LOCAL SIGNS

England has about 190,000km (118,060 miles) of public rights of way, providing many opportunities to enjoy the natural environment. Get to know the signs and symbols used in the countryside to show paths and open countryside. See the Countryside Code leaflet for some of the symbols you may come across.

KENNEL CLUB COUNTRYSIDE CODE

Wherever you go, following these steps will help keep your dog safe, protect the environment, and demonstrate that you are a responsible dog owner.
- Control your dog so that he does not scare or disturb farm animals or wildlife
- When using the new access rights over open country and common land, you must keep your dog on a short lead between 1 March and 31 July – and all year round near

farm animals – and you may not be able to take your dog at all on some areas or at some times. Please follow/abide by any official signs.

- You do not have to put your dog on a lead on public paths, as long as he is under close control. As a general rule, though, keep your dog on a lead if unsure about how reliably he will do as you ask. By law, farmers are entitled to destroy a dog who injures or worries their animals
- If cattle or horses chase you and your dog, it may be safer to let your dog off the lead. Your dog will likely be much safer if you let him run away from a farm animal without impedance from you – and so will you
- Take particular care that your dog doesn't scare sheep and lambs, or wander where he might disturb birds nesting on the ground and other wildlife: eggs and young will soon die without protection from their parents
- Everyone knows how unpleasant dog poo is, and a health hazard to boot, so always clean up after your dog and dispose of the poo responsibly – bag it and bin it (don't leave it hanging from a branch ...). Make sure your dog is regularly wormed to protect him, other animals, and people

Visit Hubble and Hattie on the web:
www.hubbleandhattie.com • www.hubbleandhattie.blogspot.co.uk • Details of all books
• Special offers • Newsletter • New book news

Appendix ii
Campsite details

(All details and prices correct at time of going to press: charges are per night)

Wales
CEREDIGION
Woodlands Caravan Park, Devils Bridge, Aberystwyth, Sir Ceredigion SY23 3JW
Tel: 01970 890 233 • email: enquiries@woodlandsdevilsbridge.co.uk
• website: www.woodlandsdevilsbridge.co.uk
Open: 1st Mar-31st Oct
N: 52.37912 W: 3.84523

DIRECTIONS
The campsite is located on the A4120, a fairly major road that feeds into the main A44, Aberystwyth to Llangurig. From the A44 take the A4120 that leads directly to the campsite entrance. Do not follow the satnav and use the minor B roads indicated, as these are not suitable for motorhomes.

CHARGES
Pitch+electric+2 adults+awning – £22.00-£27.00
Dogs – £1.00
Additional adult – £4.00
Pup tent – £3.00
Children – £3.00

DENBIGHSHIRE
Fundraising (Pet Rescue) Campsite, Llewerllyd Farm, Dyserth LL18 6BP
Tel: 07721 627 486 • email: fundraisingcampsite9@gmail.com
• website: www.fundraisingcampsite.co.uk
Open: All year
N: 53.30651 W: 342673

DIRECTIONS
M56 feeds into A494. Turn onto A55 at Ewole heading towards Conway. Exit at junction 31 signposted Prestatyn A515. Follow A5151 to Dyserth. Turn right at traffic light signposted Prestatyn A547 onto Waterfall road. Turn left at traffic lights just past New Inn on left onto

A547. Campsite entrance is wide driveway on right

CHARGES
Pitch+electric+2 adults – £20.00
Dogs – £2.00
Membership – £5.00
Other – Information unavailable: discount for OAPs

MONTGOMERYSHIRE
Mellington Hall Holiday Home Park, Mellington, Church Stoke, Powys SY15 6HX
Tel: 01588 620011 • mb: 07900 707 621 • email: info@mellingtonhallcaravanpark.co.uk
• website: mellingtonhallcaravanpark.co.uk
Open: All year
N: 52.52093 W: 3.09423

DIRECTIONS
From A489, which leads to Craven Arms in west and Newton in the east, turn south at Blue
Bell Hotel onto B4385. Continue along road over bridge round to left; first right onto long
drive up to the hall

CHARGES
Pitch+electric+2 adults+awning+TV – £30.00
Dogs – Free
Additional adult – £6.00

North East England
COUNTY DURHAM
Daleview Holiday Park, Station Bank, Middleton-in-Teesdale DL12 0NG
Tel: 01833 640 233 • mb: 07788 245 975 • email: daleviewcaravanpark@gmail.com
• website: www.daleviewcaravanpark.com
Open: 1st March-31st Oct
N: 54.61829 W: 2.08345

DIRECTIONS
From A1 (M1) take A66 to Barnard Castle, then the B6278 which feeds into the B6282 to
Middletone-in-Teesdale. Turn south over the bridge to campsite entrance on left

CHARGES
Pitch+electric+2 adults – £25.00
Dog – Free

LINCOLNSHIRE
Three Horseshoes, Shoe Lane, Goulceby, Louth LN11 9WA

Tel: 0333 456 1221 • Pub: 01507 343 909 • email: info@the3horseshoes.com
• website: www.the3horseshoes.com
Open: Feb-Dec
N: 53.29366 W: 0.12090

DIRECTIONS
From the north (Louth), take A153 towards Horncastle, passing through Scamblesby.
In half-a-mile turn right onto Ranyards Lane, signposted to the pub and Goulceby. At
T-junction turn right onto Horncastle Rd. At next T-junction turn left onto Main Road, then
first left on bend into Shoe Lane (cul-de-sac). Campsite is on the right

From the south (Horncastle), take A153 towards Louth. In approximately 5 miles (8km)on
sharp right bend turn left onto Horncastle Rd, signposted Goulceby and pub. At T-junction
turn right onto Horncastle Rd. At next T-junction turn left onto Main Road, then first left on
bend into Shoe Lane (cul-de-sac). Campsite is on the right

CHARGES
Pitch+2 adults – £20.00-£30.00
Electric – £5.00
Dogs – £2.00
Children – £2.00
Additional adult – £5.00

NORFOLK
Causeway Cottage Caravan Park, Bridge Road, Potter Heigham NR29 5JB
Tel: 01692 670 238 • mb: 07867 974 143 • email: sue32@btinternet.com
• website: causewaycottage.webs.com
Open: 1st April-31st Oct
N: 52.71269 W: 1.57604

DIRECTIONS
From Norwich take A47 to Acle, then A 1064 to Billockby. Continue along Main Rd (B1152)
which feeds to Mill Rd (B1152) through Repps. Turn left over narrow bridge onto The
Causeway. Campsite is on the left

CHARGES
Pitch+4 adults – from £15.00 (large units: price on request)
Dogs – Free
Electric – £5.00
Awning – £1.00
Additional adult – £1.00
Shower – £1.00

WEST YORKSHIRE

Upwood Holiday Park, Blackmoor Road, Oxenhope, Keighley BD22 9SS
Tel: 01535 644 242 ● email: info@upwoodpark.co.uk ● website: www.upwoodpark.co.uk
Open: 1st Mar-31st Jan
N: 53.81561 W: 1.93336

DIRECTIONS

Do NOT follow satnav. From A629 (Halifax Road) turn right from Keighley, or left from Halifax, onto B6144 (Hawoth Rd/Brow Top Rd). Take first left onto Black Moor Rd. Campsite is on left just before the bus shelter

CHARGES

Pitch+electric+4 adults+awning – £19.50-£33.00
Dogs – Free
Additional adult – £5.00
Gazebo – £5.00
Shower – 50p

North West England

CHESHIRE

Cotton Arms, Cholmondeley Road, Wrenbury CW5 8HG
Tel: 01270 780377 ● email: campsite@cottonarmswrenbury.co.uk
● website: www.cottonarmswrenbury.co.uk
Open: All year
N: 53.02751 W: 2.61168

DIRECTIONS

From the A49 west turn onto Wrenbury Rd at crossroads by Cholmondeley Arms pub, signposted. Follow signs to Wrenbury over canal bridge. Campsite entrance on left

From the M6 east exit junction 16 on to the A500. Turn left at Nantwich onto A51. Straight on at roundabout onto A530. Pass school on right in 20mph school zone, then turn right onto Wrenbury Heath Rd. Continue along road to crossroads at Wrenbury Hall. Turn left onto Nantwich Rd. Follow road into village. Campsite on right just before canal bridge

CHARGES

Hardstanding pitch+electric+2 adults – £20.00
Grass pitch+2 adults – £12.00
Dogs – Free
Shower – £1.00

CUMBRIA

Great Langdale Campsite National Trust, Great Langdale, Ambleside LA22 9JU

More wonderful walks from dog-friendly campsites

Tel: 01539 432 733 • email: lakescampsites@nationaltrust.org.uk
• website: www.nationaltrust.org.uk/holidays/great-langdale-campsite-lake-district
Open: All year
N: 54.44310 W: 3.09885

DIRECTIONS
From Ambleside follow A593. At Skelwith Bridge turn right onto B5343. Campsite on the left after approximately 6 miles (9.65km)

CHARGES (MINIMUM BOOKING 2 NIGHTS)
Hardstanding pitch+electric+1 adult – £11.00-£24.00
Dogs – £1.50
Additional adult – £7.00

LANCASHIRE
Burrs Country Park Caravan and Motorhome Club Site, Woodhlll Rd, Bury BL8 1DA
Tel: 01342 327 490 • email: via website • website: www.caravanclub.co.uk/club-sites/england/north-west-england/lancashire/burrs-country-park-caravan-club-site/
Open: All year
N: 53.6105 W: 2.30476

DIRECTIONS
Exit M66 at junction 2 onto A58 signposted Bury. Follow brown signs to East Lancs Railway. Continue on A58, passing Bury Market on right, and at traffic lights (with Bury Town Hall and Registry Office on left) continue downhill on A58, following signposts to Bolton, Ramsbottom. At traffic lights (Toyota garage on left) keep in right-hand lane and follow signposts to Tottington, Ramsbottom, and brown signposts to Burrs Country Park. Stay in the same lane through next two sets of traffic lights; 300 yards (274m) past office building turn right into Woodhill Road (brown signpost to Burrs Country Park Club Site). Follow road to end onto cobbles and over bridge into site

CHARGES
Pitch – £4.80-£16.50
Adult – £8.00-£10.30
Dogs – Free
Children – £2.00-£3.30

Central England
LEICESTERSHIRE
Globe Inn, 6 Main Street, Snarestone DE12 7DB
Tel: 05130 272 020 or message via facebook: TheGlobeInnSnarestone/
Open: 1st Apr-31st Oct
N: 52.68073 W: 1.49422

DIRECTIONS

From M42 exit junction 11 A444 Burton-on-Trent. Take 4th exit at roundabout onto Tamworth Rd, signposted Measham. Turn right at traffic lights in Measham onto B4116 signposted Snarestone. Turn right onto B4116 signposted Atherstone. Turn left at crossroads signposted Swepstone. Campsite is on right

CHARGES

Pitch+electricity+2 adults – £18.00
Dogs – Free

WARWICKSHIRE

Cottage of Content, 15 Welford Rd, Barton, Bidford on Avon B50 4NP
Tel: 0178 772 279 ● email: cofcontent@gmail.com
● website: www.cottageofcontent.com/rooms
Open: 1st Mar-31st Oct
N52: 15929 W: 1.84396

DIRECTIONS

From roundabout on the A46 at Bidford on Avon follow signs into village. At next roundabout take 3rd exit signposted Honeybourne. Straight on at traffic lights, over bridge, turning next left signposted Welford and Barton. Campsite entrance on the left on a bend

CHARGES

Pitch+electric+2 adults – £22.50-£30.00
Dogs – Free

WORCESTERSHIRE

Turbles Holiday Caravan Site, Dugger's End Lane, Castlemorton, Malvern WR13 6JD
Tel: 01684 833 234 ● mb: 07963 414 613 ● email: enquiries@turbles.co.uk
● website: www.turbles.co.uk/caravan-site
Open: All year
N:52.04481 W: 2.30610

DIRECTIONS

From Gloucester take the A417 to Staunton. Continue ahead onto B4208 signposted The Malverns. Follow the B4208 as it twists and turns; over M50. Turn first right onto Drugger's End Lane, after passing Robin Hood pub on right. Campsite entrance is on left

CHARGES

Pitch+electric+2 adults – £18.00
Dogs – Free
Additional adult – £4.50

South East England

EAST SUSSEX

Horam Manor Country Park, Horam, Heathfield TN21 0YD
Tel: 01435 813 662 • email: info@horammanorcountrypark.com
• website: www.horammanorcountrypark.com
Open: All year
N: 50.93206 W: 0.23933

DIRECTIONS

The campsite is on the A267 between Heathfield and Eastbourne

CHARGES

Pitch+2 adults+electric – £35.00-£40.00
Dogs – £2.00
Additional adult – £5.00

KENT

Hook and Hatchet Inn (Hillside Campsite), Church Rd, Hucking ME17 1QT
Tel: 01622 880 272 • email: info@hookandhatchetpub.co.uk
• website: www.hookandhatchetpub.co.uk
Open: All year
N: 51.29378 W: 0.63383

DIRECTIONS

From M20 exit at junction 7 on to A249 (N) signposted Sheerness. Turn right onto Rumstead Lane (single track) signposted Hucking, and follow to junction with pub and campsite on left

From M2 exit at junction 5 onto A249(S) signposted Sittingbourne. Turn left onto Rumstead Lane (single track) signposted Huckingand follow to junction with pub and campsite on left

CHARGES

Pitch+2 adults+electric – £29.90
Dogs – Free
Additional adult – £5.00
Children – £2.00

SUFFOLK

White Horse, Mill Green, Edwardstone, Sudbury CO10 5P
Tel: 01787 211 211 • email: edwardstonewhitehorse@gmail.com
• website: www.edwardstonewhitehorse.co.uk/staywith.html
Open: All year
N: 52.05017 W: 0.84402

DIRECTIONS

From Sudbury take the B1115. Follow road which becomes single lane to pub and campsite on right

CHARGES

Pitch – No charge
Adult – £9.00
Dogs – Free
Electric – £5.00

South West England

DEVON

Fox & Hounds Campsite, Bridestowe, Okehampton EX20 4HF
Tel: 01822 820 206 • email: info@foxandhoundshotel.com
• website: www.foxandhoundshotel.com
Open: All year
N: 50.66112 W: 4.08786

DIRECTIONS

The campsite is on the main A386 Okehampton to Tavistock road

CHARGES

Pitch+2 adults +electric – £20.00
Dogs – Free

DORSET

Bagwell Farm Touring Park, Bagwell Farm, Chickerell, Weymouth DT3 4EA
Tel: 01305 782 575 • email: enquiries@bagwellfarm.co.uk
• website: www.bagwellfarm.co.uk
Open: All year
N: 50.63346 W: 2.52902

DIRECTIONS

From Dorchester take the A354 to Weymouth. At Manor roundabout take 2nd exit, then third exit at next roundabout to Granby Way (B3157). Over next roundabout to traffic lights – turn right (B3157) and continue in Portesham/Abbotsbury direction. Campsite is at the top of the hill on the left just after Victoria Inn on the left

CHARGES

Pitch+2 adults +electric – £20.00-£42.00
Dogs – £1.00
Additional adult – £5.00
Children – £2.00

GLOUCESTERSHIRE
Red Lion Campsite Park, Wainlode Hill, Norton GL2 9LW
Tel: 01452 731810/01452 730251
Open: All year
N: 51.93091 W: 2.22248

DIRECTIONS
From Gloucester take A38(N), left fork at Norton signposted Wainlode Hill. Campsite on right in about 1 mile (1.6km)

CHARGES
Pitch+2 adults –£13.00
Dogs – £2.00
Electric+additional adult and children – £2.00

Red Shoot Camping Park, Linwood (New Forest), Ringwood BH24 3QT
Tel: 01425 473 789 (phone bookings only) • email: enquiries@redshoot-campingpark.com • website: www.redshoot-campingpark.com
Open: 1st Mar-31st Oct
N: 50.88406 W: 1.73481

DIRECTIONS
From M27 take A31(W) towards Ringwood. Take A338 at Ringwood signposted Fordingbridge/Salisbury. Turn right onto Ellingham Drive at brown campsite sign. Continue along road over cattle grid and bridge. Left at T-junction; first right signposted Linwood. In about 2 miles (3.2km) campsite is behind pub on left

CHARGES
Pitch+2 adults +electric – £26.50-£40.50
Dogs – £2.00
Additional adult – £8.00

Scotland
ABERDEENSHIRE
Braemar Caravan Park, Glenshee Road, Braemar AB35 5YQ
Tel: 01339 741 373 • email: info@braemarcaravanpark.co.uk • website: www.braemarcaravanpark.co.uk
Open: All year
N: 57.00178 W: 3.39545

DIRECTIONS
The campsite is on the outskirts of the village on the A93. Follow this road from Perth in the south or Aberdeen in the east

CHARGES

Pitch+electric+2 people – £24.00-£30.50
Dogs – £5.00
Additional adult – £10.00
Children – £5.00

ARGYLL & BUTE

Glenloin House Caravan & Camping, Glenloin House, Arrocher G83 7AJ
Tel: 01301 702 239
Open: 1st Mar-31st Oct
N: 56.20748 W: 4.74233

DIRECTIONS

The campsite is on the A83 Tarbet to Inveraray road, opposite the car park at the top of Loch Long

CHARGES

Pitch+electric+2 adults – £15.00
Dogs – Free
Additional adult – £5.00

DUMFRIES & GALLOWAY

Garlieston Caravan & Motorhome Club Site, Garlieston, Newton Stewart DG8 8BS
Tel: 01342 327 490 • email: via website
• website: www.caravanclub.co.uk/club-sites/scotland/dumfries--galloway/garlieston-caravan-club-site/
Open: 16th Mar-5th Nov
N: 54.78766 W: 4.36756

DIRECTIONS

From Dumfries take the A75 towards Newton Stewart, crossing the River Cree on the outskirts to a large roundabout. Take first exit onto A714 Wigtown Rd. Follow road into Garlieston, turning left onto Mill Rd, then right onto South Crescent. The campsite is at the very end on the left

CHARGES

Pitch +electric – £7.60-£11.40
Adult – £6.60-£9.70
Dogs – Free
Children – £2.00-£3.10

Index

Stride out with your dog from a great campsite. Follow nearby footpaths and byways to explore the surrounding countryside.

This book will guide you on *45* different walks that allow you and your dog to enjoy the diversity of the British landscape, and return to the campsite invigorated and exhilarated!

HH5045 • PAPERBACK • 152x225MM • 248 PAGES • 100 COLOUR IMAGES • 45 MAPS • ISBN 9781787220458 • £16.99*

*price subject to change

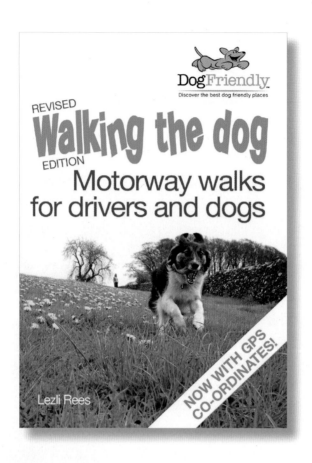

All motorway drivers will benefit from this guide to walks within 5 miles of motorway exits. All of Great Britain is covered, from Exeter to Perth and Swansea to Canterbury. Use this book to discover countryside walks for drivers, dogs and their families, with recommended family activities and suitable places to eat along the way.

HH4886 • PAPERBACK • 105x150MM • 208 PAGES • 200 COLOUR IMAGES • ISBN 9781845848866 • £7.99*

*price subject to change